the cinema of KEN LOACH

DIRECTORS' CUTS

the cinema of

KEN LOACH

art in the service of the people

jacob leigh

 WALLFLOWER PRESS LONDON & NEW YORK

First published in Great Britain in 2002 by
Wallflower Press
5 Pond Street, London NW3 2PN
www.wallflowerpress.co.uk

Copyright Jacob Leigh 2002

A catalogue for this book is available from the British Library

ISBN 1-903364-31-0 (paperback)
ISBN 1-903364-32-9 (hardback)

Book design by Rob Bowden Design

Printed in Great Britain by Antony Rowe, Chippenham, Wiltshire

CONTENTS

ACKNOWLEDGEMENTS

This book is based on my thesis and I would like to thank the Arts and Humanities Research Board for a three-year award, the School of English and American Studies at the University of East Anglia for granting me a bursary in my fourth year, Deirdre Newman, who was kind enough to give me many of her father's books on film and television, and Julian Petley, for supplying me with an unpublished manuscript for *Ken Loach: La Mirada Radical* (1992). I also wish to thank the BBC Written Archive Centre at Caversham Park, Reading, who allowed me to carry out research there, the BFI Library and its staff, and the National Film and Television Archive. Graham Fuller's book-length interview with Ken Loach and George McKnight's edited collection were published during my PhD research and these books have been valuable resources. The BECTU Oral History Project provides a precious archival source and I happily acknowledge the usefulness of several of their interviews with British film and television personnel. David Sharp of the BFI helpfully facilitated this. Ken Loach kindly granted me permission to use images from his work, as did Artificial Eye and LWT.

I am grateful to Rob Burns for introducing Loach's work to me, Harriet and Robert Dudley, who provided the spark that set the work in progress, and Karen O'Brien and Ben Cook, both of whom supplied me with copies of Loach's rare work. Thanks are also due to Charlotte Brunsdon for twice inviting me to lecture at the University of Warwick on *Up the Junction*, thus enabling me to polish that material, and to Glen Creeber, who stood in as supervisor for a year for Charles Barr. Thank you to Aileen Davies of the School of English and American Studies at the University of East Anglia for her administrative assistance. Stella Bruzzi and Jon Burrows read versions of Chapter Two, and I gratefully acknowledge their helpful comments. Juliet Smith brought her experience and her knowledge to our discussion of *Ladybird Ladybird*, helping me clarify many issues. The chapter on *Kes* was improved by comments from Andrew Klevan. Steven Marchant read an early draft of the *Raining Stones* section and offered insightful suggestions; besides this, our ongoing conversation about film and films continues to stimulate my thinking.

I am indebted especially to Jim Allen and Ken Loach, both of whom granted me invaluable interviews. Ken Loach also allowed me access to his archives at Parallax and let me watch *Questions of Leadership* there; I am thankful to Alex Reed at Parallax, who organised this. I appreciate the work of my PhD supervisor, Charles Barr, who has been consistently encouraging and supportive. Many thanks are also due to Yoram Allon and his colleagues at Wallflower Press.

I am grateful to my parents, Andrew and Margaret, for their love and assistance over many years of extended study. The book is dedicated to Sarah Guest, who translated most of the French material and proofread the thesis. Without her love and support, I would probably not have finished it.

LIST OF ILLUSTRATIONS

INTRODUCTION

This book has two aims: to describe the thematic and stylistic consistencies in the work of Ken Loach and to provide an account of the development of his career. By combining the two, I hope to present a personal aesthetic history.

Within the context of the mainstream film and television industry, Loach's linking of art and left-wing politics distinguishes his work and provides him with a consistent frame of reference, yet his politics present him with creative challenges. Themes recur in his films over a long period of collaboration with different writers, yet Loach's handling of these themes changes throughout his career. This book examines the changing methods which Loach uses to incorporate his political beliefs and those of his writers into his work. It refrains from judging his political beliefs; instead, it evaluates how his films express them – it studies his work as a film-maker. This evaluation derives from a study of mainstream, narrative fiction films, some made for television and some made for the cinema; although in Chapter 4, I write about the documentaries that Loach made during the 1980s.

The book moves chronologically through his career; each chapter studies closely one, two or three of his works. The exception is Chapter 1, which is introductory: it attaches three key themes of the book to a discussion of two scenes in *Carla's Song* (1996). The themes are realism, politics and melodrama. Chapter 2 examines works from the beginning of Loach's career, focussing on *Up the Junction* (1965), *Cathy Come Home* (1966) and *Poor Cow* (1967). In the 1960s, collaborating with writers like Troy Kennedy Martin, John McGrath, Nell Dunn, Christopher Logue and David Mercer, Loach experiments with aesthetic strategies that are indebted to the vogue for loosely Brechtian techniques.[1] Chapter 3 analyses *Kes* (1969), Loach's second cinema film. *Kes* exemplifies the director's growing interest in finding more subtle ways of expressing his political concerns artistically. This chapter scrutinises his consolidation of his methods of directing the camera and actors.

Chapter 4 discusses the impact that the writer Jim Allen had on Loach's work. Allen believed in revolutionary left-wing politics, and he influenced Loach's politics and aesthetics in the late 1960s and early 1970s. Together with the producer Tony Garnett, Allen and Loach made the four-part television serial *Days of Hope* (1975) at a time when a schism existed in cultural and political debates on the left in Britain. *Days of Hope* attempted to intervene directly in these debates. Chapter 5 finds its subject in Loach's connection to documentary. From his use in the 1960s of unspecified voice-overs and observational shots to his neo-*vérité* style in *The Gamekeeper* (1980) and *Looks and Smiles* (1981) and, beyond this, to his documentaries of the 1980s, Loach's work sometimes seems to lie between documentary and drama, often controversially so. This chapter reflects on the relationship between non-fiction and fiction in his work. The final, sixth chapter examines three films from the later phase of his career: *Raining Stones* (1993), *Ladybird Ladybird* (1994) and *Land and Freedom* (1995). It describes the style in which Loach, in what can be described as his mature period, employs genre paradigms as narrative frameworks for his films, integrating these with a developed realist aesthetic.

Overall, this book interprets and evaluates aesthetic changes in Loach's work. It claims that style and form are not equivalent. An account of a film's style and a director's style includes an account of what is expressed and how. V. F. Perkins' distinction between style and form is germane:

> We do not deduce the standards relevant to Rembrandt from the essence of paint; nor does the nature of words impose a method of judging ballads and novels. Standards of judgement cannot be appropriate to a medium as such but only to particular ways of exploring its opportunities. (Perkins 1978: 59)

This book is concerned with the 'particular ways' that Loach explores the opportunities of the medium of film. In *The World Viewed*, Stanley Cavell argues:

> You can no more tell what will give significance to the unique and specific aesthetic possibilities of projecting photographic images by thinking about them or seeing some, than you can tell what will give significance to the possibilities of paint by thinking about paint or by looking some over. You have to think about painting, and paintings; you have to think about motion pictures. (Cavell 1979: 31)

In an earlier essay, 'A Matter of Meaning It', Cavell suggests that although philosophers will occasionally write that paint is the medium of painting or words are the medium of literature, a medium is not made up simply of the physical materials themselves, but of the materials applied in characteristic ways. We can describe wood or stone as the media of sculpture, as we can describe celluloid as the medium of film but, Cavell contends, 'what needs recognition is that wood or stone would not be a medium of sculpture *in the absence of the art of sculpture*' (Cavell 1995: 221). I follow Perkins and Cavell in taking as my primary method the aspiration to interpret films as accurately as possible.

This book studies the work of a director, but it comments on his collaborations, acknowledging his work with key creative personnel, although the book does not investigate who did precisely what on which films. In an open and sustained way, Loach collaborates creatively with writers, producers, directors of photography, editors and production designers; therefore, although I write phrases like 'Loach uses', 'Loach cuts', or 'the film cuts' as shorthand, and although I do not mention every contributor by name, I do so for convenience of writing and reading and because we can assume that Loach either makes or approves of many final decisions. In addition, long-standing collaborators learn what will meet approval.

Film-makers in cinema and television collaborate; individual artists shape their relationships with their collaborators according to their personality, ambitions and circumstances, and according to the economic, social and political contexts in which they work. Loach maintains long-term relationships with both collaborators and institutions throughout his career. On the one hand, he works closely with writers, producers and directors of photography; we need only think of the reputations and contributions of producers Tony Garnett and Sally Hibbin, writers Barry Hines and Jim Allen, or cinematographers Chris Menges and Barry Ackroyd to remind ourselves that Loach is a collaborator. To account for his work is to account for those collaborations. On the other hand, despite the influence of the BBC and of Channel 4 on his career, he has maintained an autonomous distance from mainstream institutions within the film and television industry. Some of his projects have been suppressed or handled with reluctance by their commissioners; but he has never had projects taken away from him; he has always maintained the option of 'final cut': 'It's never been a problem. I've never been in a situation where anybody else has moved in. I think that would be intolerable really. That's a different business.'[2] Because of his films' low budgets, in comparison with Hollywood, his control over projects is not surprising; but this book proposes that one result of this control is that despite his frequent testaments to the contributions of his collaborators a reference to Loach suggests stylistic and thematic consistencies. On the issue of authorship and films, Cavell maintains that:

> As long as a reference to a director by name suggests differences between the films associated with that name and ones associated with other such names, the reference is, so far as I can see, intellectually grounded. (Cavell 1996: 8–9)

This book recommends reasons that a reference to Ken Loach suggests differences from the work of other film-makers; I hope that the following chapters make these reasons evident.

CHAPTER ONE

clear notes in the concert

Carla's Song: the rhetoric of the unplanned shot

In Loach's 1996 film *Carla's Song*, written by Paul Laverty, one scene exemplifies a failure to resolve a problem that has consistently confronted the director. The film is set in Glasgow in 1987. George (Robert Carlyle) has stopped his younger sister, Eileen (Pamela Turner), on her way to school in order to talk to her. He has recently met and romanced a beautiful Nicaraguan refugee called Carla (Oyanka Cabezas). Initially intrigued by Carla, George discovers, after she attempts suicide, that her refusal to talk about herself is linked to a past trauma. George wants to help Carla tackle this trauma and in order to achieve this he accompanies her, later in the film, back to Nicaragua. Now, though, he wants to ask Eileen about Nicaragua. Loach uses a shot/reverse-shot sequence to present their conversation (figure 1).

Eileen:	There's a war. I've been doing it in modern studies.
George:	There's a wee bit a trouble, right enough.
Eileen:	A wee bit a trouble?
George:	Alright, a war.
Eileen:	A war. You've just no got a clue.
George:	Aye well, more or less.
Eileen:	More or less?
George:	Ach, Jesus Christ, can you stop repeating everything I say. It's really annoying.
Eileen:	George, this is embarrassing. There's the Contras. Contra means against. Against what? Against the revolution. Against the

Figure 1: *Carla's Song*

	Nicaraguan … government, who are led by the Sandi … nistas. Sandinistas are who kicked out the dictator, Samosa, in 1979, and this is what's confusing Father Murphy.
George:	What's confusing Father Murphy?
Eileen:	The US are calling them communists, but there's three priests in the government. And they're gonna screw the Sandinistas.
George:	The priests?
Eileen:	No you dumpling, the US.
George:	Oh, for fuck's sake, this is fuckin' confusin'.

Eileen appears to be no more than 14 or 15 years old; yet she clarifies the history behind Carla's trauma; apparently a priest at her school has provided her with this history.

While we could regard these things as plausible, other features of the scene and of its relationship to the film strain against expectations. Neither Pamela Turner nor Robert Carlyle appear comfortable with their lines. Eileen delivers her rhetorical question 'Against what?' with a practised ease that contrasts strongly with her delivery of the lines that follow, in particular with her hesitation between 'Nicaraguan' and 'government', and her stumble when she first mentions 'Sandinistas'. The hesitation and stumble are perhaps purposeful – they mean to reflect the character's efforts to remember the correct words, rather than the actor's; but Turner's abrupt veering between a confident delivery and a marked hesitation suggests instead that, struggling to handle some unwieldy lines and yet simultaneously imply that her character lacks confidence about her memory, she finds the exertion too much to control within a convincing performance. The excessive earnestness that George's nodding head and facial expression convey in the reverse-shot after Eileen stumbles on 'Sandinistas' compounds the sense of unwieldiness; Carlyle appears to encourage Turner not Eileen.

The laboured quality of the exchange increases when Loach and Laverty – they are responsible – interpolate the joke about Father Murphy. Carlyle and Turner can do little with this, and their helplessness only further exposes the scene to a derision that distances us from the characters and the film.

The distance originates in Loach and Laverty's use of a crude device to inform their imagined audience: Eileen functions as a cipher, used as a means of delivering information; George's supposed ignorance provides the occasion for that delivery. In his comprehensive essay on Loach and Jeremy Sandford's *Cathy Come Home* (1966), John Corner calls this kind of dialogue 'leaky', in that a conversation between two people 'leaks' information to the audience in a manner he finds familiar from British wartime propaganda and documentary films. He writes: 'There is often a tension between the requirements of the dramatically plausible and the requirement to get certain facts (and often figures) across to the viewer without resorting to graphics or commentary' (Corner 1996: 96). Corner's comments apply because the scene in *Carla's Song* represents a moment where the need to inform audiences overrides Loach and Laverty's concern with plausibility, dramatic or otherwise.

In the same film, however, another scene reverses this dynamic – plausibility, in the sense that what happens appears to happen not just for the camera – endows the scene with intense feeling and encourages closeness to not distance from the characters. George and Carla arrive in Nicaragua and search for Antonio, Carla's partner, whom Contra soldiers attacked and crippled. Carla witnessed this attack, and the Contras also wounded her; these events have since traumatised her (the film flashes back to these events with her nightmares). On their quest for Antonio the couple travel into the countryside on top of a bus, in the company of some Nicaraguan peasant farmers – *campesinos*. George speaks no Spanish, and he relies on Carla to translate; despite her trauma, Carla, speaking her own language, emerges as a more open and confident person than she appeared in Glasgow, with only a few words of English. At the start of their journey, the farmers ask George what he grows in his country. Following a long shot of the bus moving along a country road, a medium shot shows Carla sitting between two Nicaraguan men and one woman (figure 2). As Carla finishes translating the question into English, the camera pans to frame George, sitting on the opposite side of the bus. Mildly baffled, he replies: 'I dunno.' The *campesino* next to George asks him something. Carla translates: 'Any corn?' and the film cuts to a closer shot of her speaking. George replies off-screen, 'No'; Carla echoes this. The conversation continues, as does the shot/reverse-shot alternation. George is asked if beans or melons are grown in his country, to which he answers no, this time in a slightly closer shot. He then remembers that his country does produce something and, reaching into his bag, he retrieves a half-bottle of whisky, which he passes round to the *campesinos*, who are warmly appreciative.

Already in this scene of strangers becoming less strange to each other, Loach combines long takes and pans with shot/reverse-shot alternations. In the first shot of Carla the camera pans from her to George, as if following their conversation in an

Figure 2: *Carla's Song*

unplanned way: they talk and the camera responds to them. Yet immediately after this, a shot/reverse-shot alternation presents their conversation, with its ten shots becoming gradually closer to the characters. Loach establishes that the camera possesses the freedom to respond to the direction in which the characters take the conversation, but to avoid this device becoming repetitive and obtrusive he returns to a conventional shot/reverse shot alternation to present the rest of the conversation. The alternation breaks when two truckloads of cheering Sandinistas pass the bus; after this a long shot shows the bus stopping in a village. In a point-of-view shot taken from the top of the bus, young women approach, reaching up to sell refreshments to the passengers. The film cuts to George looking down, then to another point-of-view shot showing the women. Off-screen a man begins talking, and a subtitle translates his Spanish: 'We run a co-operative. Show your friend. He'll see how title deeds work here.' Loach cuts to Carla and the *campesino* that is speaking. The speaker passes the deed to her, and she looks at it before passing it to George. She translates for the *campesino*, but George is puzzled and he asks, framed in a medium close shot now, how the farmer got the land. Someone speaks in Spanish, and Carla translates: 'The revolution give the people, for the country.' The *campesino* sitting next to George speaks and two subtitles translate: 'It had one Somocista owner'; '… now we're 40 families'.

Other *campesinos* join in, and Loach continues to alternate between medium close shots of Carla and the men next to her and George and the man at his side. When George asks, 'What happens if the rich bastard comes back, the one guy?' Carla translates (off-screen), and the farmer on George's left answers. The camera pans slightly right to film him. Subtitles translate his answer: 'If the owner comes back, we're all united. We'll fight him with rifles and we'll beat him off again.' He gestures with his fist; and George smiles, commenting: 'I know what he's saying: they'll tell him to fuck off.' Now, the film introduces a woman who we have not yet seen, though she sits on the same side as George, closer to the camera. She says something – seemingly unprompted, joining in the conversation – and she too gestures with her fist. At first, her left hand enters the frame from the bottom right corner (figure 3); the camera responds to her gesturing hand by panning slowly right, until it frames only her in a close profile shot. She speaks quickly and intensely, and looks at Carla. A cut to a shot of Carla confirms that she listens attentively. She begins to translate.

The slow pan from George to the unknown woman enacts the film-makers' principle of endowing the camera with the potential to move responsively; the camera begins its pan as a response to her interjection and gesturing fist. The woman appears to lose her inhibitions and start describing her own experiences. The cut to a reverse-shot of Carla shows immediately that the woman's words affect her: sombre absorption replaces the lightness and jokiness of her earlier demeanour. While the woman speaks, the camera frames Carla, who listens intently. She pulls in her lips, nods her head slightly and pauses before translating for George: 'And she says that now everybody happy, because, because, everybody, they, *compañeros* give the *sangre*, give the blood, for the revolution and now everybody defend this revolution.' Carla stumbles as she translates for George: the Nicaraguan woman had said '*la sangre des compañeros*' and Carla, moved by these words and the feeling with which they are spoken, forgets, momentarily, to translate them. As she talks, she hesitates; her voice becomes tremulous and her eyes fill with tears. Unlike Pamela Turner's mannered stumbles and hesitations when she tells George about Nicaragua, here Oyanka Cabezas seems to forget that she is acting for a camera; instead she responds to the woman's words almost involuntarily, with what looks like a genuine expression of feeling. The way these words move Cabezas appears unplanned: the sense of this stems from both Cabezas' affecting response and the camera's revelation of the Nicaraguan woman as it pans round to discover her. The camera's ability to respond to accidents of conversation has already been established, for the pan from Carla to George which opens this scene

Figure 3: *Carla's Song*

prepares us for the larger, more significant discovery that it now makes when it pans from George to the unknown woman.

The film cuts from Carla translating to George listening; it then cuts back to her before panning slightly left to another man, who says in Spanish: 'We'll resist because it's our revolution and nobody can take it away from us.' Before Carla can translate, someone else says something. The camera pans back to her and, as she starts to translate, tears run down her right cheek. Loach then cuts back to the woman on George's left, who is shot so that the bottom of the frame underlines her outstretched arm. As this woman talks passionately, the camera pans back to Carla, who again translates: 'And she says now everybody defend this revolution because this revolution is for people, young people, children, old people – and everybody can't forget, every, everybody, *todo compañeros*, all *compañeros*, that give the life for this revolution, and everybody together.' As she momentarily forgot to translate the word '*sangre*', here Cabezas initially forgets, or struggles to remember, how to translate '*todo*'. It is the act of translating the woman's Spanish, which is to say it is the act of speaking these words herself, that provokes Cabezas' tears; while she translates, she continues to cry unselfconsciously. It appears that Cabezas as much as Carla responds here; again, the sense of this derives from her performance and the film's presentation of her response in its pan to her before she translates. A final cut to George reveals him reaching across the bus to clasp Carla's hand and kiss it. Carlyle's eyes indicate that he too is close to tears, that Cabezas' response has moved him: he tilts his head slightly, purses his lips and looks directly at her, as if offering support. The scene ends by panning back to Carla.

The combination of long-take pans and shot/reverse-shot alternations is important in this scene. Loach, the director of photography, Barry Ackroyd, and the editor, Jonathon Morris, create this combination with care. Crucially, the two shots that reveal Carla responding emotionally to what she hears and then says both begin as pans to her from the speaker who moves her to tears. Loach and Ackroyd seem to discover Carla's reaction and then pan to include it in the film. This does not explain the emotional intensity of the brief scene, however. That intensity begins when the farmer takes out the deeds and shows them to George – this, one imagines, was scripted and planned: as the point of the scene with Eileen was to leak to an imagined audience a brief account of the war in Nicaragua in 1987, so the point of this scene is to show something of the revolutionary spirit of collectivism and how it benefits the peasant farmers – yet only when the conversation shifts to the human losses incurred does Carla begin to respond emotionally.

This moment of emotional intensity enables us to feel close to the people in the film, to feel that we are empathising with them; and throughout this scene there is a powerful sense of the film-makers witnessing the feelings and spirit of Oyanka Cabezas and the other Nicaraguans. Central to our understanding of this intensity is the degree to which we respond to the sense of authenticity that the people on top of the bus bring to the scene: these are not professional actors drafted in to play Nicaraguans, but real Nicaraguans to whom the words that they speak mean something. The Nicaraguan woman asserts her independence in the presence of the film-makers and says what she feels; apparently, she interjects spontaneously into a scripted conversation. The cameraman's and the director's prepared ability to respond to this kind of interjection facilitates the creation of a sense of authenticity. This scene and the earlier one with Eileen exemplify the characteristic strengths and weaknesses of Loach's work.

It is unsurprising that artists whose political beliefs differ from those of dominant ideologies often experience difficulties creating works that are coherent and complex, and that resonate with their political beliefs while avoiding didacticism. As Andrew Britton observes, 'uncertainties of realisation ... are in fact very commonly to be found in works of art which have the courage and integrity to project a radical utopia beyond the existing reality principle' (Britton 1992: 59). A continuing challenge for Loach has been to discover how to inform *and* to entertain audiences, yet ensure that the artwork does not resemble a manifesto; avoiding, for example, moments where the characters make speeches as if they are mouthpieces for his or his writer's views. Loach is a socialist, and a creative problem that he and his writers have encountered has been the question of how to dramatise issues that they feel strongly about in ways that incorporate a sense of social and political forces, and make arguments about those forces in films that remain attractive to large audiences. Distinguishing between personal and impersonal narrative causality is not straightforward; nevertheless, much of this book examines the diverse methods Loach employs in trying to film relationships between individuals and the social and political forces which, he believes, influence our lives.

In the scene in *Carla's Song* with George and his sister, Loach and Laverty leak historical information; but for the sake of clarity they sacrifice nuance, plausibility and authenticity. Conversely, the scene on top of the bus is nuanced in its combination of long takes and shot/reverse-shot alternations, plausible and authentic, to the extent that the camera appears to document Cabezas' true reactions. Loach claims that he was mixing documentary and fiction when he shot this scene: the *campesinos* recounted their real experiences, and their words upset Cabezas and Carlyle. As he tells Graham Fuller: 'The scene on the bus touched Oyanka particularly, because of the transparent honesty of the *campesinos* and the fact that many had lost family members in the war' (Fuller 1998: 107). To Susan Ryan and Richard Porton, he says:

> Among the Nicaraguans, there's only one actor. The rest are just people, extraordinary people. The woman who plays Carla's mother, for example, had been in the Sandinista army and was then working on community projects. Almost all the people we met had relatives killed during the war. There was a feeling of being very close to the carnage. For example, the scene on top of the bus was not even like a reenactment. People were just talking about the revolution; the only sense in which it was a reenactment was that people were talking about the present, whereas these events had occurred in the past. The

boundaries of what was real and what was invented for the film were very loose. In a way, this made it difficult to keep a tight rein on the film's structure. It was nice to be open to whatever came our way, but the problem with that approach is that you're liable to lose the shape of the film. (Ryan & Porton 1998: 26–7)

Carla's Song is a fiction film, yet Loach describes how he employs the strategies of a documentary film-maker; for example, he takes a camera to places rarely seen in mainstream cinema fiction; he brings people into the film and encourages them to speak: these things in themselves can produce vitality and richness. Alluding to this potential for richness, Stephen Frears points to the entrance of the games teacher, Sugden (played by Brian Glover, a teacher at a school near the location and a friend of the film's writer, Barry Hines), in *Kes* (1969):

> I can't think of any better entrance in a British film – now I'll make a preposterous claim; well, that's like Orson Welles in *The Third Man*, isn't it? It's on that sort of level. Just one moment, and a whole sort of world is exposed; that whole world, that teacher and that wonderful man arrived. Well that's extraordinary.[1]

Loach's decision of where to film and whom to film contributes to the rendering of moments that can expose a 'whole sort of world'. One variable in his style is the degree to which he integrates this potential for richness, which is present in his earliest work, with control of the shape and structure of his films; more attention to these elements allows him to develop metaphors for his politics, the games lesson scene in *Kes* being an example of such a metaphor.

The intensity of the scene on the bus in *Carla's Song* only partly comes from the sense that the film documents real people and real places. Loach discusses the benefits of leaving oneself open to respond to 'whatever came our way'; yet he also identifies the difficulty of achieving a convincing sense of the characters' autonomy from their authors while keeping a 'tight rein' on them and on the structure to which they relate. In an essay on Alexander Dumas the younger, Henry James writes about this issue of autonomy:

> His characters are all pointed by observation, they are clear notes in the concert, but not one of them has known the little invisible push that, even when shyly and awkwardly administered, makes the puppet, in spite of the string, walk off by himself and quite 'cut', if the mood takes him, that distant relation his creator. (James 1949: 275)

Differences exist between characters in plays and characters in films, yet we can transfer James's use of the metaphor of puppets for characters, manipulated by their creators, between the two media: the metaphor encapsulates some of the problems with the scene in which Loach and Laverty pull Eileen's 'strings' to ensure that her dialogue with George leaks the necessary information.

In her largely favourable review of Loach and Laverty's follow up to *Carla's Song*, *My Name is Joe* (1998), Judith Williamson criticises Loach in terms that recall those in which James criticises Dumas the younger. She directs her readers to a scene in which circumstances relating to his involvement with drugs and crime force the central character, Joe (Peter Mullan), a recovering alcoholic, to confront the woman, Sarah (Louise Goodall), with whom he has recently begun a relationship. Williamson writes: 'The moral [of the film] is contained in Joe's keynote speech (in Loach films there is always a keynote speech) to Sarah in which he tells her that he doesn't live in a "tidy wee world" like hers, and asks her what she would have done' (Williamson 1998: 58). Williamson's reference to the 'keynote speech' in Loach's films typifies a recurrent criticism of his work; it correlates, for example, with my own criticism of the scene between Eileen and George in *Carla's Song*, except that Mullan and Goodall are considerably more experienced performers than Pamela Turner and this scene and *My Name is Joe* are more effectively written and shaped.[2] We can summarise the recurring issue, though, as the problem of how to incorporate politics into mainstream fiction films without making the speeches sound as 'clear notes in the concert'. In his book on James and revision, Philip Horne expounds the James quotation thus:

> The wit of 'cut' is relevant here, for James admits that the 'string' can't be severed while asserting that the artist's created character, even if only through the dictates of consistency with himself or herself, can put up an authentic resistance to the artist's will. It will always be open to the reader to take the author's creation of the illusion that the characters walk off by themselves as sinister, but for James and his sympathetic readers it is morally valuable. (Horne 1990: 66)

That we occasionally feel that the characters might 'walk off by themselves', beyond the camera's frame, is one way of considering the realism of Loach's best work. Horne additionally introduces an important idea: unsympathetic readers or viewers might regard the creation of realistic characters as a sinister illusion.

Politically orientated accounts of mainstream fiction films frequently describe the illusion of realism as sinister: critical responses to Loach's work often doubt the efficacy of realism in promoting political activism. As a critical term, realism has been so widely used that it can be meaningless unless qualified; a brief account of its use in relation to Loach's work is necessary. In 1975, there were several published responses to the four feature-length episodes of *Days of Hope*.[3] Two articles, one written by Colin McArthur and the other by Colin MacCabe, raised issues that were to recur.[4] In an earlier piece, MacCabe describes the features of the 'classic realist text': the illusion of transparency, narrative closure, a concentration on individual drama and, therefore, an inability to deal with the complexities and contradictions of a world in which ideological forces determine lives. MacCabe's list of examples of classic realist texts includes *Middlemarch* (George Eliot, 1871–2) and, as books and films, *Toad of Toad Hall*, *The Grapes of Wrath* and *The Sound of Music*.[5] There can be, he argues, progressive content in classic realist texts – he cites as examples the films of Costa-Gavras or 'such television documentaries as *Cathy Come Home*' (MacCabe 1974: 16);[6] yet, for MacCabe the form of classic realism itself undermines radical political intentions.

In his short critique of the four films of *Days of Hope*, Colin McArthur draws on MacCabe's formula of the classic realist text. Both critics argue that Loach, Allen and Garnett's commitment to the form of the classic realist text inhibits their radical intentions. MacCabe advocates modernist techniques of self-reflexivity and Brechtian principles of epic theatre.[7] He follows Brecht's definition of epic theatre in the programme notes to Brecht's and Kurt Weill's *Rise and Fall of the City of Mahagonny* as that in which there is a radical separation of the constitutive elements of the text, proposing that only critical distance politicises audiences. Much of his argument reduces complex issues, and numerous critics have since outlined the limitations of the concept of the classic realist text.[8] Julian Petley distinguishes between two uses of the term realism in film studies:

> The first is wide-ranging: here a work is considered realist simply if it is a lifelike or a faithful copying of reality. Since most films ask us to believe that their diegetic world is 'real', these films can all be considered, in Colin MacCabe's phrase, as 'classic realist texts'. The second use is narrower and more or less synonymous with the term 'naturalist', indicating a searching out and detailed observation of elements of the social environment frequently excluded from systems of representation. In cinematic terms this normally means an emphasis on working-class or 'problem' subjects, like *Saturday Night and Sunday Morning* (Karel Reisz, 1960) or *Poor Cow* (Ken Loach, 1967). (Petley 1992a: 101)

Petley's second use of realism includes Loach's work and the Italian neo-realist films of Roberto Rossellini, Vittorio De Sica and Luchino Visconti.[9] MacCabe's concept reduces and limits because it fails to distinguish between the uses of the term realism that Petley identifies.

As a theoretical model within film and television studies, the classic realist text is soon overtaken by the notion of the classical Hollywood film – although this too raises problems:[10] Christopher Williams argues that both the classic realist text and the classical Hollywood film are two 'parallel fantasy monoliths' (Williams 1994: 276). Andrew Britton criticises the 'inane formalism' of MacCabe's model (Britton 1982: 95), while George M. Wilson discusses the problems of the classic realist text in detail, concluding:

> It is in classical narrative film alone that a more or less determinate fictional history is portrayed by visual narration, which can simultaneously sustain both

a salient, standard perspective and a distinct, oblique perspective, both of which may be equally and continuously coherent. (Wilson 1996: 198)

In her article on Loach, Deborah Knight builds on Wilson's comprehensive untangling of MacCabe's ideas to suggest that Loach is a 'critical realist' (Knight 1997: 68). Nonetheless, despite criticism of the classic realist text model, in writing about Loach, arguments about realism continue, and the formula of the classic realist text demonstrates a surprising longevity: Colin McArthur, John Caughie, Derek Paget and John Hill all use it as a theoretical model.[11] In *Sex, Class and Realism: British Cinema 1956–63*, for example, Hill cites *Days of Hope* as an example of the political inadequacy of films where there is new content but no new form:

> It was an adoption of the form of realism which effectively militated against an explication of the social and economic forces leading to the collapse of the General Strike. The film's formal logic (with its dependency on the visible and hence the interpersonal) inevitably led towards conspiracy theory, the attribution of the strike's failure to the betrayal of trade union leaders. (Hill 1986: 60)

Hill endorses MacCabe's claims about the applicability of the classic realist text, using a wider concept of ontological realism (the image as transparent) to judge and criticise work often thought to fall within a narrower definition of realism (a subject not necessarily filmed before).[12]

Hill later concludes that 'Loach is a formidable film-maker whose continuing commitment to using film for political purposes places him in an uniquely important position in British cinema. As such, his work demands both attention and respect' (Hill 1997a: 139). However, this comes at the end of an essay in which Hill argues that Loach consistently fails to find a form for expressing his political beliefs. Hill describes Loach and Trevor Griffiths' *Fatherland* (1986) as a confused European art film and labels Loach and Jim Allen's *Hidden Agenda* (1990) pejoratively as a genre thriller.[13] He recapitulates arguments about politics and realism, comparing the films of Jean-Luc Godard, which 'demonstrated an insistence on the need for revolutionary messages (or content) to be accompanied by an appropriate revolutionary form', and the films of Costa-Gavras, which 'sought to bend mainstream Hollywood conventions to radical political ends' (Hill 1997a: 131). The spectre of the classic realist text advances when Hill claims that films with a 'revolutionary form' are preferable, because, 'Hollywood's narrative conventions encourage explanations of social realities in individual and psychological terms, rather than economic and political ones' (Hill 1997a: 132). Hill claims to be only revisiting the criticisms of realism and the political thriller, rather than advocating an ideal Godardian or Brechtian model of political cinema – he points to the shortcomings of the 'traditional critique of [classic] realism' (Hill 1997a: note 33, 142–3); nevertheless, he judges *Hidden Agenda*'s 'tendency towards personalisation' negatively, arguing that as a political conspiracy thriller it dramatises individual actions, rather than 'underlying social and economic forces' (Hill 1997a: 132). What George Wilson calls MacCabe's 'dark allegations about their [classical narrative films'] putative limitations' (Wilson 1996: 194), and what Philip Horne conveys with his 'sinister' illusion (Horne 1990: 66), Andrew Britton regards as tendentious:

> Hollywood movies are indeed 'obviously' character-centred, but it is by no means obvious that 'personal or psychological causality' is *therefore* 'the arma-ture of the classical story.' *Why* should 'character-centred' narrative causality necessarily imply *personal* causality? – and why should it be by definition incompatible with that 'causality of institutions and group processes' for which Soviet films of the 1920s strike Mr Bordwell as being so supremely remarkable? (Britton 1988–89: 52)

Rightly, Hill observes that Loach, particularly in his later films, 'bends mainstream Hollywood conventions to radical political ends'; but those conventions are not in themselves sinister.

Critics have used various methodologies and terminologies to discuss the aesthetic conventions in Loach's work. The combined use of the long take and pan in the scene on the bus in *Carla's Song* seems to guarantee the authenticity of the scene and the autonomy of the people who perform for the camera. In a 1977 interview Loach describes the responsiveness of his camera in *Days of Hope*:

> If you are making a documentary and there was just a cameraman in the room and he was following the conversation, he would never be at somebody when they started to speak. He would follow the conversation. That's what we tried to do really, to let the conversation call for the cuts, rather than the camera knowing who was going to speak next and, therefore, always being in at the start of a sentence. (quoted in O'Hara 1977: 301)

John Caughie takes up Loach's comments. Before quoting them he writes:

> The point of interest is that all of these strategies of the documentary look rely less on the guarantees of their own reflection of the real world and more on a reference to other formal conventions which are associated with reflection. At another, and I think more fundamental level, the documentary look finds its consistency in the rhetoric of the 'unplanned' shot or 'unpremeditated' shot: the camera surprised by the action. (Caughie 1980: 28)

Caughie, like MacCabe, is more sceptical than I am about the ontological basis of the medium of film – its capacity, that is, not to reflect the world, but to reveal it; yet, his phrase 'the rhetoric of the "unplanned" shot' powerfully evokes a key visual trope in Loach's work. Rather than anticipating the movements or dialogue of the characters, the camera appears to respond to them.

John Corner, writing about *Cathy Come Home* in his book on documentary, identifies similar camera and performance strategies when he argues that Loach films Cathy and Reg's story with 'some of the stylistic markers of action-led camera' (Corner 1996: 99). He detects its use when bailiffs evict Cathy and Reg:

> Stability of frame and composure of *mise-en-scène* give way to a visualisation appearing to have caught a real incident and filmed it within the limitations which such filming entails in respect of camera positions, steadiness of composition, the following of action, a soundtrack containing 'incidental' sounds, and so on. (Corner 1996: 99)

Whether one describes it as the unplanned shot or the action-led camera, Loach uses this technique throughout his career; and, as Caughie notes, the unplanned shot belongs to a rhetoric, often an aggressively emphatic one. Nevertheless, as Stephen Frears observes, Loach's work does occasionally expose, in a moment, a 'whole sort of world' in what frequently feels like an unplanned way. When Carla cries on the bus, one senses unresolved issues of anger, loss and grief opening up; one feels, as Loach puts it, 'close to the carnage'. Some of the anxieties that have bedevilled critical writing on Loach's work begin with scepticism about the 'sinister' illusion of being close to an event that appears to have been filmed in an unplanned way.[14]

Loach's films often try to convince viewers of a political belief; they also strive to convince one of their authenticity. Renowned for spending a lot of time casting his main actors, the director usually tries to cast in the lead someone whom he feels can bring to the part the requisite experience. He justifies this process as follows:

> There are really two sorts of acting. There's theatre acting and there is film acting, I think, which can be something different, where somebody can be taken through a story and experience the story and put themselves in that position and respond as they would respond. So that you're really experiencing that person in that story. And I guess that's what we've tried to do, over the years. I mean that's developed into a way of working ... So that, in a way ... when we make the film, they'll obviously be going through the experience of the character, and the character as written, but in a sense it may be, in part, a sort of documentary about them as well.[15]

When Carla cries it can seem as if Cabezas is not performing, but is moved to tears by the Nicaraguan woman's words; a large part of the scene's power comes from its plausibility and its authenticity. Yet this is an isolated moment in a film that, on the whole, inclines towards the implausible and the inauthentic. A more sustained and integrated performance of emotional power and authenticity is that of Crissy Rock in *Ladybird Ladybird* (1994). In this film Loach combines emotional intensity and plausibility with a more crafted narrative structure: at no point do he and the film's writer, Rona Munro, resort to 'leaky dialogue' of the kind that *Carla's Song* features.

Robin Wood, writing of Hitchcock's films with Ingrid Bergman, discusses emotional authenticity in terms that could describe many of the performances in Loach's films. He writes:

> Again, it needs to be stressed that one is speaking of a construction rather than a reality – of something that is *acted* but which gives the impression of transcending 'mere' acting. One variation of this is the 'Method' school, with its emphasis on entering into, 'becoming', the character. More generally, it is manifested in the acting of emotional extremes, 'tearing a passion to tatters'. One thinks at once of Anna Magnani, and recalls that it was Magnani's performance in *Rome, Open City* [1945] that first inspired Bergman to seek a (professional) relationship with Rossellini. (Wood 1989: 315)

Wood's phrase 'the acting of emotional extremes' invokes a quality on which Loach's performers often depend. Wood also evokes the cycle of Italian neo-realist films to which Loach's films are linked (and to which Loach links his films): continuities exist between Magnani's performance in *Rome, Open City* and those of Rock in *Ladybird Ladybird*, David Bradley in *Kes*, Bill Dean and Sandy Ratcliff in *Family Life* (1971), Rosana Pastor and Ian Hart in *Land and Freedom* (1995), and Pilar Padilla and Elpidia Carillo in *Bread and Roses* (2000). However, the authenticity of these performances depends upon the careful orchestration of emotional crescendos. These crescendos, built into a film through the interaction of different elements, connect Loach's work to the narrative structures of melodrama.[16]

Loach is not a realist film-maker if one takes that phrase to evoke a film-maker who presents the action of his films from an 'objective' viewpoint; on the contrary, his films usually direct our attention to events on screen from a sharply defined perspective. John Hill writes:

> Indeed, much of the power to unsettle in Loach's work derives from the apparent impassivity of his cinematic style in relation to the disturbing events in front of the camera. But though his films are shot from a distanced observational standpoint, many of them rely on the dramatic machinery of melodrama: impossible choices, misjudgements, coincidences, a foreshortened sense of cause and effect. (Hill 1998: 20)

Referring to melodrama, Hill calls attention to a significant feature of Loach's work, even though he still hints at allegations of a 'dark' and 'sinister' emotional involvement with films centred on 'interpersonal relations'. He argues, for instance, that, 'what separates Loach's work from conventional melodrama is the way it discourages too strong an emotional identification with the characters while insisting on the economic and social underpinnings of their actions' (Hill 1998: 20). Hill praises Loach's work, but his words betray dissatisfaction with 'conventional melodrama', to which he alludes without offering examples. The implication of a negative evaluation of melodrama hides in the phantom insinuation that 'conventional melodrama' can encourage an identification with characters that is excessively and undesirably emotional. Moreover, the suggestive phrase 'the dramatic machinery of melodrama' opens out negatively: Loach's films, according to Hill, 'rely' upon what he evokes as a mechanical handling of the conventions of melodrama. Hill apparently uses the term melodrama in its pejorative sense. He confirms this when he writes, 'For all Loach's reputation as a political film-maker, his films tend to be played out on the melodramatic terrain of domestic and family relations' (Hill 1998: 21). Skirting the issue of whether or not the 'terrain' of domesticity and family life is a political one, Hill's comments assert that Loach's reputation is essentially undeserved.[17]

Apart from the misleading equation of 'cinematic style' with the formal techniques of the camera, excluding from an account of style the 'disturbing events in front of the camera', Hill's suggestion about the 'impassivity' of Loach's photographic style is still inaccurate: there is nothing impassive about the 'cinematic style' in the two sequences discussed from *Carla's Song*. Hill proposes that 'Loach's films rarely ask us to identify with characters so much as to observe, and understand their predicaments' (Hill 1998: 19). He thus invokes the dichotomy between identification and understanding that lies behind MacCabe's classic realist text. In fact, as I argue throughout this book, Loach goes to considerable lengths to encourage us to share the epistemic and emotional perspective of characters, of Billy in *Kes*, of Maggie in *Ladybird Ladybird* or of David in *Land and Freedom*. The director attempts to encourage audiences to observe and to understand the characters in his films, and to do so by generating empathetic feelings, by having us feel close to, and emotionally engaged with, the characters. Hill is uneasy with this mode, which he appears to regard as a virtual prison from which one is incapable of understanding one's position in society and culture.

We can roughly separate melodrama criticism in film studies into two strands: that which analyses expressive codes, and that which analyses narrative structures. The separation is convenient rather than wholly accurate because it is difficult to maintain a convincing distinction between a narrative event and the filmic expression of that event; it reflects, though, dominant trends in film studies.[18] Thomas Elsaesser provides an example of the former approach, describing melodrama as 'a particular form of dramatic *mise-en-scène*, characterised by a dynamic use of spatial and musical categories, as opposed to intellectual or literary ones' (Elsaesser 1987: 51). Elsaesser argues that regarding melodrama as a 'dramatic narrative in which musical accompaniment marks the emotional effects' is useful 'because it allows melodramatic elements to be seen as constituents of a system of punctuation, giving expressive colour and chromatic contrast to the story-line, by orchestrating the emotional ups and downs of the intrigue' (Elsaesser 1987: 50). Some critics have questioned Elsaesser's approach, but his description remains relevant and it influences this discussion of Loach's work.[19] Nonetheless, judging melodramas by their formal excess can limit attention to films that exhibit an apparently 'excessive' style. The notion of excess is problematic because it presupposes something already fixed and understood (a plot or the action) of which the film's 'form' can be in excess. As V. F. Perkins emphasises, because every part of a film is potentially significant, that we cannot make a 'neat distinction' (Perkins 1990b: 1–2) between the action of a film and the expression of that action before we consider and evaluate what is significantly expressive in a film.

Christine Gledhill summarises film melodrama in her introduction to an anthology on the subject:

> Melodrama utilises narrative mechanisms that create a blockage in expression, thereby forcing melodramatic enactments into alternative and excessive strategies to clarify the dramatic stakes. Characteristically the melodramatic plot turns on an initial, often deliberately engineered, misrecognition of the innocence of a central protagonist. By definition the innocent cannot use the powers available to the villain; following the dictates of their nature, they must become victims, a position legitimated by a range of devices which rationalises their apparent inaction on their own behalf. (Gledhill 1987: 30)

Gledhill too posits a separation between 'narrative mechanisms' and the 'excessive strategies' of melodrama, but her characterisation of melodramatic plots supports the argument about Loach's work because of the way that so many of his characters are misrecognised innocents; for example, Cathy in *Cathy Come Home* (1966), Billy in *Kes* (1969), Janice in *Family Life* (1971), Bob in *Raining Stones* (1993) and Maggie in *Ladybird Ladybird* (1994). Steve Neale, in 'Melodrama and Tears', his insightful essay on narrative structure and the affective pleasures of melodrama, draws on work by Franco Moretti to discuss 'the pleasure of being touched and giving way to tears' that is such a crucial feature of watching melodramas (Neale 1986: 6). Neale develops Moretti's notion of the importance of disproportion as a key melodramatic convention for promoting outrage and tears in the audience:

> In as much as there is little causal preparation for the way events unfold, the generic verisimilitude of melodrama tends to be marked by the extent to which the succession and course of events is unmotivated (or undermotivated) from a realist point of view, such preparation and motivation as does exist is always 'insufficient'. There is an *excess* of effect over cause, of the extraordinary over the ordinary. (Neale 1986: 6–7)

The notion of narrative disproportion pertains because Loach's films often restrict the presentation of narrative information, privileging one view of events.

Another critic who writes about misrecognition and disproportion and in doing so links Loach's work to the history of melodrama in American cinema is Michael Walker. Developing work done by Robert Heilman and James Smith on stage melodrama, Walker uses melodrama as a neutral, descriptive term rather than as a derogatory one. Robert Heilman proposes that tragedy and melodrama are two alternative structures. He writes: 'In tragedy the conflict is within man; in melodrama, it is between men, or between men and things' (Heilman 1968: 79). Heilman suggests that melodrama is the realm of social action and tragedy the realm of private action; in the former the world is divided, while in the latter the self is divided. Walker summarises Heilman's 'divided world' theory:

> The hero of melodrama is himself undivided, 'whole', free from the tensions of choosing between conflicting loyalties, imperatives or desires. The forces with which such a hero must grapple are external: oppression, corruption, villainy in general, 'natural' disasters. (Walker 1982: 2)

Walker's summary of the forces which a hero or, as Gledhill formulates it, a victim, faces corresponds to the range of impersonal, institutional and ideological forces that a number of Loach characters confront; and he connects the misfortunes that befall characters in Loach's melodramas to a history of melodramatic structures.[20] Walker points out that considering melodrama as a narrative structure allows us to apply it to a range of settings, although certain settings, he contends, are more inherently dramatic than others: upper-class settings allow opulence to lead to 'intrigue, decadence and vice'; lower-class settings allow poverty to lead to 'suffering, crime and violence'. One advantage of regarding melodrama as a genre structure is that it attempts to avoid the word's qualitative overtones; attempts only, because, as Walker points out, the tragic structure of a divided character often permits greater complexity.

In defining melodrama, a crucial consideration for Walker is ideology, and he argues:

> To achieve 'full tragic awareness', the characters must in some sense come to understand the nature of the forces which impel them, the choices which confront them. Otherwise they remain characters of melodrama, acting 'blindly', to a greater or lesser extent at the mercy of ideological forces. (Walker 1982: 4–5)

Loach's characters rarely achieve 'full tragic awareness'; frequently his characters remain at the mercy of the ideological forces that impel them. His films scrutinise the way that ideological forces, apparently existing at an abstract level, can determine people's lives, to the extent that his heroes often have no powers to resolve their problems or to change their lives. Extending his discussion of the role of ideology in melodrama, Walker introduces James Smith's distinction between melodramas of triumph, of defeat and of protest (Smith 1973). Walker discusses the paradigmatic structures of climax and suspense in D. W. Griffith's melodramas, and points out that *Cathy Come Home* 'reprises Mae Marsh's helpless fight to keep her baby' in *Intolerance* (1916) (Walker 1982: 6). He concludes that what makes the comparison germane, beyond the fact that the separation of a mother and child is apt to upset audiences, is that both films are melodramas of protest. Smith identifies the melodrama of protest by its aims: 'to stimulate awareness, question established values, expose injustice, champion reform, fuel argument on ways and means and sometimes to incite direct support for bloody revolution' (Smith 1973: 72). Following Smith, Walker proposes that films like *Cathy Come Home, Intolerance, Rome, Open City* (1945), *Battleship Potemkin* (1925), *One Flew Over the Cuckoo's Nest* (1975) and *Dances with Wolves* (1990) continue to use the structure of the melodrama of protest, and he finds that one of its basic devices is the death of an innocent. Loach and his writers employ this device in several films, either literally (*Hidden Agenda* (1990), *Land and Freedom, My Name is Joe* (1998), *The Navigators* (2001)) or metaphorically (*Cathy Come Home, Kes, Family Life, Ladybird Ladybird*). In the melodrama of protest, Walker argues:

> The world depicted is completely polarised, and our sympathies are enlisted unequivocally with a group of people – defined by race, nationality, class or political creed – who are 'innocents', victims of persecution, exploitation or oppression … Like all melodramas of protest, these films are in effect propaganda. They all use the death of the 'innocent', or indeed, innocents (in *Battleship Potemkin*, both Vakulinchuk's death and the Odessa steps massacre are focal points) as an emotional device to rouse not just the people in the film, but those in the audience as well. (Walker 1982: 14)

The melodrama of protest attempts to rouse the audience, to activate a sense of outrage at the injustices or atrocities of the authorities against an innocent protagonist. Loach has made melodramas of protest throughout his career, from *Cathy Come Home* to *Bread and Roses* (2000), using a range of strategies to bring political and social protest into mainstream fiction films. The degree to which we *experience* his films as political propaganda depends upon the extent to which the director and his collaborators have been able to integrate the devices of the melodrama of protest with characters and stories that carry conviction and plausibility. Eileen's talk with George exemplifies a moment in Loach's work where the edifying and instructive impulses of the melodrama of protest overwhelm other considerations; at this moment in *Carla's Song* the director seems unwilling to risk ambiguity or vagueness, yet in his best work he succeeds in avoiding such didacticism.

CHAPTER TWO

what to do with a camera

This chapter examines the aesthetic strategies of Ken Loach's early work by focusing on *Up the Junction* (1965), *Cathy Come Home* (1966) and *Poor Cow* (1967). Understanding Loach's type of authorship depends on acknowledging two things: first, he is a strong collaborator, and I will discuss his collaboration with Nell Dunn in adapting her books; second, his style changes radically throughout his career. *Up the Junction*, *Cathy Come Home* and *Poor Cow* take as their general themes the way that ideological forces often shape the lives of working-class women. These three films, two made for the BBC's celebrated *Wednesday Play* series and one made for the cinema, express this theme with a striking combination of the diagrammatic and digressive. All Loach's work of the mid-1960s shows the equivocal influence of Brechtian techniques. I will trace this influence by examining the use of music and the varying narrational modes in *Up the Junction*, *Cathy Come Home* and *Poor Cow*.

In 1962 the Pilkington Report authorised the launching of BBC2, and the BBC, in preparation for the launch of its second channel in April 1964, employed many new members of staff, including Ken Loach. The director recalls the experience:

> There was a six-week course at the BBC for new directors from all departments: documentary, news, films and even radio. But above all we learnt how the BBC worked. A wardrobe assistant, for example, came to explain that we had to fill in forms requesting costumes three weeks in advance, otherwise we wouldn't get them in time. There was only half a day entitled 'What to do with a camera'. The majority of the course consisted of wandering the corridors of the BBC trying to find your way. (Ostria 1994a: 37)

Loach's first assignment was directing one episode of a drama series called *Teletale*. In the run-up to the start of BBC2, the drama department produced short dramas that provided opportunities for new writers and directors fresh from the trainee course. The Head of Drama, Sydney Newman, commissioned *Teletale* from producer James MacTaggart and writer/script editor Roger Smith. Smith would become a significant collaborator of Loach's, working as a script editor on his *Wednesday Play* films, and then thirty years later as a script consultant on *Land and Freedom* (1995), *My Name is Joe* (1998), *Bread and Roses* (2000) and *The Navigators* (2001). In directing his episode of *Teletale*, called 'Catherine' (1964),[1] Loach also met another collaborator – Tony Garnett, who was acting in it. Garnett would become his producer for 15 years, from *Cathy Come Home* until *Black Jack* (1979).

Roger Smith and Christopher Williams wrote a proposal for the Deputy Head of Drama, Elwyn Jones, suggesting 13 30-minute stories for *Teletale*:

> The stories will be told with maximum economy and condensation. The juxtaposition of scenes and the cutting between them will be crucial to the narrative. The style of narration will be fluid, using and exploring the resources of framing, camera mobility and studio space. Narrative and camera will select the relevant 'information' in each scene. We hope that this method will allow us to liberate the action from the accepted necessities of naturalism, while not detracting from the interest of the story.[2]

Two points can be made about the writers' desire 'to liberate the action from the accepted necessities of naturalism'. The first is aesthetic in that their aims connect with the interest in loosely Brechtian stylistics in the 1960s that attracted Loach at the beginning of his career. The second is technological in that Loach began directing television drama during a transitional period, when shooting on film was replacing live studio broadcasts; although despite the technological advances, the television industry remained committed to live television drama for some time.[3] The writers' desire for liberation is partly a desire to escape from the studio and to abandon a tradition they perceive as artificial; this desire for realism galvanises Loach and his contemporaries into shooting television drama on film. Rebelling against the live studio broadcast motivates some of Loach's early artistic decisions. Smith and Williams seek more realism, but their 'accepted necessities of naturalism' refers to the tradition of live studio broadcasts. It was the same perceived constraints of television naturalism that Troy Kennedy Martin and John McGrath sought to shake off when, following their departure from *Z Cars*,[4] they wrote *Diary of a Young Man* in six episodes, for which Loach directed episodes one, three and five.[5]

Diary of a Young Man chronicles the adventures of two young men, Joe (Victor Henry) and Ginger (Richard Moore), who travel to London from the North of England looking for work. Joe keeps the 'diary' and his voice-over communicates his entries. Episode one mixes studio-shot material, still photographs, archive footage and film shot on location; its makers experiment with techniques in an effort to jolt the audience. Kennedy Martin accompanied the programme with a repudiation of past efforts, setting out his ideas for radical television drama, in opposition to 'boring naturalism', in an article entitled 'Nats go Home: First Statement of a New Drama for Television' (1964), published in the 'vital theatre' magazine, *Encore*, a month before the transmission of *Diary of a Young Man*.

After the broadcast of the first episode, Sydney Newman sent this memo to its production team:

> The first episode of *Diary of a Young Man* will be regarded in the years to come as a major breakthrough in television storytelling as *No Trams to Lime Street* [Newman's *Armchair Theatre* production] was five-and-a-half years ago. From what I understand of the remaining five episodes this is a dead cert. I could be wrong, but for sheer variety in the total use made of live action, film and stills combined with the highly original and imaginative use of words, music and sound effects, this is television of the first order. If you watch the 'bloodies' and the bed scenes, etc. – in short avoid getting into trouble over irrelevancies as you prepare your single plays for the next calendar year [1965] we will win, hands down, in the single drama stakes.[6]

Newman holds this team in high esteem, and his memo indicates his plans to use this group for his flagship single drama slot, *The Wednesday Play*.[7] Newman favoured work that would reflect his own aesthetic preferences. These preferences were grounded in notions of realism, and formulated through his experience of working for John Grierson at the National Film Board of Canada in the 1940s.[8] As a young man in the 1930s, Newman had been interested in left-wing theatre, particularly in the work of Brecht and Kurt Weill, and of American playwrights Irwin Shaw and Clifford Odets. He recollected, 'I was somewhat influenced by art in the service of the people, that kind of ideology' (Swallow and Lawson 1990); and he cited Grierson's influence:

> He was crystallizing a whole sense of teenage jumbled thinking into almost a concrete pattern or art, which is useful, in this case, the cinema ... He crystallized, in my mind, art that had to leave a residue of conscious thinking on the part of the audience, so that the art would stir them into action the following day, the following days. And so, when I got into drama at the CBC [1955], this thing was strong in me, and I knew very well that it's no use us doing plays by Ibsen or Shakespeare particularly, as fine as they were, because they wouldn't touch my Canadian audiences: my Canadian audiences should be seeing plays about themselves. (Swallow & Lawson 1990)[9]

The BBC hired Newman at time of expansion and his ideas about 'art in the service of the people' are close to statements by the Controller of the BBC during the 1960s,

Hugh Greene, and what Garnett and Loach later say of their own work.[10] Certainly, Newman's support for *The Wednesday Play* team and his enthusiasm for 'art in the service of the people' is an important context for Loach's early career.[11] In 1965, Loach directs six of the thirty-three *Wednesday Plays* broadcast during the series' first year. By far the biggest impact was made by his adaptation of Nell Dunn's first book, *Up the Junction* (1966).[12]

Up the Junction: addressing the audience

Dunn's book of *Up the Junction*, sections of which she first published in the *New Statesman*, collates accounts of episodes in the lives of a group of young working-class women living in and around Clapham Junction and North Battersea.[13] The first of the *New Statesman* stories, 'Out with the Girls', becomes the first chapter in the book and the first scene in the television film. 'Out with the Girls' opens with three young women meeting three young men in a pub. One of the men asks the women if they come from Battersea. Rube replies: 'Yeah, me and Sylvie do. She don't though. She's an heiress from Chelsea' (Dunn 1966: 10).[14] Dunn the author apparently refers to herself as a narrating presence here, because the writer was an 'heiress from Chelsea'. In Dunn's book, the narrator is a reliable mediator between the reader and the narrated events: she meets people in Battersea and Clapham, and her descriptions of her experiences link the episodes in the book.

Peter Collinson's 1967 feature film version of *Up the Junction* develops this narrator figure – the 'heiress from Chelsea' – as a central character, focusing on the topical frisson of a cross-class romance between Polly (Suzy Kendall) and Peter (Dennis Waterman). Polly replaces Dunn's narrator, and Collinson and the film's writer, *Wednesday Play* script editor Roger Smith, make more of her movement between Chelsea and Battersea, emphasising her journey across Albert Bridge. Loach and Dunn drop this narrator figure almost completely, preserving only a trace of her in the tallyman sequences. In their version, Eileen (Vickery Turner) replaces the narrator, and she has a social background equivalent to the other women in the film. However, although the television version of *Up the Junction* loses the figure of a journeying stranger discovering a new social milieu, and the consequent framework she provides for the fiction to follow this witness, it retains the dynamic of a witness reporting on experiences and events in many of its dialogues and monologues. Dunn lifts much of the dialogue straight from her book, a large part of which consists of vernacular.[15] The television film also retains Dunn's episodic narrative structure, although it focuses loosely on three young women: Rube (Geraldine Sherman), Sylvie (Carol White) and Eileen.

'I'd love to make you into a really bad girl' (Dunn 1966: 111). So says Barny, the tallyman, to the narrator of Dunn's original book of *Up the Junction*. Considering that Dunn seems to base the narrator on herself, one wonders whether while researching her book someone propositioned Dunn in this way. The 'heiress from Chelsea' has just met Barny as she sits with Sylvie, Jeannie and three men (Bob, Dick and Barny) in a Brixton nightclub. The television version of *Up the Junction* opens with a scene in a pub similar to this; before that, though, a song plays over the credits that recalls this proposition. Nell Dunn wrote the lyrics for 'Bad Girl'; Stanley Myers composed the music. The lyrics are as follows:

Oh, oh little girl, pretty little girl
You're such a good little girl
Why don't you let me make you a bad girl?
Oh, oh yes I could
Make you such a bad little girl
You'd be a glad little girl if only you were a bad girl

Oh, little girl, pretty little girl
I wouldn't let you be sad
I would make you so glad

Hear me babe
Oh, little girl, pretty little girl
You're such a good little girl
Why don't you let me make you a bad girl?
You'd be such a glad girl
If you were a bad girl

Oh, little girl, pretty little girl
I wouldn't make you feel so sad
I would make you so glad

Hear me babe
Oh, little girl
Pretty little girl

A close-up of Norton York singing directly to the camera follows the generic *Wednesday Play* credits. From the studio, we cut to a montage sequence that John Caughie describes:

The play opens with a studio close-up of a singer belting out a rather conventional 1960s pop song; it then cuts to a sequence of shots with an ASL [average shot length] of 9.5 seconds showing the industrial landscape of Clapham (railway train, smoke stacks, kids playing on wrecked car). (Caughie 2000: 115)

Caughie judges 'Bad Girl' to be 'a rather conventional 1960s pop song', but it performs a significant function. While York continues to sing 'Bad Girl', the credits appear over the montage of images of South London, ending with shots of Sylvie, Rube and Eileen standing by Clapham Junction Station, laughing and chatting. The film cuts from a close shot of Eileen back to the studio interior and four shots of women dancing, while York finishes 'Bad Girl'. It returns to the close-up of York as he sings, 'You look so tame but what a hurricane – hah – hah – hah'. From there, we cut to Terry (Michael Standing) inviting the three women for a drink as they enter the pub in which York is singing.

The cut to York singing the first line of 'You look so tame' after the last line of 'Bad Girl' can make it seem, especially on first viewing, as if the two lines belong to the same song, when they are in fact from two songs. (Sound and image quality change noticeably on the cut back to York, marking the change from location to studio, and from film to telerecording.)[16] As Ron (Ray Barron), Dave (Tony Selby) and Terry talk to the three young women, the band finishes 'You look so tame', and plays two more songs: 'Have a Heart' and Georgie Fame's hit, 'Yeh, Yeh'. Myers and Dunn's 'Bad Girl' purposefully adapts the conventions of these 1960s pop songs, but it is not the 'rather conventional' song that Caughie alleges. It possesses an energy typical of the pop music of the period, as does the lively *Wednesday Play* theme music itself, 'Dead Beat, Dead Pan, Dead Cert', composed and played by Manfred Mann, who also composed and performed the music for Peter Collinson's feature film version of *Up the Junction*. Importantly, though, 'Bad Girl' connects thematically with the rest of the film; and the way in which the opening segues Dunn's introductory 'Bad Girl' into York's 'You look so tame' condenses appositely the film's larger strategy of integrating pointed observation about the ideological implications of some popular music with a celebration of the culture in which that music plays a part.

The opening song corresponds to one of the film's major themes: sex. Terry will later seduce Rube; by having sex outside marriage, Rube becomes a 'bad girl', according to what was then a pervasive but increasingly challenged contemporary morality. The song's narrator, like Barny in the book, invites a 'pretty little girl' to become a 'bad girl'; he indicates that she will enjoy being made a 'bad girl'; and the song thus evokes some of the social confusions and contradictions about sex which *Up the Junction* seeks to expose. Terry insists on having sex with Rube (Rube: 'Does it mean a row?' Terry: 'Yeh.' Rube: 'All right then, but I'm keeping my coat on.'), but when she feels forced to have an illegal abortion he calls her 'nothing but a cheap thrill'. When Terry, Dave and Ron meet Rube, Sylvie and Eileen in the pub, nothing leads us to imagine that the young women would not like to have sex as much as the men do; however, the film later makes clear that the young women do not want to be marked out as 'bad girls'.

They leave the pub with the three men, and go for a swim. The film shows the clinch between Dave and Eileen, who promises that she 'hasn't been with anyone before', after Dave has said that he does not love his wife 'because [he] wasn't the first'. We cut away from them, but the film implies that Eileen and Dave have sex in a derelict house, which, Dave explains, was where he used to live and which is about to be pulled down as part of slum clearances. As they kiss, Loach introduces Johnny Kid and the Pirates' song 'Ecstasy' onto the soundtrack:

> Oh never let me go
> Let that love light show
> Come on now
> Take me by the hand
> And lead me to the land of ecstasy
>
> First time that I saw you
> You showed me the door to ecstasy
> Now I just keep praying that we'll always stay in ecstasy
> Whoa, don't you go away
> For a single day
> Come on now
> Take me by the hand
> And lead me to the land of ecstasy

One more verse plays, but at this point Loach cuts from a big close-up of Eileen and Dave kissing at night to a sequence of shots which show a building being demolished.

The song conceives of sexual satisfaction as a utopian place, to which one can be led by the hand; the ensuing cut to the shots of old buildings being pulled down creates a contrast between the 'land of ecstasy' in the song and the images: the juxtaposition is characteristic of the pointed way that Loach and Dunn use music in the film. Another instance of this kind of juxtaposition occurs after the 'Wedding Anniversary' scene, when there is a single, interpolated shot of a train passing under a bridge, accompanied by a brief excerpt from The Kinks' 'I Need You'. The quick shot acts as punctuation before the next scene, but the song is also an ironically appropriate one with which to follow a scene that shows a wedding anniversary being celebrated by a fight between the estranged husband and wife.

Throughout *Up the Junction*, Loach and Dunn present the recurrent themes of pop songs – love, romance and sex – in a significant relationship to the women whom these songs address, juxtaposing the songs and the romantic aspirations they celebrate with the reality of the women's lives. By far the most disturbing use of a 'conventional' pop song occurs during the scenes of Rube's illegal abortion. MacMurraugh-Kavanagh argues of this scene that Garnett 'hijacked' the writer's 'message' (MacMurraugh-Kavanagh 1997b: 254); yet although, through the use of a voiceover, the film introduces an overt protest missing from the book, much of the scene derives from Dunn's original. Both the chapter on which these scenes are based and the film itself feature women discussing pregnancy and childbirth, planned and unplanned: in her book Dunn places quotations from romantic pop songs next to women talking about pregnancy, and having abortions; the film extends this juxtaposition into a protest against the law and social attitudes.[17]

In the chapter 'The Deserted House', Dunn quotes from the song 'Ecstasy'; Loach, taking his lead from Dunn's writing, mixes this song onto the soundtrack as Dave and Eileen kiss. Similarly, in the chapter 'Bang on the Common', Dunn describes Rube's protracted miscarriage, brought on after several visits to an abortionist, Winnie (Ann Lancaster). She quotes Ben E. King's song 'Yes', which is playing on the radio in the background:

> *Oh yes, she said yes, and she opened her arms.*
> *Oh yes, she said, yes and she closed her eyes.*

> When I came back from ringing, Rube was shrieking, a long, high, animal shriek. The baby was born alive, five months old. It moved, it breathed, its heart beat.
>
> Rube lay back, white and relieved, across the bed. Sylvie and her mum lifted the eiderdown and peered at the tiny baby still joined by the cord. 'You can see it breathing, look!'
>
> Rube smiled. 'It's nothing – I've had a look enough meself.'
>
> 'I reckon she had some pluck going seven times,' said her mum.
>
> Finally the ambulance arrived. They took Rube away, but left behind the baby, which had now grown cold. Later Sylvie took him, wrapped him in the *Daily Mirror*, and threw him down the toilet. (Dunn 1966: 71)

In the film this sequence begins with a close-up of Rube saying, 'When you love a boy you wanna give him the best thing in the world and there is only one thing.' Following this she and Eileen go with Annie (Gilly Fraser) to visit Winnie. While they walk across the common, anonymous women's voice-overs describe their attempts to terminate their own pregnancies. Then a male voice speaks:

> In my surgery I see at least one woman a week who is seriously contemplating an abortion. Quite apart from the 35 deaths a year that we know are directly attributable to the back street abortions, the most common and seriously disturbing result must be that this girl is unable to have any more babies. She may not be able to have any. She may be unable to have a family.

As Rube walks across the common, alone now, Loach dubs Terry's voice onto the soundtrack after the doctor's: 'Rube? Nah, she was nothing but a cheap thrill.' After this the film cuts to Rube's home.

Close-ups of Rube screaming and writhing in agony dominate the scene of her miscarriage.[18] Over the last of these shots, the doctor's voice is again heard: 'Take the lowest figure: 52,000 abortions a year. That's 1,000 abortions a week. Something like five or six every hour of every day. And that's taking the minimum figure.' Loach cuts from the Doctor's voice-over to 'Yes':

Yes, she said yes
And she held me so tight
Oh yes, she said yes
With all her might

Oh yes, she said yes
And smiled up at me
Yes, she smiled up at me
And said yeah, yeah, yes

Yes you can hug me
And yes you can squeeze me
And yes you can have my caress.

While the song plays, a montage sequence shows images of Rube from previous scenes. Like 'Bad Girl' and 'Ecstasy', 'Yes' is about sex; and Dunn and Loach's use of the line 'Yes, she smiled up at me' after Rube has just had a miscarriage is brutally ironic, even crude. There is no doubt that Loach, Dunn and Garnett aimed to disrupt viewers' engagement with the character.

Using an expert's voice-over is a documentary technique but, in Brechtian 'epic' terms, one could argue that the doctor's voice-over disrupts our emotional involvement with the individual character by reminding us of the statistics; the voice-over introduces a social and political perspective on Rube's experience. Garnett recalls their intentions:

At the time we were making it [*Up the Junction*] and in fact at the time it was actually transmitted, [David] Steel's Bill about abortion law reform was going through Parliament. And when Ruby – Ken and I both hit on this device, which was, I don't know, I suppose it was a bit Brechtian at the time, but it served its purpose – of when Ruby was having the illegal abortion on the kitchen table, Don Grant, who was my GP, did the voice-over; just quietly and authoritatively giving the statistics of deaths from illegal abortions.[19]

The voice-over disseminates general information about a specific narrative event: as a method of incorporating politics into dramatic fiction it addresses the audience far more directly than Eileen's potted history of Nicaragua in *Carla's Song* (1996).

The doctor's voice-over matches the style of *Up the Junction* and the style of Loach's work during the mid-1960s, but it exemplifies a technique that he abandons relatively early in his career, suggesting that he found it unsustainable. Nonetheless, while he abandons the technique he continues trying to make popular films that protest against institutional practices and ideological principles. Throughout his career he explores ways of making films that are about individuals, but which also have something to say about society; he remains concerned with the connections between the unique and the general. This concern clearly comes from his belief in socialism and his Marxist understanding of history: Loach's work follows historian E. H. Carr's dictum that 'those who insist so fervently on the moral condemnation of the individual sometimes unconsciously provide an alibi for whole groups and societies' (Carr 1985: 78).

All Loach's work of the mid-1960s reveals a loosely Brechtian influence; Julian Petley (1997a) and Paul Kerr (1986) both note that long before the controversy over *Days of Hope* (1975), Loach experiments with Brechtian strategies for combining individual drama and social analysis. The range of techniques in *Up the Junction* typifies Loach's experimentation in the mid-1960s. The experimentation was common in theatre and film then, a time when the work of Brecht was influencing British theatre, and when films by European directors, particularly those of Jean-Luc Godard and Michelangelo Antonioni, were exploring modernist ideas of self-reflexivity, alienation and distance.[20] Loach and the writers, script editors and producers with whom he worked belonged to this trend. He recollects:

> It was the time of the French new wave, it was the time of a great interest in Brecht and exposing the mechanism of drama was something we talked a lot about. Troy [Kennedy Martin] and John [McGrath] wrote a series called *Diary of a Young Man*, which told the narrative in a very fractured way with stills and with music and with voice-overs, and turned everything upside down, and that was very interesting. But the danger of it as a technique to sustain for a long time was that it could become mannered.[21]

One of the most Brechtian of Loach's works is his curious musical, *The End of Arthur's Marriage* (1965). It commences with Arthur (Ken Jones) being given £400 by his father-in-law to put down as a deposit on a new house. Instead, accompanied by his daughter Emmy (Maureen Ampleford), Arthur goes on a spending spree. The whole film uses satirical ballads, written by the composer Stanley Myers and the poet Christopher Logue, to comment on their day out.[22]

The first ballad is heard as a crane shot shows Arthur and Emmy leaving his father-in-law's house. As they walk along the street, the camera moves upwards to reveal rows of suburban terraced houses. Simultaneously, we hear a song:

We are the little investors
We are the decent people
We have spent our lives working
We are obedient politician lovers
We are the image of people like you
This is a country of homeowners
It represents a lifetime of work
When you lock your front door
We are not very likeable
Desperate for security
We own our own homes
How easy it is
To tell the truth
We do not care for ourselves

The song satirises the aims and aspirations of 'obedient politician lovers' and 'little investors', and the stylised basic cadence of the verse and the insistent declamatory mode of singing calls to mind the style of Brecht and Weill's operas, particularly *The Rise and Fall of the City of Mahagonny*, first performed in 1930 but revived by Norman Tucker and Colin Davis at Sadler's Wells in January 1963 and broadcast on BBC2's *Opera 625* in February 1965. When Arthur and Emmy leave a Piccadilly department store an unusual scene unfolds. A documentary camera crew asks Emmy if she likes spending money. A shot then follows that reveals Loach directing another camera crew and trying to prevent the two crews from having an argument. The moment is surprising: Loach reveals not only the 'mechanisms of drama', but also himself. However, despite this apparent interest in self-reflexivity Loach indicates that he always had reservations about 'exposing the mechanism of drama':

> There was never an interest in getting actors to behave unnaturally, stylisti-
> cally, for me; it was – perhaps you might take a series of stills, but you would
> still try to make the content of the still as realistic as possible, or the perform-
> ance as authentic as possible. I mean, I may not have been very good at it,
> but that was the intention; it wasn't to produce some heightened stylistic kind
> of performance. And gradually those techniques of fracturing the narrative
> became, I think, less interesting. And what became a bigger challenge was to
> put something in front of the camera that was absolutely authentic.[23]

While other film-makers, notably Godard, have employed and adapted distanciation techniques, Loach is uneasy with them and finds, in particular, that Brecht's 'epic' style of acting, which stresses the idea of an exposed distance between actor and character, does not interest him.

We can understand the limitations that Loach imposes on his fractured narratives and the difference of his use of direct address to the camera from its use by Godard, by studying the performance of George Sewell in *Up the Junction* and the adaptations of dialogue and action from the book in the sequence featuring Barny the tallyman. In one sequence, transposed from Dunn's original, various narrational modes are used. In Dunn's book, a chapter title identifies Barny as 'The Tallyman'. When the narrator meets him in the Brixton nightclub, this man invites her to join him on his rounds. The next morning the narrator recounts:

> I go up the road to meet Barny – twelve o'clock on the corner. He still wears the same shiny suit in the sunlight. There are black scoops under his small eyes. 'Jump in!' Into the new Austin van with the grating over the windows; in the back are the goods – sheets and shirts and petticoats in cellophane and black and yellow boxes. (Dunn 1966: 114)

The film has no comparable narrator: as discussed above, Eileen replaces her. Instead, this sequence opens by cutting from Terry and Rube deciding to stay in to a shot of an elderly woman walking along a street. She is photographed with a long lens, as if without permission, for she looks inquisitively at the camera, while the background is out of focus. From her, the film cuts to a big close-up of another woman; the camera then pans left, blurring the picture before finding a third woman. All three frown, their faces creased with concentration. During these three shots, a male voice talks: it is not an authoritative, upper-class voice like the doctor's but one with a working-class London accent:

> See you get your foot in the door and you start off with a few soft goods: couple of shirts for Dad, pair of shoes for Johnny, underset for Mum.[24]

Now we cut to a shot of Barny (George Sewell) inside his van. The back of his head and shoulders occupy the right of the frame. No one else is in the front seat, so it is unclear to whom he is talking. As he drives past rows of run-down, inner London Victorian terrace houses, visible through the windscreen, he continues his monologue: 'Then 'fore long you're selling them everything.' Barny glances over his shoulder in the vague direction of the camera, gesturing with his hand as he does so.

His comments deride his customers, yet he confides his scorn to his listener with bravado. These women to whom he sells, and whom he implicitly invites his listener to acknowledge as easy prey for his sales techniques, could be the three anonymous women we have seen in close-ups. Barny concludes his summary: 'Kitchen sets, bedroom suites, curtains, cardigans: the lot. Once you've got your foot in the door, you've got to keep it there. You hold onto them and you never let 'em go.' On this phrase, the film cuts to a shot of a thin old woman shuffling slowly along the street. The shot frames her alone; she stares down at the pavement, looking fleetingly towards the camera as it passes her. Her mouth is set in a grimace; and her look at the camera, her slow progress along the street, her hunched posture and her decrepit appearance give her a ghostly, insubstantial appearance, suggestive of the potential solitude and poverty of old age. She looks profoundly sad, yet we have no way of knowing her other than this brief shot, and we are as distant from her as is Barny, who comments: 'Some of these old dears, it's the event of the week. They don't have no other social occasion.' The next shot reveals another old woman, also looking frail. Like the preceding one, it lacks contrast and is grainy; but one can still perceive her stare at the camera. Barny continues: 'When you go in the teapot's already laid out for you.' Evidently, Loach wants these observational shots of anonymous women to represent the 'old dears' to whom Barny refers.

Back inside the van, Barny talks about his wife who is, apparently, 'as good as gold'. Loach then cuts to a shot of two black women looking in a shop window. Their presence is another putative prompt for Barny. He moans:

> See 60 per cent of my calls are black. I'm like the great white hunter. Down the bottom of the street you can practically hear the tom-toms going ... I'm sick of these coloureds. I want some nice young housewives to cheer me up on a Tuesday morning.

While Barny speaks, one of the women turns away from the shop window, seemingly distracted by something along the street: she sees the camera and looks directly at it. The film places Barny's 'old dears' next to images of two old women; here it shows the subjects of Barny's racism while he describes himself as a 'great white hunter'. Barny assumes that his attitude towards his customers will not repulse his listener. He continues, 'I got this nurse you see'. As he says this, he turns round and looks, for the first time, directly at the camera, indicating that he feels he has something even more conspiratorial to say. His look at the camera confirms that it represents a first-person narrator, an adaptation of Dunn's book, in which Barny takes the narrator on his round; as she says, 'I go up the road to meet Barny'.

Barny continues his rounds, stopping to take money from a mother and child on their doorstep, after which we return to inside the van, now stationary. Barny faces the back seat, looking directly at the camera as he talks. He does not acknowledge the camera as a camera, with a listener sitting next to it; he beholds it as his listener. Gesturing emphatically, he invites this listener into his confidence (figure 4):

> Pair of good blankets she's owing. Well I can't take 'em back. I mean I wouldn't dare put them in the back here. The van would crawl away. Anyway, she's what we call a pawnshop call. Y'see we sell her a pair of blankets and ten minutes later she goes and sells them for cash to some old woman down the street. And then she's paying me five bob a week for the rest of the year for something she hasn't even got. You dunno how stupid they are. They think

Figure 4: *Up the Junction*

they're being clever. They've got four or five different tally men. They get something different off of each one. 'Which one are you?' they say, when you going in. They don't know what they're paying for or when the debt's done. And the more they get into debt the dirtier they become. You don't know the filth they get into. I smell that filth as soon as I go, go in the front door. They live more like animals, animals! I have to keep smoking all the time I'm, y'know, writing in me book.

George Sewell hesitates during his soliloquy, stumbling on 'go in' as if he planned to say something other than 'the front door', but then changed his mind or remembered the correct line. When he recounts how he 'smell[s] that filth' he screws up his face and brings his fingertips up to his nose, underlining forcefully the apparent odour of his clients' houses. The gesture precedes the stumble in the flow of his words; following it, he repeats the word 'animals' with an ugly aggression, and then mimes smoking vigorously as he explains how he copes with the smell.

Barny speaks to the camera as if he has walked to the front of a stage: away from the other characters and momentarily privileged in that he can direct his speech out from the dramatic world, he discloses himself to his audience. When he addresses the camera, there is an acute sense of the deliberate and rhetorical use of clichés to evoke the limited vocabulary of the unpleasant tallyman. Sewell strives for a naturalistic performance of Barny's cadences, but there is still a feeling of exaggeration in his voice, his gestures and his facial expressions; this exaggeration, together with the stumble, means that the whole soliloquy produces an effect of Sewell 'working up' his performance. The actor addresses the camera, and has to exert himself to enable his performance to suggest that he chats informally to a listener. The effort is apparent. The character is meant to be an extrovert with an imposing personality, but his stumble is unexpected from a fluent talker; together with his over-emphatic hand gestures, the ensuing moments hint that Sewell is trying to recover his relaxed demeanour in the face of the camera.

V. F. Perkins writes of a moment in *Johnny Guitar* (1954) when a character, Sam (Robert Osterloh), appears to address a remark to the camera:

> To have the actor head for and speak into the camera is to compromise the integrity of the fictional world and to unsettle our confidence in the identity of performer and role. Since there is no camera in the world of the characters, the actor (who can be aware of the camera) is distinguished from his character (who cannot). (Perkins 1996: 227)

Godard is renowned for using the convention of separating character and actor in order to unsettle our confidence in the identity of performer and role. In one scene in his *Une femme est une femme* (1961), Angela (Anna Karina) and Emile (Jean-Claude Brialy) start to argue at home. Before they argue, they turn and bow to the camera. In doing so, the actors distance themselves from the characters, and the technique distances the film from its viewers. As Gilberto Perez argues, Godard draws a line between the person and the impersonation (Perez 1998: 339–40). James Naremore describes the purpose behind this kind of Brechtian acting:

> The antirealistic Brechtian player is more like a comic than a tragedian, concerned less with emotional truth than with critical awareness; instead of expressing an essential truth, she or he examines the relation between roles on the stage and roles in society, deliberately calling attention to the artificiality of performance, foregrounding the staginess of spectacle, and addressing the audience in didactic fashion. (Naremore 1988: 3)

Although Loach wants to foreground the relation between the fictional role and the social role, he nonetheless demands that his actors carry complete conviction in their performances; his actors must *be* their characters.

Sewell's performance as Barny is representative: in spite of his momentary stumble, his remarks to the camera are not meant to distinguish actor from character, in the way that Karina and Brialy distance themselves from Angela and Emile. Loach and Dunn want to reveal how ordinary Barny's prejudices are by pretending to document a real person; yet despite the naturalness of Sewell's performance, in particular the manner in which he shares professional secrets with his listener, his direct address to the camera imparts a rhetorical, exaggerated quality to the photographic representation of Barny. An uneasily simultaneous sensation of closeness and distance exists in both the dramatic representation, whereby Barny invites us to share a confidence but his attitudes repulse us, and the photographic representation, whereby Barny addresses the camera as if it is a listener/narrator but this address demands of Sewell an oratorical pretence with which the actor remains uncomfortable. The sensation becomes acute when Barny next turns to the camera. Barny recommences his commentary during travelling shots of run-down houses. Then, inside the stationary van again, Barny says: 'Only a couple more calls and we'll go and 'ave a drink. You look as if you could do with one. I know it gets a bit hot back there.' As he invites his listener for a drink, he turns his head three times to look at the camera at the beginning of each of the three sentences. His invitation confirms that we are meant to understand that Barny is talking not to a camera, but to a narrator.

The action moves to the interior of a pub; Barny is having a pint of beer and some food, describing the 'floozies' he has 'had' in his time. It is apparent immediately that Loach shot this scene in a television studio. The footage shot on location has sharply defined contrasts in the images, with saturated blacks and bright whites; in the interiors, where the image is produced electronically, there is less brightness or contrast in the image and greys dominate. Not only has the image quality changed, but Barny's relationship to the camera has also altered. Throughout the scene the camera is placed opposite Barny, yet he directs his eyes to the right of the camera as if there is now a second person there, to whom he addresses his comments. It is a significant shift, for although Barny talks as before, the film changes its mode of narration as it returns to the television studio.

A similarly abrupt change in the relationship of character to camera takes place when Barny sells a suit to a black man (George Webb). In his van, Barny, casually racist, invites his listener: 'Come on, I'm selling a suit to a darkie.' In Dunn's book, the narrator and character relationship continues as before, with Barny, the narrator and the customer present in the scene that the narrator establishes: Dunn writes, 'He lived in one bow-faced room and I looked the other way while he tried it' (Dunn 1966: 119). Loach abandons this dynamic though and telerecords the scene as if Barny's listener is not present, despite having just been invited. On location, Loach films in a moderately inventive way, experimenting with the mode of narration (albeit by reproducing the dynamic of the book); in the studio, he chooses not to stray outside the parameters of live studio broadcasts, even though this confuses the visual equivalent to the first person narration that the film has attempted to establish in the scenes in the van.[25] One feels the shift in narrational mode more acutely because Loach and Dunn have already adapted the novel's narrator into the character of Eileen.

Loach employs a range of techniques in *Up the Junction*: while some scenes are observational in the style of a documentary, others, like the tallyman's scenes in the pub and the flat, exemplify Loach's negotiation of the tradition of live television, his attraction to loosely Brechtian techniques and his reliance on Dunn's book. Despite the film's periodic return to Rube, Eileen and Sylvie, *Up the Junction* has no central storyline; throughout the film, documentary-style shots observe unspecified people in Battersea and Clapham, similar to those with which the film opens and to those used during Barny's monologues. While these montage sequences do not always advance a linear narrative, common themes (work, pregnancy, marriage) unite them. The voice-overs that accompany these montage sequences often sound like taped interviews with residents of the area where *Up the Junction* is set. This combination of observational shots of people and places shot on 16mm film and 'wildtrack' or 'vox-pop' interviews was made famous by Denis Mitchell in television documentaries like *Eye to Eye: Night in the City* (1957), *Morning in the Streets* (1959) and *A Soho Story* (1959).[26] Lindsay Anderson also uses the technique in *Every Day Except Christmas* (1957), while Karel Reisz uses it in *We are the Lambeth Boys* (1959).

One such sequence in *Up the Junction* focuses on pregnancy. A young woman's voice-over begins:

> I never once lay down with him. I used to meet him in a back alley off the Latchmere. I never really knew what he was at. I never got no pleasure out of it. I didn't know I was carrying till I was five months. I kept thinking it would pass off. He wasn't half handsome. All the girls used to say, 'What a handsome chap'.

As this woman speaks, a sequence of shots shows pregnant women: one stands in a doorway, looking directly at the camera; another walks through a playground; four more shots continue the theme, one of which features a woman looking in a shop window while a voice-over says, 'It'll be nice to be looked at again. I'm gonna make meself a new dress, tighter than tight, like a second skin.' Combining shots of anonymous pregnant women and unspecified voice-overs elaborates the theme of teenage sex and pregnancy; these sequences connect associatively with Rube's abortion and with Sylvie's personal history ('I was the youngest bride in Battersea'). The associative connections imply that Rube and Sylvie's stories exemplify a social problem, one that changes in legislation, education and social attitudes would relieve. Caughie makes this point in reverse, arguing that in *Up the Junction* 'typicality is dramatized rather than simply observed' (Caughie 2000: 119). The film achieves the connections between typicality and individual drama by adhering to principles of association and juxtaposition rather than integration. Loach develops this strategy in his most famous *Wednesday Play – Cathy Come Home*.

Cathy Come Home: fictional journalism

Although it is now over 35 years since Loach made it, not only is *Cathy Come Home* one of the works for which he is best known, but it continues to be the work of his to which critics concerned with drama documentary most frequently return. John

Corner's essay on *Cathy Come Home*, in his book on documentary, *The Art of Record*, analyses it as a drama documentary and he describes it as having a 'mixed aesthetic':

> *Cathy* develops both as 'story' and 'report', the latter being produced through the use of images and speech which generate a documentary referentiality around the main line of action, thereby connecting this to contemporary reality in a way which differs from conventional drama. (Corner 1996: 92)[27]

Many people regard it as a quintessential work of the 1960s, seeing in it an expression of the anxieties and energies that a generation of film-makers and audiences felt.[28] The issues that it raised are still, for some, relevant in discussions of Loach's work; and the way his work has developed since *Cathy Come Home* has had little tendency to diminish its reputation.[29] Ever since 1966, some critics have accused Loach of deceiving viewers by mixing the conventions of fiction and non-fiction, drama and documentary;[30] while others have argued that his work presents only individual drama, personalising what are social and institutional problems. Within film and television studies, some on the left have berated Loach for relying on social realism (with its allusion to Stalinist propaganda) and classic realism, both regarded as incapable of offering analyses of wider political and socio-economic issues.

Despite its reputation, *Cathy Come Home* is the product of a tradition in broadcasting, indebted to the research methods and narrative strategies of the drama documentaries of the 1950s, or 'dramatised documentaries' as they were then institutionally defined.[31] Like most other programmes before 1960, television drama documentaries were broadcast live, relayed electronically from the studio.[32] Scripted, rehearsed and acted, and using filmed inserts for continuity or short location sequences, they covered issues of social concern.[33] A writer and producer would conduct intensive research: Caryl Doncaster spent months interviewing teenagers for her drama documentary *The Rising Twenties*.[34] She then transformed her research into a story. As Paddy Scannell writes: '[a] generalised topic was gradually changed into an ideal-typical representation distilled into a narrative line' (Scannell 1979: 107). Jeremy Sandford developed and wrote *Cathy Come Home* in a similar manner, basing it on research for his radio documentary *Homeless Families*.[35]

While Nell Dunn apparently bases *Up the Junction*'s narrator on herself, Sandford, Dunn's husband and presumably also a resident of Battersea, uses the same structure of a mediating witness reporting on what she experiences for his script of *Cathy Come Home*. However, the witness in *Cathy Come Home* is the central character, Cathy (Carol White). Cathy's journey comprises a series of humiliating degradations as she and her husband Reg (Ray Brooks) find their accommodation deteriorating, culminating in separation, homelessness and the taking into care of their three children. At each stage of Cathy and Reg's downfall they talk to people as if they were researching information about the situations in which they find themselves living, thus reproducing the dynamic of a writer interviewing people; for example, when they move into a caravan and when Cathy moves into the 'Part III' accommodation, inhabitants tell them about the conditions there. Loach and Sandford assemble their report on the environments Cathy experiences around a framework of Cathy's decline. They dramatise Cathy and Reg's experiences by having them listen to people they meet and by using montage sequences of unspecified voice-overs and observational shots to protest against the widespread nature of a social problem.

As marked as this narrative structure is, what distinguishes *Cathy Come Home* is that it was filmed mostly on location with a documentary style. Following *Up the Junction*, Sydney Newman promoted script editor Tony Garnett to producer. Garnett produced *Cathy Come Home*, and he worked with Loach until *Black Jack* (1979). Shooting on film was a move that Garnett wanted television drama to make; as he declares in an internal memo in August 1967, all his productions for the following season's *Wednesday Play* series will be 'one hundred per cent film': 'We are therefore virtually within reach of the ambition, which is to make feature films.'[36] Loach shot *Cathy Come Home* almost entirely on film: there are only five short scenes recorded electronically.[37] In his next *Wednesday Play*, *In Two Minds* (1967), and from then on, he films only on location.

More generally, as improved technology in the late 1950s and early 1960s increases flexibility in filming on location, wholly filmed television documentaries begin to replace the old, studio-based drama documentaries.[38] In television, this is part of a broad shift to greater and more flexible use of film. Using a small tape-recorder, documentary crews filming on location can achieve a more intimate relationship with interviewees; it no longer matters if interviewees hesitate, mumble or repeat themselves, the film-makers can edit the soundtrack later. *Cathy Come Home* uses an interview format throughout: Cathy's voice-over presents her perspective on the story as if someone is interviewing her; yet, her voice-over does not always connect logically to the story. As Corner points out, a key principle of the film's organisation as story and report is Cathy's regular first person, past tense voice-over, which comments reflectively on the present tense visual unfolding of the story.

During the opening, a lorry picks up Cathy, hitching on a motorway. As the lorry drives away, the song '500 Miles' fades out and Cathy's voice-over comes in:

Well, I was a bit fed up, y'know. There didn't seem to be much there for me; y'know how these little towns are, one coffee bar. It was closed on Sunday. Didn't even tell 'em I was going. I sent 'em a card when I got down there. That house over there, yeah, that one with the broken steps; that's where I went for a room. The fella kept touching me. Where did I get a room in the end? Oh yeh, down there, Mantua Street, three pounds a week. That's where I got my first job. Petrol-pump girl. Mad.

Cathy explains vaguely why she left her hometown, and, although the film presents her voice-over as an interior monologue, in that it represents her ruminations as she seems to sit silently in the driver's cab, her address to an implied second person resembles a response to an interviewer or reporter. When she specifies a place that this implied listener might be able to see ('That house over there, yeah, that one with the broken steps') what the film shows in a travelling shot is a parade of shops. From this shot we cut to a close-up of an anonymous old woman crossing the road, which begins a montage sequence of observational shots that resembles sequences in *Up the Junction*. Cathy's voice-over continues, before Loach dubs in Reg's voice-over, talking to Cathy ('We're going along in these hearses, y'see') during a close-up of an old man. The film cuts to close-up of Reg, which pans to Cathy and then cuts to a two-shot of Reg and Cathy walking together.

Cathy Come Home combines Cathy's voice-over with voice-overs other than those of the central characters as a way of alternating between a unique and a general perspective. After a brief courtship, Cathy and Reg get married and move into a relatively expensive apartment. Unfortunately, Reg is injured in an accident while driving his lorry, and he loses his job. They are then forced to look for a cheaper flat. A sequence shows Cathy out looking for a flat, while a male voice reads statistics. It sounds official yet sympathetic; it also sounds like George Sewell, though the credits do not confirm this.

> There's 200,000 more families in the London area than the houses to put them. [cut] And in addition there's 60,000 single persons living without sinks or stoves. In seven central London boroughs at least one in ten of all households is overcrowded; that is to say, living more than one and a half people [cut] per room.

Two cuts occurs during this voice-over: the first moves from Cathy walking along the street to a shot of a man in a doorway talking to her; the second is to a shot of Cathy talking to a woman on her doorstep about her room. Cathy's brief conversation with the landlady interrupts the male voice-over. Three more shots show Cathy and Reg flat hunting, while the voice-over recommences:

> The present target of 500,000 set by the government is not high enough. Even if it is reached there's still people living in slums ten years from now. What's needed is a government that realises that this is a crisis and treats it as such.

The sequence ends by cutting to a shot of Cathy and Reg walking together; Reg says that they will have to move to his mother's, even if her flat is already overcrowded.

The male voice-over is diagnostic and programmatic; it tells us that housing problems constitute a crisis affecting thousands of people, not just Cathy and Reg; and while the statistics impress upon us authoritatively the seriousness of the problem, the voice-over challenges the government to tackle this problem. Later, when Cathy is looking for a place to live in Birmingham, after they have been served with an eviction notice, Loach again alternates between this male voice-over delivering statistics about homelessness ('Birmingham, 39,000 families on the waiting list. Leeds, 13,500. Liverpool, 19,000. Manchester, nearly 15,000.'), and Cathy's voice-over ('It wasn't long before I realised something – we'd been lucky to get the old place. There didn't seem to be anything for us anymore'). As with the combination of Rube's abortion and the doctor's voice-over in *Up the Junction*, *Cathy Come Home* juxtaposes individual drama with an account of a problem facing thousands of people.

Apart from the use of official voice-overs, the other feature of *Cathy Come Home* that relates to documentary conventions is the use of montage sequences of observational shots that depict unspecified people and places filmed on location. As Corner points out, these observational images 'are edited together into a representation of a peopled environment in which space and place are observed by the camera as *significant* independently of any narrative line' (Corner 1996: 97). One example is the sequence in which Cathy and Reg move in with Reg's mother, Mrs Ward (Winifred Dennis). It begins, after Cathy has given birth, with a fade-in upon lines of washing stretched across the courtyard of a tenement block. In the background, Mrs Ward begins climbing the iron stairs. As she makes her way up, the camera follows her movement from a distance, slowly zooming in on her, then panning as she climbs the stairs so that objects near the camera often obscure her progress. The shot lasts approximately one minute and 15 seconds.

During the shot, six voice-overs (one male and five female) describe conditions in the flats. An elderly male voice begins, but they all segue into each other:

1. This is what you call 'the island of paradise'. Kids here have seen rats running round the place nearly as big as cats.
2. Anytime the children 'ave accidents, nine out of ten times all the mothers come down to see if they can do anything to 'elp ya.
3. They're so old, damned old places. They want pulling down.
4. You've got plenty of company and I think we're reasonable people that can all get on together. We 'ave our ups and downs. You can fight over the kids but, erm, apart from that we're lucky I suppose, better off than some people.
5. I don't like one half of the people in it. What's more there's none of them neighbourly. They always got somat t'say about ya, behind ya back.
6. I had a friend lived next door to me, she really would have give a thousand pounds, as she used to say, to move out a 'ere. But now she's gone – she's got a brand new maisonette – she said she'd still like to come back, if she could bring her flat back 'ere. She likes the company 'ere and the friends.

The alternating negative and positive accounts of life in these flats, conjoined with the long take of Mrs Ward, impart an impression of what it is like to live there. The film does not use these voices again; they are anonymous and unidentified. Their accents sound authentic and what they say and how they say it conforms to expectations about what inhabitants of these flats might say if a documentary maker or writer such as Sandford had interviewed them. They may be actors but they sound like real people, and their use suggests, as Corner notes, a documentary report. While in *Cathy Come Home* the status of the reporting voices remains ambiguous, in his *Wednesday Play The Golden Vision* (1968) Loach does interview real people, in this case members of the 1968 Everton squad, including Alec Young, Brian Labone, Ray Wilson and trainer Wilf Dixon, whom captions identify.

The voice-overs end as the film cuts to a shot of Cathy cooking inside Mrs Ward's tiny flat. Mrs Ward, whom the camera has revealed in a pan left, talks about Reg's uncles. The film then cuts to an exterior long shot that looks down into the courtyard. The camera pans upwards, with a revelatory slowness, following a group of boys playing football and showing the lines of washing that criss-cross the courtyard. A similar shot of girls playing with a pram follows. During these shots, another anonymous woman grumbles: 'When I first came 'ere, we never 'ad none of this lot. We never 'ad no children in 'ere. This was only for a married couple or one on their own. No children. You 'ad ladies 'ere then.' A long shot of a pregnant young woman looking sullenly at the camera follows, then a shot of three older women talking, one of whom holds a baby. A new voice-over commences: 'There was rats under the floorboards, and I 'ad the council down to take the floorboards up and put all the poison down for the rats. And they said that definitely rats had been there but they'd probably gone somewhere else, to annoy somebody else like.' The camera zooms in on one of the three women, then cuts to a long shot of a small boy drinking milk from a bottle. A new voice-over starts, 'Eh, Reg, we got a new girl at work'; and Loach cuts to a close-up of Reg's sister, Eileen (Adrienne Frame), at the dinner table.

Having shifted back again from the report to the story, Loach uses a shot/reverse-shot couplet to present the dinner-table conversation between Eileen, Reg and Cathy, ending it by zooming in on Cathy as she laughs at one of Reg's jokes. The brief scene of the Ward family meal begins with the overlapping of Eileen's voice with the shot of the boy, and it ends similarly with Loach returning to the report by dubbing an anonymous voice-over onto the last few frames of the shot of Cathy: 'I think this is the only tenement block in Islington where you can sit in your toilet with your door open and cook your breakfast at the same time.' After 'Islington' Loach cuts to a close-up of a large woman leaning silently against the railings, looking into the courtyard. A medium long shot of two women standing in a doorway talking follows this, while another voice commences:

We've only got one bedroom. I mean you've got no married life. You're sort of, erm, half your questions and half your rows is over sex because your husband thinks that they ... y'know and course you're always on nerves with the chil-

Figure 5: *Cathy Come Home*

dren. I don't think it's fair to a man or if you're married 'n' that, and if you got children. I think you're entitled to 'ave another room.

Before 'fair' there is a cut to a shot of a woman with a pram through some railings; then, after 'room', the film cuts to a shot of some washing being pulled in. A new female voice says: 'You can look out your door up the other one's passage. You can't do that in any new flats, can you.' Meanwhile, the camera pans right, and instead of finding an anonymous woman taking in the washing, the camera discovers Cathy and Mrs Ward, standing by the railings and bickering about whether or not frozen chips are good for Reg (figure 5). Loach dubs in Cathy's voice before we see her; as with Eileen at the dinner table, it is an example of the director juxtaposing Cathy's story with the report on the conditions in this Islington tenement building.

Cathy and Mrs Ward's voices begin as unsynchronised voice-overs, like those of the other residents; but in panning right to reveal them Loach unites their voices with the real tenants' voices. After the pan along the washing, the alternation between story and report quickens. The arguments between Cathy and her mother-in-law increase. The quickening pace of the alternation between their arguments and the increasingly fleeting shots of the other residents corresponds to the escalating tension between Cathy and Mrs Ward. The quarrels culminate when Cathy shouts that they will move out. The film fades to black, and the next sequence begins on a close-up of Cathy's children playing in a yard; about two years seem to have passed;[39] Cathy's voice-over explains: 'We moved right away from the parts we'd been living in.'

The sequence with Mrs Ward epitomises Loach's early style: the director juxtaposes story and report in other sequences, notably in the opening and the sequence in Birmingham; but the Islington sequence is the most sustained and self-enclosed. It contains all of Cathy and Reg's experiences while living with Reg's mother, encompassing a whole episode in the series of episodes that depicts their decline. It exemplifies Loach and Sandford's attempt to locate their fictional characters in a context that allows us to perceive that what happens to Cathy and Reg is not an isolated occurrence but, as Corner argues, a particularisation of a systemic problem. *Cathy Come Home* protests against homelessness and the methods used to deal with it in Britain in the mid-1960s. It combines images and sounds that seem to document the real conditions facing homeless people, with a focus on the experiences of one person, Cathy. With this focus on an unjustly persecuted individual struggling against ideological systems (legislation, local authority practice and class prejudice) in a divided world, *Cathy Come Home* qualifies, as Michael Walker argues, for consideration as a melodrama of protest. The portrayal of the housing officials as punitive and unsympathetic, the rapid succession of short episodes depicting Cathy's decline, and the worsening situations that she falls into, concluding in the final separation of mother and children, all exemplify the paradigmatic conventions that Walker discusses.[40] At times, though, it is mechanistic in the negative sense that John Hill evokes when he notes the reliance on 'the dramatic machinery of melodrama' (Hill 1998: 20).

One problem is that Cathy and Reg never develop as characters beyond the way that Loach and Sandford use them as ciphers in a diagrammatic story of decline. Loach and Sandford's concentration on the general experiences of homelessness partly accounts for this; they fail, for instance, to discover a way of conveying Cathy's point of view, despite using her voice-overs. Performances contribute to the problem: Ray Brooks is unconvincing as Reg, often grasping for authenticity, while Carol White does not always meet the demands that the story places on her. The problems of White's uncomfortable fit as Cathy stem from her limitations as an actor. The scenes in which Cathy is meant to be emotionally authentic in a grandly demonstrative manner fall flat; in particular, her teary confrontation with the social workers, when she calls them 'runts', fails to carry conviction. Appreciation of the film depends heavily on White's performance as Cathy; without a feeling for her acting, and a belief in the character, it is difficult to empathise with her predicament, although the film can nonetheless be appreciated as a piece of cultural history. Nevertheless, White has a noteworthy iconic presence which Loach exploits fully in his next film with her, *Poor Cow* (1967).

Poor Cow: the limitations of digression

Towards the end of *Poor Cow*, Loach's first cinema film and his second collaboration with Nell Dunn, on whose book it is based, its lead character, Joy (Carol White), walks aimlessly around the area where she lives. Tom (John Bindon), her husband, has just hit her, and her voice-over tells us that she is thinking about her life and whether or not to leave him. At one point, Joy crosses a street and in the background of the shot Battersea Power Station is visible (figure 6). Simultaneously, Joy's voice-over articulates some sense of self-knowledge when she asks, 'Whoever heard of girls like me making it?' The shot reproduces an almost identical one from the credit sequence of *Up the Junction* (figure 7). The combination of her rhetorical question and the shot of Carol White on a street in South London condenses the issues of class and gender that are central to both *Up the Junction* and *Poor Cow*. The visual link between the two films calls to mind the links that Nell Dunn, Battersea and White provide. As a teenager in the late 1950s and early 1960s White appeared in several British films, yet it was only with *Poor Cow* that she created sufficient impact for *Variety* to register her as 'potential marquee bait' (Otta 1967: 6).[41] The trade paper recognised star presence in her performance as Joy, though it was as Cathy that she made an impact on 'the consciousness of the nation'. She fails to convince in *Cathy Come Home*, but she finds in *Poor Cow*'s digressive tale of three years in a young mother's life a project that suits her ability to project relaxed confidence and a spontaneous, flirtatious warmth; she and her co-star, Terence Stamp, make an attractive couple.

 Poor Cow was Terence Stamp's third film for producer Joseph Janni, made just as the actor was reaching the peak of his 1960s fame as a working-class star; his presence in *Poor Cow* underscores its links to mainstream commercial British cinema of

Figure 6: *Poor Cow*

Figure 7: *Up the Junction*

the 1960s. Janni produced it for Vic Films, and Nat Cohen at Anglo-Amalgamated financed it, with Warner-Pathé distributing. Cohen and Janni's records as producers linked them with the 1960s 'kitchen-sink' and 'swinging London' cycles.[42] Before Loach, Janni had plucked another director from BBC television, John Schlesinger, who, like Loach, had been at Oxford University following National Service.[43] For Janni, Schlesinger directed *A Kind of Loving* (1962), *Billy Liar* (1963), *Darling* (1965) and *Far From the Madding Crowd* (1967), the latter three of which starred Julie Christie.

Just before the release of *Poor Cow*, Cohen announced in the trade press that, in collaboration with Anglo-Amalgamated, Janni's Vic Films had signed contracts with Carol White and Loach to make two more films for him.[44] Following *Far From the Madding Crowd*, Schlesinger had left the UK for Hollywood to direct *Midnight Cowboy* (1969); and Janni was perhaps trying to reproduce with Loach and White the partnerships he had enjoyed with Schlesinger and Christie. This was not to be: despite the initial box-office success of the X-rated *Poor Cow*, Janni and Loach parted company.[45]

As *Variety* notes, White dominates *Poor Cow*, and the press compared her with Stamp's co-star in *Far from the Madding Crowd*, Julie Christie: one critic described *Poor Cow* as 'a sort of *Darling* of the working-class' (Hirshhorn 1967).[46] *Poor Cow* has slight, but suggestive, similarities with *Darling* (1965): both films describe the lives of flirtatious women over a period of three years, albeit women who come from different classes; both focus on young women whose central assets, as portrayed in the films, are their attractive appearances.[47] Whereas Julie Christie in *Darling* uses her looks in advertisements, Carol White in *Poor Cow* finds work as a pornographic model: rather literally, one is a 'darling', the other is a 'poor cow'. The aspirations of the attractive young women played by White and Christie partially correspond also: as Joy admits near the start of the film, the things that matter to her are 'plenty of clothes and money'; although as she perceives at the end of the film, girls like her rarely 'make it'. Like *Up the Junction*, *Poor Cow* takes as its central theme the lives of working-class women; in developing this theme, Loach's first cinema film is similarly sensitive to issues of class, sexuality and gender. The director remembers only that he 'did a very bad job of it' (Petley 1982: 10–11); but he succeeds in filming a gently rumina-tive portrait of Joy; this achievement results partly from Dunn's book and script and partly from the aptitude of White in the role of Joy.

The film opens with a pre-credit sequence of Joy giving birth. Loach and editor Roy Watts cut between close-ups of Joy and close shots of a bloody birth. Already, the film asserts its realism, for we see the baby's head emerge. As Joy cradles the baby, the opening song begins and the film cuts to the credit sequence. While the song plays, Joy walks through streets crowded with shoppers, her baby in her arms. Donovan accompanies himself on guitar:

Be not too hard
For life is short
And nothing is given to man.

Be not too hard
When he is sold and bought
For he must manage as best he can.

Be not too hard
When he gladly dies
Defending things he does not own

Be not too hard
If he tells lies
And if his heart is sometimes like a stone.

Be not too hard
For soon he dies
Often no wiser than he began.

Be not too hard
For life is short
And nothing is given to man.

Donovan wrote all the scored music for *Poor Cow*; John Cameron, who would later compose the music for *Kes* (1969) and *After a Lifetime* (1971), arranged and conducted it. Donovan also wrote the music and lyrics for two of the songs heard in the film, 'Poor Love' and 'Colours'. However, it was Loach's collaborator from *The End of Arthur's Marriage*, Christopher Logue, who wrote the words for 'Be not too hard', while Donovan wrote its music. Logue's lyrics earnestly exhort the listener to refrain from judging too harshly the man who is given nothing, who is 'sold and bought' and who dies 'defending things he does not own'. It is sung just after a baby has been born, and it accomplishes an establishing function comparable to Dunn and Myers' 'Bad Girl' in *Up the Junction*. *Poor Cow* covers approximately the first three years of the life of Joy's son, Jonny. Joy's husband and Jonny's father, Tom, is a thief, and when he is imprisoned for robbery, Joy takes another thief, Dave (Terence Stamp), as a lover. The song seems to urge that we 'be not too hard' on the central character, Joy, and her husband and lover; but the fact that it is played immediately after his birth suggests that Loach and Dunn also want us to consider the environment into which Jonny is born.

As they do in *Up the Junction* and *Cathy Come Home*, Loach and his collaborators experiment on *Poor Cow* with narrational strategies. Although *Variety* emphasises the potential box-office attraction of Carol White, national press and magazine film reviewers are almost unanimous in commenting on what they divine to be the twin influences on Loach's first feature film: Jean-Luc Godard and television.[48] Typical is David Robinson, who writes: 'More unhappy is Loach's apparent hero-worship of Jean-Luc Godard, which comes out in unassimilated Godardian effects – including the familiar title device and the direct-to-camera (improvised?) statements which end the film – whose misuse here only serves to revive one's appreciation of Godard' (Robinson 1967: 28).

Adapting Dunn's novel and attempting to present the story of *Poor Cow* from Joy's perspective, Loach employs a range of techniques, including some of the more Brechtian ones he had used on *Up the Junction*. In the novel, Dunn writes Joy's voice as an occasional interior monologue, marked by her use of present tense verbs and first person pronoun reference; in the film, Loach and Dunn adapt this interior monologue into a voice-over, justifying it in two ways. One is the conventional strategy of editing a character's voice-over with images of that person writing a letter, and I comment on this below; the other resembles the use of a character's voice-over in *Up the Junction* and *Cathy Come Home*, in that a character speaks ruminatively about their life, as if to an unseen interviewer.

Soon after Johnny' birth, Joy and Tom move to Ruislip; Joy introduces herself in a voice-over while walking Jonny's pram in a park:

My name is Joy. I'm about five foot three. My measurements are 36, 24, 36. And English. My little baby's name's Jonny. He's quite a chubby little baby and he cries a lot, most of all in the night.

As we hear her voice, Joy sits on a park bench next to two old women. Loach cuts in their chatting voices for a moment, then cuts back to Joy:

> I've got long hair and green eyes. My legs are a bit skinny, actually. Don't like me legs. The things I like are plenty of clothes and money. Well, I was born in Fulham. And, er, my mum had quite a few of us. She spent most of her time in the pub. My dad's a scaffold erector, and he likes the women. Well, I fell in the family way when I was 18. And I got married, to a right bastard. Well, I didn't think so at the time, but I do now.

Joy describes herself to a listener in her own words; her manner is part self-conscious introduction and part interior monologue. Dunn's novel treats its subject empathetically, shifting frequently from third person narration to first person. The novel opens thus: 'She walked down Fulham Broadway past a shop hung about with cheap underwear, the week-old baby clutched in her arms, his face brick red against his new white bonnet' (Dunn 1968: 9). The second chapter, 'In the Money', having begun with five short paragraphs in the third person, switches the mode of narration:

> I've always been a daydreamer, me Joy – Joysy as my Auntie calls me. Daydreamed about – oh, loads of things – just to have something, to be something. I don't want to be down and out all the time I want – I don't know what I do fucking want but I dream about driving a car, that I'm in this big car driving around. (Dunn 1968: 11)

Joy's interior monologue in the novel reveals her thoughts as if directly to the reader; the intermittent first person account contributes to the sense the reader has of the novel's narrative being organised to reflect Joy's point of view. In adapting the novel and in trying to achieve the same intimacy with the central character, Loach and Dunn import the novel's narrative dynamics into the film, as they did with *Up the Junction*.

Most scenes in *Up the Junction* and *Cathy Come Home* are short and self-contained; the same is true of *Poor Cow*: as in the two television films, *Poor Cow*'s scenes do not always have an immediately obvious causal relationship to each other. Besides Joy's voice-overs, one further way that Dunn and Loach try to impose causality is by using intertitles to introduce scenes. The first two intertitles appear after Joy returns home from the hospital: 'When Tom was in the money the world was our oyster...'; 'And we chose Ruislip'. The two intertitles, written in the first person plural and with past tense verbs, narrate a past event to an implied listener. The first implies that Tom was not always 'in the money', and yet when he was he and Joy – for the intertitles represent her 'voice' – could choose where they lived and how. They chose a stereotypically unadventurous place, and in delaying the disclosure of their choice until the second intertitle the film invokes a comparison between the apparently unlimited

Figure 8: *Poor Cow*

'the world was our oyster' and the conservative reality of a suburb on the outskirts of London. The ellipsis and the second intertitle deliberately suspend the revelation of Tom and Joy's choice and construct an ironic retrospective awareness in the central character's 'voice' of how much Ruislip represents a cliché of an unadventurous choice. A long, slow pan across a red-roofed suburban housing estate, presumably Ruislip, follows the two intertitles (figure 8). The shot is steeply angled; it is perhaps taken from the high-rise flat where, we discover, Tom and Joy now live. The area is relatively green; a park is visible and wide grass verges border the roads; in the early morning mist it looks pleasant. But the slowness of the pan declares the uniformity of the architecture; and the shot embodies the distancing view that Joy takes as she reflects on her past, the disappointment she expresses with 'And we chose Ruislip'.

Overall, the causal looseness of *Poor Cow*, like that of *Up the Junction*, entails a felicitous digressiveness in the way that the film communicates its themes through building patterns of association. One typical example of an associative montage sequence set to pop music presents close-ups of the customers in the pub where Joy works; another shows holidaymakers eating ice-cream on a cold day at the seaside. More developed digressions reveal the decrepit state of the block of flats where Dave lives. When Dave first takes Joy to his flat, shots of the courtyard convey the grimy drabness of the location. After Dave and Joy enter the stairwell, for example, an overhead shot shows dustmen pulling a large dustbin out through the courtyard. It is followed by a long shot of the courtyard, criss-crossed by washing lines, and a medium shot of an Italian woman leaning out of her window. These shots do not offer Joy or Dave's view. They are establishing shots in that they present the location of Dave's flat, but their duration and the accompanying music separates them from Joy's story. They link associatively with later shots of the courtyard, however.

When Joy is washing Dave's back in a tin bath in his living room, shouting from the courtyard catches their attention. Dave has been talking about a robbery and what time he will be home; this robbery is a significant narrative event, but Loach shows neither the robbery nor any aspect of its preparation and outcome that Joy does not witness. As she bathes him, they hear shouting. A high-angled overhead shot looks down on the courtyard. There, a man hits a woman hard and chases her towards the dustbins. After this, Loach cuts to Joy and Dave standing by their window looking down: the preceding overhead shot can be understood as representing their viewpoint. Another shot of the fighting woman and man ensues: the man passes a group of women looking on and shouts at them: 'It's nothing to do with you.' The framing of the fight in the courtyard is unstable; the camera seems to discover an event in the world; there is a sense of Loach leaving the filming open to whatever comes his way. But it is difficult to see how he could stage this scene without planning; although significantly, unlike most others, this scene is not based on one in the novel. As Dave, looks down at the fight, he laughs callously and comments: 'He's giving 'er a right wallopin' in't 'e.' His laughter underlines how accepted the abuse is, even though the domestic violence contrasts with the tender relationship that we have just seen between Dave and Joy and relates to the film's penultimate scene, in which Tom hits Joy.

The film looks at gender relations in working-class lives in a number of sequences. Following Tom's arrest, Joy and Jonny leave Ruislip and move in with Joy's Aunt Emm (Queenie Watts) in her poky London flat. An intertitle announces, 'At Aunt Emm's', and the film continues with a shot of Joy helping Emm bring in her washing. As Emm prepares to go out, the film alternates between her talking and radio commentary and pop music. Emm tells Joy about her experiences with men in a way that recalls the witness structure of *Cathy Come Home*; for example, she describes to Joy how she 'took the landlord in for half an hour' when she had no money for the rent. Later she observes: 'They want you to think they need them. You know, to pay for the bread, and see the rent's done and all that. It's all a big lie. You go up the Assistance Board anytime. They'll give you the money.' Joy receives comparable advice from Beryl (Kate Williams), her colleague at the pub where she works while both Tom and Dave are in prison. Beryl instructs Joy on her first night how to flirt with male customers who appear rich; later on, she chastises Joy for 'giving it away', telling her to ask for something. With both husband and lover imprisoned, Joy has a series of affairs; the film introduces this sequence with the intertitle: 'I need different men to satisfy my different moods.' At the same time, through Beryl, Joy finds work as a pornographic model, and Loach films the modelling session with many close-ups of sweaty middle-aged men, the camera inspecting their leering faces.

While she is staying at Emm's, Joy takes up with Dave, and then moves in with him at his neglected flat. The film depicts their developing relationship in one of its most extended montage sequences, setting it to Donovan's hit song 'Colours', taken from his 1965 album, *Fairy Tale*. The song is a gently musing celebration of love; a man commemorates his happiness with his lover by beginning each verse with a meditation on the appealing associations of colours: 'Yellow is the colour of my true love's hair'; 'Blue is the colour of the sky'; 'Green is the colour of the sparkling corn'. Loach introduces the song when Dave and Joy kiss tentatively on Dave's bed. Several shots follow of them cuddling; in three brief shots, Dave feeds Jonny, who now looks about two years old. There is then a long take of the three of them walking across the roof of the tenement block where Dave lives. The camera pans slowly from right to left, stopping as Joy looks down over the courtyard. The next shot shows Joy leaning out of Dave's window and hanging washing on a line that stretches across the courtyard.

The film indicates that some time passes during the 'Colours' sequence by fading in and out to black at the beginning and ending of each shot. The fade-outs also give the sequence a moderate rhythm that duplicates the rhythm of Donovan's song. All the shots show either moments of tenderness and intimacy between Dave and Joy or Dave being a 'father' to Jonny. Joy's hanging out of the washing implies that she and her son have set up home with Dave, and left Aunt Emm's flat. The final shot of the sequence fades in on Dave's living room, with Dave sitting at Joy and Jonny's knees singing and playing the guitar.

When the three of them go to Wales for a holiday, an intertitle introduces the episode as part of Joy's continued remembering of the events that the film is depicting. However, unlike the ironic account of her life with Tom, regret and longing suffuse her recollection of life with Dave:

> I love you always and as days go by
> I'll love you more and more…
> Oh God I'll never forget WALES
> It was terrific

Joy does not address an implied yet anonymous listener; she tells Dave that she loves him; her promise to remember the happy experiences they shared asserts the continuing reality of her commitment to him. But this recollected happiness is about to happen in the unfolding present of the film's world, and a narrative framework has not yet been established for Joy's recollection of a past event. The film cuts from the intertitle to Joy and Dave camping in Wales. From there, it cuts to a sequence of Dave and Joy walking, and then kissing while standing underneath a waterfall. As they walk, Joy's past-tense voice-over continues the intertitle's mode of remembering:

And then we came across this great big waterfall. I don't know what the place was called. And it really was, oh it was fantastic. And all the water came from the mountains like a great big rushing cascade. It wasn't a dream, it really did. And we had it right on the top of this waterfall.

The narrational mode of the voice-over differs from that of the intertitle which introduces the Wales episode: Joy describes the same happy experiences, but she tells them to someone other than Dave.

As they do with the shifts in narration in *Up the Junction* – from Barny talking to the camera, to him talking to an implied second person next to the camera – in the intertitles and voice-overs of *Poor Cow*, Loach and Dunn frequently shift the distinction of personal address. This shifting appears to be a conscious strategy of the filmmakers, an attempt to employ the loosely Brechtian strategies of distanciation and alienation then popular in theatre and cinema. Dunn uses the same techniques in her books; and the likeness supports the impression that Loach not only collaborates extensively with his writers, but also, at the beginning of his career, relies upon them. The Wales intertitle, for instance, adapts a line from the novel, in which Joy closes one of her letters to Dave in prison with: 'Oh God I'll never forget the Water Fall in WALES it was terrific' (Dunn 1968: 40). In the novel, the line invites Dave to recall, as she does, a past event; however, in the film the placement of the intertitle has the potential to confuse this narrative logic, for it occurs before Dave and Joy's experiences in Wales, and before Dave goes to prison.

Loach and Dunn reproduce the novel's shifts to Joy's subjective, first person narration by adapting into intertitles, voice-overs and the final interview what are thoughts, dialogue or letters in the novel. In two scenes in *Poor Cow*, Loach edits Joy's voice-over with images of her writing a letter to Dave, in prison for robbery. The first occurs when Joy returns with Jonny to Dave's flat in order to retrieve her belongings. After Joy has finished packing, and is sitting by a window writing a letter, Loach cuts from a Donovan song to Joy's voice-over: 'Well, my love, I'm now sitting at number eight, writing this letter. Oh God, I've never felt so lonely in all my life.'[49] Her voice-over continues, explaining to Dave how she is selling the things that they bought for the flat. The second scene in which writing justifies Joy's voice-over occurs on the seaside trip with Jonny. It begins with an intertitle that imitates Joy's idiomatic style of writing: 'Well love, I'm sitting on the beach listening to the wireless – the one from home. It's nice and sunny very cold so no bikin [sic].' While we see Jonny playing by the water's edge and Joy writing, her voice-over recalls shared experiences to Dave. Both the letters and voice-overs foreground Joy's perspective.

The issue of whose perspective we take on Dave's criminal activities – Joy's or society's – is brought abruptly to the fore when Dave robs an old woman in her home and is subsequently caught and imprisoned. The opening song has urged us not to judge what we are about to see and hear and the film provokes thought about the relationship between Joy's young son and the environment in which he grows up, in particular the contact that he has with his criminal father, Tom, and with Joy's criminal lover, Dave; it contextualises this by referring to Dave's history.

Immediately after the robbery, Dave enters his and Joy's bedroom and wakes Joy up to show her the jewellery he has stolen, including a necklace that she tries on. He explains that the robbery went well:

Dave: But, er, she was there unfortunately. We locked her up in the cupboard.
Joy: Oh, you didn't.
Dave: 'Ere, that's for you.
Joy: Hey, that's nice. Oh, I like that. What is it, amber or something?
Dave: Something like that.
Joy: How's that?
Dave: Fine. She's all right though; we gave her a cup of tea afterwards.
Joy: Did you?
Dave: Yeh.
Joy: How smashing. Oh, that's a nice one, I like that. Let's put it on.
Dave: Fantastic, i'n' it.
Joy: I think that one really suits me, don't you?

Joy and Dave's immorality emerges; Dave was the perpetrator, yet Joy's delighted reception of the stolen jewellery implicitly condones his actions; the scene tests our agreement with *Poor Cow*'s opening exhortation not to judge too harshly. Joy's voice-overs constantly make her perspective known; and the sequences depicting her relationship with Dave emphasise the mutually felt tenderness and intimacy that comes to unite them. Yet Loach cuts abruptly from Joy observing, 'I think that one really suits me, don't you?' to a big close-up of a judge declaring: 'You all three stand convicted of a craven and cowardly assault on a defenceless old lady.' In his summing up, the judge describes how Dave and his two colleagues hit the woman on the head and, while she was unconscious, locked her in the bathroom. The effects of the blow to the head, the judge explains, mean that the woman is now almost blind.

The sharp placing together of Dave's version of events, Joy's response to his account, and the judge's summary highlights the extent to which Loach and Dunn generally organise the film to reflect Joy's perspective. She unquestioningly accepts Dave's story; trying on the jewellery absorbs more of her attention than concern for the victim. In contrast, the judge's summing up offers a normative perspective on the crime that Dave has committed; a cut to the judge introduces this perspective, disrupting our involvement with Joy and Dave in a manner that flaunts film's potential for shifting perspective. Significantly though, the judge adds that Dave has been entrenched in crime since his childhood; and he lists Dave's previous convictions, many of them for violent robbery. Dave and Joy are not 'lovers-on-the-run', but *Poor*

Cow relates to a tradition of depicting young criminals as outlaws from a hostile society, people to whom society has, by its systems of organisation, denied opportunities.

Nicholas Ray's *They Live by Night* (1948) exemplifies the genre; like the opening song of *Poor Cow*, the opening pre-credit subtitles of *They Live by Night* provoke us to consider what happens to the young outsiders at the film's centre. They declare, in mitigation for what the film will show: 'This boy ... and this girl ... were never properly introduced to the world we live in.' As Joy's husband, Tom, John Bindon projects none of the sympathy that Terence Stamp does as Dave; yet both men are role models for Jonny.[50] Dave is humorous and sensitive, but he is also a violent criminal. The film initially shows him only from Joy's perspective; when Loach introduces society's view of him he does so in a decisively disjunctive way. The last scene of *Poor Cow* confirms that the film is meant to express Joy's perspective. She talks to an unseen interviewer about topics signalled by intertitles – 'The Future', 'My Perfect Life' and 'Thinking of Dave' – and the film then ends with a freeze-frame of her. This interview with the protagonist mimics a documentary, yet though it retroactively places the rest of the film in the past, it does not bring a coherent or logical narrative structure to what we have seen and heard.[51]

When *Up the Junction* introduces the Doctor's voice-over during Rube's miscarriage, Loach, Dunn and Garnett want to jolt us out of emotional empathy with her painful experience and alert us to the social problem that exists. Both Loach and Garnett recall the influence of Brechtian methods of 'fracturing the narrative'; but Loach also remembers how uneasy he was with these techniques. In *Poor Cow* Loach and Dunn use a similar tactic of juxtaposing two perspectives with the aim of unsettling and prompting us to think about what social and economic factors provoke people to commit crimes. *Poor Cow* opens and closes by focusing on Joy's son, Jonny, and the effect of environment on the socialisation of a child is central to the concerns of the film-makers. This theme, which Loach had explored in his *Wednesday Play The Coming Out Party* (1965), becomes the central topic of his next two feature films, *Kes* (1969) and *Family Life* (1971). However, although the theme recurs, the Brechtian strategy of juxtaposing perspectives using both unspecified voice-overs and jump cuts is abandoned. *Poor Cow* and Loach's early television dramas, *Diary of a Young Man*, *Up the Junction*, *The End of Arthur's Marriage* and *Cathy Come Home*, are all tentative, experimental works, embarked upon with youthful energy and vigour, which, in formal terms, they generally embody. In spite of these qualities though, only with *Kes* does Loach begin to develop a more sophisticated style and discover what best suits his own ambitions, leaving behind both the tentativeness and the influences of Brecht and Godard.

CHAPTER THREE

sympathetic observation

After his unsatisfactory experience with mainstream film production on *Poor Cow*, Loach and his producer, Tony Garnett, helped set up an independent production company in order to make films for cinema and television – Kestrel Films, named after the novel, *A Kestrel for a Knave* (1969) which Loach, with the help of its author, Barry Hines, and Garnett, adapted into his second feature film, *Kes* (1969).[1] This chapter examines the changes in Loach's work at the end of the 1960s: it considers photography and performance, and assesses what Loach's direction of these brings to the adaptation of a novel. Working with an independent production company afforded Loach increased artistic freedom, albeit one related to the economic, social and political constraints of the British film and television industry. Loach could now choose projects and collaborators, and the visual style of *Kes* owes much to his choice of director of photography, Chris Menges.[2]

Menges operated the camera on *Poor Cow*, under its director of photography, Brian Probyn. Loach promoted Menges to director of photography on *Kes*. In between *Poor Cow* and *Kes*, Menges operated for a Czech director of photography, Miroslav Ondricek, on Lindsay Anderson's *If…* (1968). Ondricek shot one of Loach's favourite films, Milos Forman's *Loves of a Blonde* (1965),[3] and Loach attributes the development of his own photographic style to the influence of Menges:

> As far as filming is concerned, it's Chris Menges who taught me most about lighting and filming. Since the end of the 1960s, from my film *Kes*, we put together an unsophisticated style, with quite harsh lighting. Chris had previously worked with a Czech master cameraman, Miroslav Ondricek, and had been influenced by some of his ideas. It was important to us that the camera

could spontaneously react to everything which took place during filming. Nothing could be locked up from the beginning. The focusing itself isn't premeditated, it's done in a way that those acting can freely move in front of the camera. But the images must be pleasing to look at, of course. If a certain amount of spontaneity is maintained on camera, the frames will be pleasing and the lighting correct. (Ostria 1994a: 38–9)[4]

Menges photographed documentary reports for *World in Action* during the 1960s, under Denis Mitchell's supervision. His collaboration with Loach epitomises the director's consistent collaboration with directors of photography who have a background in documentaries: Tony Imi worked on documentaries at the BBC before shooting Loach's *Wednesday Play* films; the *Days of Hope* photographer, John Else, shot reports for *Man Alive*; Loach first worked with Barry Ackroyd, his regular director of photography in the 1990s, while directing the documentary *The View from the Woodpile* (tx: Channel 4, 12 June 1989). Ackroyd also shot Nick Broomfield's documentaries *Too White for Me* (1992), *Aileen Wournos: The Selling of a Serial Killer* (1992) and *Tracking Down Maggie: The Unofficial Biography of Margaret Thatcher* (1994).

The director's choice of photographer affects the visual style of his films, and Loach recognises the importance of his first collaboration with Menges:

Until then it had been seen as like fictional journalism: you get a 16mm camera and grab the action, so that you really felt like you're on the street with everybody and there's a sense of actuality and it's like the camera's running with the participants. And it was Chris Menges, really, who I certainly owe a lot to. His contribution was to say, look, we just need to observe it more, let the action happen. And we just need to observe it and not be so busy all the time with the camera: just let the camera reflect on it, rather than pursue it.[5]

Of the camerawork in *Kes*, Loach remarks:

I was aware at that time of not trying to let the camera do the work, but let the people in front of the camera tell the story, so that the camera was a sympathetic observer. And you had to get what was in front of the camera absolutely right and true, and if it was right and true, and you photographed it sympathetically, then it would work.[6]

The most common strategy that he and Menges use is to have the camera follow the action. From a distance, with a long focus lens, usually about seventy millimetres, the camera seems to discover its subject and frame it in a medium close shot. The use of a long lens for close shots and long shots, panning and re-focusing between framings, flattens space and minimises perspective; there is often a shallow depth-of-field in Loach's films, with only one plane in focus. This aspect of his photographic style remains generally consistent in his career. The photography in *Kes* is a noteworthy development in Loach's work; but other advances contribute to the equilibrium of the film. These advances are the result of directorial decisions beyond the choices of subject matter and collaborators; among them are decisions about narrative structure, theme and the balance between making clear political statements and creating nuanced stories. Perhaps most importantly, on *Kes* Loach refines his treatment of character perspective and point of view. In 1994 he reflects on this while differentiating between *Cathy Come Home* (1966) and *Ladybird Ladybird* (1994):

> *Cathy* was a campaigning film about homelessness, while *Ladybird* is about the relationship between Maggie and her new partner Jorge. In a way, *Ladybird* is much more like *Kes*, because it's about someone who presents a different face to the authorities from the one we see in the film. (Allen 1994: 15)

Like *Cathy Come Home*, *Kes* censures institutional practice, yet it achieves this political aim by observing a side of Billy different to the one that his teachers perceive. In *Kes*, Loach refracts politics through personal relations, through the family; instead of explicitly articulating a political programme, *Kes* uses metaphors to give significance to the power struggles of school and home.

Kes: implying shared experiences

The opening shot of *Kes* discloses a dark bedroom; two people are asleep in bed. After a few seconds an alarm goes off. An arm reaches out to switch it off. More time passes; the camera remains still; the wakened body reverts to slumbering stillness. Finally, after what feels like a long time, a voice calls out the first word of the film: 'Jud.' 'What?' comes the reply. Neither speaker moves beneath the covers. 'You'd better get up.' A young voice responsibly reminds Jud to heed the alarm: 'The alarm's gone off y'know.' Jud (Freddie Fletcher) retorts sarcastically: 'Do you think I don't know that?' The young voice repeats its reminder to Jud that he will be late. Finally, Jud gets slowly up and sits on the side of the bed, holding his head. Early morning grumpiness dominates the ensuing exchange: 'Set clock on for me, Jud, for seven'; 'Set it yeself'; 'Go on, you're up.' Jud stands up and heaves the covers from the bed. He flicks the light on, revealing a young boy, Billy (David Bradley), scrambling to get under the covers again.

Billy: You rotten sod, just because you' to get up.
Jud: Another few weeks lad and you'll be getting up with me.
Billy: I'll not.
Jud: Won't ya?
Billy: Nope, 'cause I'm not gonna work down the pit.

Jud: Where thou gonna work then?
Billy: I dunno, but I'm not gonna work down the pit.

After Billy repeats his resolution not to work as a miner, the film cuts to Jud, who is standing by the bedroom door pulling on his shirt. He finishes dressing and leaves. Billy switches the light off, and returns to bed. The credits begin.

During this long take – lasting nearly two minutes – of the two brothers in bed, and then of Billy under the covers, the camera does not move. The alarm goes off a few seconds after the shot begins, yet another half minute passes before the first word of the film is spoken; and the camera is appropriately still in its presentation of the stillness of the reluctant early riser. This opening shot introduces narrative expectations and deadlines: Billy and Jud share a bed; maybe they share a fate – as Jud threatens smugly: 'Another few weeks lad and you'll be getting up with me.' Jud's comment indicates that his brother has only a 'few weeks' left at school; it assumes as an inevitability that Billy will work 'down the pit'. The name of Billy's kestrel hawk, 'Kes', gives the film its title, yet the centre of interest in *Kes* is not the bird but Billy himself; the drama of the film is the drama of his consciousness and his personality, the 'different face' of which Loach speaks. The first word of the film though is 'Jud', spoken by Billy; it is significant because the relationship between the two brothers shapes much of the drama. This opening shot, and the fraternal altercation it portrays, subtly intimate the theme and structure of the film.

Barry Hines based *A Kestrel for a Knave* on his own experiences and those of his brother: born near Barnsley in 1939, the son of a miner, Hines taught at a local secondary school as a physical education teacher, following an attempt to become a professional footballer. He dedicates his novel to his brother, Richard, who was a falconer and who served as technical adviser for the film.[7] The novel and the film tell the story of a 15-year-old-boy's experiences during his last term at school: without qualifications and apparently destined for the colliery or for manual labour, Billy captures and trains a fledgling kestrel hawk. In directing the film, Loach follows the novel closely, as he does with Dunn's *Up the Junction* and *Poor Cow*; but differences exist between novel and film that testify to his increasing willingness to attend to questions of narrative structure. He avoids the direct transposition of a novel's dynamics that marks his versions of Dunn's books. *Kes'* credits state that the novel is 'Adapted by Barry Hines, Kenneth Loach and Tony Garnett', and Loach, we know, always collaborates intensely with his writers. The novel's themes, dialogue and structure resemble those in the film, yet this does not necessarily imply that Hines took the majority of creative decisions in adapting the book. Loach attributes his photographic style to Menges, but he chose to work with Menges; similarly, although the subject of *Kes* comes from Hines' imagination and experience, he (and Garnett) chose to film Hines' novel. The 'tight rein' that the director keeps on the structure of *Kes* only partly grows out of the novel's structure; the film benefits from a responsive handling of elements other than the script, particularly, as we will see, in the casting and directing of actors.

In contrast to the film, at the start of *A Kestrel for a Knave* Billy already has the bird. After his paper round, he goes to the shed to feed it. Talking to the bird about his arguments with his mother and brother, he reflects, 'An' our Jud, he's t'worst o't' lot, he's allus after me … allus has been. Like that day last summer when I fetched you, he was after me then' (Hines 1969: 21). Billy's comments introduce a 23-page flashback of him going nesting, seeing the kestrel nest, meeting the farmer, going to the library, stealing the book, arguing with Jud and then, after Jud returns home drunk, going to capture the fledgling. The sequence of events contained within the novel's flashback resembles the sequence of events in the film, but the film integrates this sequence into a new timescale.

Kes has three parts. The first contains the weekend: on Friday, after his paper round, Billy goes to school; he spends Saturday nesting, at the library and the book-shop in town, then at home reading while his brother and mother are at the pub; on Sunday morning, after Jud returns home drunk in the early hours, Billy takes the kestrel from its nest. The second part has three sections of Billy training the hawk; it ends with the games lesson and the showers. The third part begins with Jud walking to work in the early morning; the rest of the film depicts moments from a full day at school. During this day, the headmaster, Gryce (Bob Bowes), canes Billy and five other boys; Billy's English teacher, Farthing (Colin Welland), encourages him to speak in class; Billy fights with MacDowall (Robert Naylor) in the playground; he receives a lunchtime visit from Farthing; he fails to put Jud's bet on (it is important that this day opens with Jud going to work, and therefore unable to place his own bet); he sees the youth employment officer (Bernard Atha); and he returns home to discover that Jud has killed Kes.

In adapting the novel into a film script, Hines, Loach and Garnett eliminate the novel's flashbacks and introduce a dual temporality. The middle part of the film is the shortest, but chronologically it covers the most time: the three short sequences of Billy training Kes are set in a domain of emotional intimacy with Billy; his endeavours with the kestrel reveal his acquired skill and knowledge. This part depicts the time of Kes's growth from a fledgling to an adult hawk, covering Billy's last term at school, the 'few weeks' that Jud mentions in the opening shot. In its first and third parts, the film delineates time more sharply: the rhythms of a weekend and a school day set the pace of these parts. *Kes* unfolds during the last term of Billy's school life: it moves from the first scene and Jud's comment, 'Another few weeks lad and you'll be getting up with me', to Billy's interview – as an 'Easter leaver' – with the youth employment officer; yet, opening *Kes* with Billy's early morning activities before school and ending it at teatime after school produces a diurnal temporality based on Hines' original novel. The film depicts Billy's last term, but its organisation imitates one school day. This imitative diurnal structure offers a straightforward alternative to transposing the novel's temporal structure into a film.

The concentration on revealing the 'different face' of which Loach speaks, presenting the dramatic world from the perspective of the protagonist, aligns *Kes* with the melodrama of protest. *Kes* protests against an educational system which fails to recognise individual talent, and it suggests that this is a consequence of a capitalist society which demands a steady supply of unskilled manual labour. *Kes* admonishes a practice that reproduces society's requirement for a class of children to be destined from an early age for manual labour, whatever their potential. Yet, whereas *Cathy Come Home* criticises the punitive attitudes of local authorities by having a separate report on housing that it places next to Cathy's story, *Kes* builds its critique by revealing a private side of Billy; it pits him, as a misrecognised innocent in the divided world of melodrama, against an institution and an ideology which, the film proposes, determine his life. Importantly, the intimation about Billy's future – that he may become like Jud in employment and temper – exists concurrently with a note of ambiguity at the end of the film. From the beginning, *Kes* presents its dramatic world from Billy's epistemological position, though it does so without always adopting Billy's optical perspective.

George M. Wilson describes this mode of narration as a form of restricted narrational authority, where 'the audience sees just the situations that he sees but, again, not from the places that he occupies' (Wilson 1996: 88). *Poor Cow* (1967), attempting to present its events from Joy's point of view, introduces shifts to Joy's subjective first-person narration by adapting the novel's interior monologue (whether verbalised thoughts or letters) into intertitles, voice-overs and the interview. *Kes* uses less disruptive methods than these to align the viewer with Billy and to reflect his subjectivity indirectly. Vital to the achievement of *Kes* is the presentation of its world in ways that connect it to classical narrative film. Loach and his collaborators employ realist techniques to ensure that the film seems to offer us direct access to its dramatic world; but they use strategies that present the film's world from Billy's perspective. This allows Loach to recall that 'it's about someone who presents a different face to the authorities from the one we see in the film' (Allen 1994: 15); and this feature links *Kes* to the melodrama of protest.

Billy is a misrecognised innocent, yet the film does not portray him as entirely unresponsible for his life. He is a resilient character, at times mischievous and belligerent. In the newsagents, where he picks up the newspapers for his morning paper round, his mental agility emerges behind his employer's back. Billy runs to the newsagents, as Jud has taken his bike. On arrival, Mr Porter (Harry Markham), the newsagent, greets him:

Porter:	I thought you weren't coming.
Billy:	Why? I'm not late am I?
Porter:	Very near.
Billy:	I nearly was though.
Porter:	What do you mean?
Billy:	Our Jud, he's taken bike.
Porter:	Well, what you gonna do then?

Billy:	Walk it.
Porter:	Walk it? How long do you think that's gonna take?
Billy:	It'll not take me long.
Porter:	Eh. There's a waiting list a mile long for that job of yours. Good lads too, most of them. From up Firs Hill, round there.
Billy:	I haven't let you down have I?

At this point a customer comes in, interrupting their conversation. Porter moves seamlessly from the patronising mistrust that characterises his dealings with Billy to obsequious attentiveness. As he finishes serving the customer, Billy, unseen by Porter, pockets a couple of chocolate bars. We exclusively share narrative information with Billy; the film's alignment of its own narration with Billy's experience allows us to appreciate his revenge on Porter's mistrust. After the customer exits, Porter turns to Billy; without pausing for breath after his 'Cheerio, good morning sir', he continues his harangue:

> You know what they said when I took you on, don't you? They said you'll have
> to keep your eyes open now, you know. They're all alike off that estate up there.
> They'll take your breath if you're not careful.

Wily Billy protests: 'I haven't taken nowt of yours yet, have I?' Porter replies: 'I haven't given you a chance yet, that's why.' His smugness creates an irony of which he is unaware. Although Porter seems right not to trust Billy, his hostility and prejudice influence how we understand the exchange and justify Billy's theft: if he is not going to be trusted, he might as well steal something. *Kes* steers us towards Billy's epistemological position, presenting its dramatic world in ways that encourage empathy for him. His straight-faced protestation of innocence only adds to the amusement.

Unlike *Poor Cow*, *Kes* presents its world from a character's perspective, yet it does so in ways that assert its realism. The scene in the newsagents offers a typical example: the images are darkly lit, and muted tones of brown, green and grey dominate the scene's colouring. The lighting scheme upholds on film the natural light of the location: the interior looks as if it is lit only by the daylight coming through the shop's windows. The image is highly contrasted, with shadowy areas that lack detail; the dark corner where Billy stands as he pockets the chocolate bars, for example, contrasts strongly with the almost 'burned out' windows. In *Moving Pictures*, Anne Hollander traces the history of what she calls 'proto-cinematic art', painting, which, long before photography was developed, employed realistic, chiaroscuro depictions of light. Hollander draws attention to the importance of light-filled windows or doors in the paintings of Velásquez and Vermeer, from where light appears to enter the scene:

> Painted light, imitating the action of seen light, can give this sense that the
> world of the picture is momentarily actual and in uncertain motion – becoming

seamlessly part of our own shifting world, even while remaining a painting in a frame. It does not fool or please the eye; it is like part of the eye's usual experience. (Hollander 1991: 16)

Menges and Loach set the exposure and lights to film the interior of the shop. Another director might prefer to light the interior so that it would not be 'underexposed' and the day-lit exterior would not be 'overexposed'; but Loach insists on having as few lights as possible, partly to avoid crowding the set, but also to achieve an observational, realist style.[8]

The lighting scheme for the film does not imitate how we see light in the world, because the eye adjusts to extremes of dark and light rapidly enough to be imperceptible in a day-lit room. A camera does not adjust this way, and, whatever scheme Loach and Menges chose, they had to light scenes sufficiently to expose the film at all. Gilberto Perez comments on this type of photography when he describes the work of Jean-Luc Godard and Raoul Coutard on *A bout de souffle* (aka *Breathless*, 1959):

The newsreel look of *Breathless*, central to its sense of life as improvisation in the midst of action – in the midst of a bedroom no less than in the streets – was itself not an improvisation but a calculated effect for which Godard and Coutard took pains to get the right film stock. (Perez 1998: 337)

Loach and Menges' manipulation of contrast between dark and light areas of the images in *Kes* imparts, likewise, a sense of the images having been filmed spontaneously, without pre-planning; the light of a scene appears to be 'imitating the action of seen light'. Perez observes that classical film-making disallows these techniques because they call attention to the artifice of the image; but in *Kes* the 'calculated effect' is one which contributes to the sense of a realistic or naturalistic presentation.

Billy's scenes with the newsagent typify the way that the protagonist interacts significantly with other characters, but *Kes* also reveals Billy during his private moments. One such sequence occurs during his paper round. Having chatted with the milkman, Billy climbs down a grassy bank and sits down to read a comic. Menges and Loach have carefully photographed the landscape: light green fields and dark green hedgerows provide a background from which we can barely distinguish Billy, who is dressed in light blue corduroy trousers and a khaki jacket. The countryside bordering Barnsley is present throughout the film, often in the background of shots; but this is no idealised rural landscape; it is a part of South Yorkshire dotted with collieries and pit villages, and as Billy leaves the quiet road, a colliery's winding gear is audible. He clambers down the grass verge, and the camera is there before him. As he sits, the noise of the colliery increases. Billy looks up. Only then do we see what Billy sees: the clanking pithead winding gear and smoking chimney. This shot frames Billy from behind, so that he appears small, almost hidden in the long grass on the left foreground: in his drab clothes, he almost merges with the landscape (figure 9). One colliery occupies

Figure 9: *Kes*

the middle ground; another is visible in the distance; both pump out smoke from tall chimneys; a small fire burns near one. The winding gear knocks away steadily, but Billy ignores the pit, flicking the pages of his comic to find the cartoon strip he wants. It is appropriate that Loach does not use an optical point-of-view shot from his position here; for although the mine is near to Billy – it is part of what he knows – it holds no interest for him. The shot is depressing and ominous: it is the first occasion on which *Kes* shows us the place to which Billy swears he will not go.

The film cuts to a brief close-up of Billy, and then, as he begins reading the Desperate Dan comic strip, to an approximation of his optical point of view, accompanied by his voice-over. The cartoon frames fill the film frames as the camera pans along the strip. The combination of voice-over and point-of-view shots reinforces the presentation of his perspective. In the last comic frame, when Dan punches his opponent into 'the middle of next week', the camera zooms forward into the frame of the comic strip, following the trajectory of Dan's opponent. As the framing changes, a low whistle emanates from the colliery, presumably signalling a break or shift change. The whistle connects the climax of Billy's moment of private pleasure with the colliery: its duration and pitch neatly accompany the zoom forward into the cartoon frame, but the whistle primarily reminds us of what exists for Billy beyond the comic. Throughout his reading, the low sound of the winding gear has remained present on the soundtrack; the scene juxtaposes Billy's pleasure with the sound of what he most hates. As he finishes reading, the whistle calls him and the film back to school and work.

Loach organises character perspective in *Kes* to manoeuvre the viewer's sympathies towards its protagonist, but Billy's personality is decisively important to our understanding of him, and his idiosyncratic personality dominates the film. This partly results from the achievement of David Bradley, the young actor who plays him. Bradley performs Billy so that he is not a victim of circumstance, but someone who can, given the moment, act wilfully, even be as much of a bully as his peers. Importantly, Bradley, despite his wiry frame and his unimposing physical presence, creates an air of confident social intelligence. Billy perceives instinctively the boundaries of his relationships with adults; he is generally astute when dealing with them, aware of what he can get away with. Loach's casting of Bradley indicates the transformation of his methods of casting and directing actors that takes place at the end of the 1960s. In his London films of the mid-1960s, he relies mostly on professional actors; but on *Kes* he employs mainly local people from Barnsley.

In November 1969, Loach and Garnett described to G. Roy Levin how they shot *After a Lifetime* (1971), which Loach had just finished shooting, and *Kes* with professional entertainers – club comics or musicians – rather than professional actors, thus enabling them to negotiate Equity rules. Loach observes:

> These people have got the ability to make a fictional situation believable in front of a camera. We try to get people who can draw on their own lives, on their experience – so they bring it in, they're not emoting, not a blank sheet of paper on which you and they write the part. You try to find people who have it in their own experience. (Levin 1971: 99)

Interviewed by Paul Madden in July 1976, Loach comments on his work with actors:

> The degree of improvisation depends on the emotional content of the film and who is doing it. I've never been involved in literary films, apart from my Chekhov film [*A Misfortune*, part of the BBC's *Full House* series, tx: BBC2, 13 January 1973], so exact words are not terribly important – the important thing is what's happening. Obviously, the writer puts down dialogue which is accurate and to the point, and often that ends up being said. But these words are the tip of the iceberg – it's everything else you've got to get right. When you've got actors in a film, obviously their personalities are involved, so, for instance, some will take longer to get angry. You've got to build it, so the exact words don't matter. You've got to have three-dimensional characters, which otherwise don't exist in the script as paper. (Madden 1976: no page numbers)

Words matter for Loach, but the performances and his ability to use his actors' personalities matter more. Sixteen years later, he says:

In the same way the emotions of people who are struggling to hang on to a decent life are powerful, but they are still ignored for animation or dinosaurs. People are still moved and shocked by human experience. It's always more involving than anything film-makers can invent. The most extraordinary location is someone's face and what's happening on it. That's the stuff of drama and it doesn't change, does it? (Birch 1993: 59)

When Levin asked Loach and Garnett in 1969 if they would use Carol White and Ray Brooks again if they were making *Cathy Come Home* now, they replied that they would not, 'unless we were forced to' (Levin 1971: 100).

Loach shot *After a Lifetime* in Merseyside a year after shooting *Kes*, using the same crew. *After a Lifetime* was the last of his films to be broadcast as a single play: up to that point, Loach had made eleven films for BBC1, ten for *The Wednesday Play*, and one for its replacement, *Play for Today*. *After a Lifetime* was the first film he directed for the BBC's rival, ITV. Neville Smith, who had acted in several of Loach's *Wednesday Play* films, wrote *After a Lifetime*.[9] He explains its origins:

My Dad died and I was very affected by it. I felt I wanted to do something for him. I was asked by Ken and Tony if I'd like to write it as a film for them – the result was *After a Lifetime*. My original idea was to praise ordinary men (which sounds like pseuds' corner) in a sense not to be heroic, not to say that you are celebrating the death of a hero, because that's not true, but the death of an ordinary working-class bloke, and from him you can extrapolate other men like him. You're saying he's dead, and this is what his legacy is – the continuity of experience, and the politics. Hence the photographs of my father in the credit stills at various stages of his life. I felt so strongly about it that I thought I might as well act in it, although I didn't sit down to write myself a part. I think also Ken and Tony realised how much I was involved on a personal level. It wasn't an enjoyable experience acting in it – because it meant re-living my father's funeral. I suppose I treated it as a catharsis really, but it didn't turn out that way. Obviously you are aware when you film that it's artifice and not life. But there are some things that deeply affected me in the film, which are still included – one or two parts where I wasn't acting and Ken just turned the cameras. (Madden 1976: no page numbers)

Smith recalls that there are moments where he 'wasn't acting' and yet Loach continued to film. He refers presumably to moments when he felt his grief for his own father overwhelm him during his performance of a character grieving for his father. Smith's comments provide an insight into the way that Loach takes advantage of ambiguous features of dramatic and photographic representation. Like Loach's comments about the scene in *Carla's Song* when the conversation with the *campesinos* upset Oyanka Cabezas, Smith's comments draw attention to the director's practice of documenting the actor, who, in the service of a fiction, may experience emotions close to those required by the fiction.

It was on *Kes*, which was shot on locations in and around Barnsley including St Helen's School where Barry Hines had taught, that Loach began this practice. Apart from Colin Welland as Farthing, whom Loach had directed on *Z Cars*, none of the actors were professionals: all the pupils and most of the teachers came from St Helen's, including Bradley. The real St Helen's headmaster, Bob Bowes, plays Gryce, Billy's headmaster; Brian Glover, who played Sugden, the PE teacher, was a teacher at another school, a semi-professional wrestler and a friend of Barry Hines; Lynne Perrie and Freddie Fletcher as Mrs Casper and Jud were Barnsley club entertainers; they would later feature in *Coronation Street*. Other incidental players were comics, including Bill Dean, Joey Kaye and Bernard Atha. Justifying his casting strategy, Loach argues that film actors, no matter how skilled, will always find it difficult to disguise their regional and class origins.[10] He says of his casting:

> If a part has to carry a lot of information, then you need someone who can learn their lines well, yet deliver them with spontaneity. If it is a part which involves a primarily emotional exchange with somebody, then you want someone whose emotions are very available, and who can respond in that right way. You also cast for authenticity of age, class or region. (Hacker 1991: 302)

Elsewhere, he comments on the acting in his films that 'it relies on instinct, not intellect. The actor must have a gut reaction' (Ostria 1994a: 40). Loach casts, in British documentary director Harry Watt's terms, 'natural actors' (Watt 1974: 116).[11] He employs actors who are natural in that their class, regional origins, age and temperament fit the role; and natural in that they are confident and extroverted enough to perform for the camera. This kind of typecasting attends to accent and to personality; it is a vitally important aspect of Loach's work, for the conviction that his actors carry in their performances contributes strongly to his films' realism.

The brief scene featuring Bill Dean as Floyd, the fish and chip shop owner, provides an example of the rewards that Loach's casting strategies bring. As Billy waits for his chips, he taps the bottom of the counter with his foot. Floyd reprimands him in a deep-voiced, gruff Merseyside accent: 'And stop kicking will ya; we only put that in today.' Dean's delivery has a deadpan grouchiness that suits his character. When Floyd's wife says that she's 'getting rid of these chips, it's getting late now' – that is, she is giving Billy extra scraps – Floyd grumbles: 'Aye, well don't be going mad.' As Billy departs, Floyd carps indifferently – without looking up from the paper spread out on the counter – to an old man who stares absent-mindedly out of the window: 'These kids, I don't know Mr Glover, they're just all the same.' Dean brings such a convincing authenticity to his portrayal of a grumpy shopkeeper that he manages to make it both comic and credible. *Kes* is concerned with whether or not 'these kids' are all the same;

and Loach succinctly contrasts Floyd's attitude with that of the butcher, who gives Billy a scrap of beef in the following scene.

The combination of comedy and credibility in many of the performances and situations is central to the achievement of *Kes*: the film 'sympathetically observes' its characters, and introduces a perspective that reflects Billy's own perspective. Andrew Britton, writing about realism and Max Ophuls' *Madame de …* (1953), brings a characteristic clarity to his discussion of a related issue:

> This dialectic of insideness/outsideness from the dramatic world is not 'Ophulsian' *tout court*: it is the characteristic mode of significant mimetic art, and its formal means are infinite, but it is – it must be insisted – a fact of the *writing* of the work. It testifies to that possibility which is open to mimesis of constructing critical metaphorical models of reality, and its tendency is not to solicit but to resist and disturb identification. (Britton 1982: 99)

Kes combines realist techniques with dramatic and performance strategies to create a 'metaphorical model of reality' that it presents predominantly from its protagonist's point of view. The use of comic stereotype is central to its construction of this model of reality. Andrew Klevan writes of the realism and comic melodrama of *Kes*, discussing the caning scene:

> The film's pursuit of the real leads into the comic melodrama of figures such as the headmaster. *Kes*' realism of character and setting is achieved through familiar idioms, clichés, tics, accents, haircuts and fashions, all of which afford the viewer pleasurable jolts of recognition … Furthermore, the film's realistic specificity goes hand-in-hand with the construction of melodramatic typage. The headmaster *plays* up to all the clichés we would expect from a melodramatic type; but the film's conception of the real world is precisely one inhabited by institutional and familial figures who play up to type, and the injustices it unearths lie in the rigidities which stem from that typage – here the oppressive formalities which close Casper down. (Klevan 2000: 42)

Klevan's suggestion that *Kes*' realism goes 'hand-in-hand' with melodramatic typage offers a useful way of understanding the humour that the film provides. For Loach and Barry Hines, though they produce a melodrama of protest, use clichés in dramatic situations and in performances. The pleasures that these 'jolts of recognition' afford are largely humorous pleasures, and we feel these pleasures even in situations that are thematically quite sad; as Brenda Davies writes perceptively of *Kes*: 'Infinitely sad in its total implications, it is also immensely funny in much of its detail' (Davies 1970: 75). Many of the scenes in *Kes* derive from Barry Hines' novel; but the dominant tone of humour comes from the casting and performances.

Freddie Fletcher perfectly portrays Billy's older brother, the preening and bullying Jud, 't' cock of estate', as Billy later calls him. Following the opening pre-credit sequence, Jud next appears in the film when he snatches Billy's stolen book from his brother's hands on Saturday evening at home. The scene opens with a medium shot of Billy reading in the dark living room. Jud enters the room from behind the sofa and takes the book from Billy: 'What's tha got this for when thou can't read?' he asks, adding, 'You must be crackers. I could understand if it were money, but chuff me, not a book.' Billy chases Jud, and the two brothers stand silhouetted by the window while they argue. When Billy jumps at Jud in an effort to retrieve the book, Jud throws him off and then throws the book at him. Billy picks it up and sits down again, the camera panning right with him. Jud, observing that Billy's reading re-absorbs him, walks into the frame and harasses him again, this time asking him where he is going to find a kestrel, twisting his arm until he tells him. Satisfied with his bullying, Jud walks across the room to comb his hair. Mrs Casper then enters the living room and a series of shot/reverse-shot patterns presents the remainder of the scene: of Billy and Jud, of Mrs Casper and Jud, then of Mrs Casper and Billy.

When Mrs Casper enters, the familial hostility increases:

Mrs Casper:	You had your tea yet Billy?
Billy:	No.
Mrs Casper:	Well get some then. You know where t' pantry is.

Billy's mother speaks sharply to her son, but he ignores her and continues reading his book. While she is brusque with Billy, with Jud she begins pleasantly by asking him how his horses have 'gone on'. Their conversation quickly degenerates into a row, however, focused around Mrs Casper's boyfriend, Reg (Joe Miller), whom Jud despises. As they quarrel, other issues surface, such as whether or not Jud is 'too big to have a good hiding', or who will eventually own their house. Mother and son continue their ugly bickering for a few minutes until Jud examines his hair one last time in the mirror: 'Some bird's gonna be lucky tonight.' Mrs Casper remarks sarcastically: 'God's gift to women.' Then, after a pause, as Jud is leaving the room, she asks: 'Fancy buying me a brandy and pep' tonight?' Jud answers, 'I hope it keeps high for ya'. He then leaves, whistling. Mrs Casper, regretting that her patent white shoes could 'do with a bit of a polish', leaves Billy 'two bob' for 'some pop, some crisps', then says goodnight and leaves. The scene ends with a close-up of Billy reading, and an over-the-shoulder shot of the illustrated guide to rearing kestrels.

This scene exposes Billy's family life, and, like many in *Kes*, it is remarkable for its performances and dialogue. Both Freddie Fletcher and Lynne Perrie achieve sharply defined personalities for the characters of Jud and Mrs Casper. Fletcher is thickset and blond, in contrast to the wiry and dark Billy. The burly young miner, squeezed into his smart Saturday night suit, has a proprietary manner; he acts as if he is already the 'man of the house', as he predicts that he will be. His deep, slow voice, his heavily built physique and his swaggering gait quickly convey his personality. Mrs Casper has brushed her fading bleached blonde hair back and up; her face seems haggard with tiredness; and she gives the impression of being constantly harried. Perrie flawlessly enacts a tired middle-aged woman who has been working all week and who is now desperate to go out on Saturday night and have a few drinks. As Loach says, he cast the actors in these roles with their experiences in mind, and he comments on the importance of accent; but personality and appearance also matter. He casts in order to match actor with character according to type: the benefit of this is that actors like Dean, Fletcher and Perrie can evoke personalities within brief scenes through their distinct voices, postures, ways of moving, appearances and facial expressions.

Lynne Perrie and Freddie Fletcher speak with strong Barnsley accents. As their argument develops, Perrie's voice becomes increasingly high-pitched, strained and astringent, while Fletcher's gruff and mordant voice becomes more flatly threatening and unpleasant. The scene depicts the lack of affection within Billy's family, illustrating the power struggles of home. The animosity between Mrs Casper and Jud taints the scene, yet for Billy this is normal; he responds in a similar fashion to both his mother's nonchalance and his brother's malicious bullying. Thus, the scene reveals his ability to concentrate. Nonetheless, it would be easy to read too much significance into the portrait of the family. The quick switches that they make, the sudden flare-ups and the abrupt cool-downs, modify the impression of hostility. When Mrs Casper enters the living room, getting ready to go out, it is the first time we meet her. Perrie, like many of the actors in *Kes*, attains an indelible quality in her performance. Part of this permanence originates in the dialogue.[12] 'What trout you been going with lately then?' she asks Jud. 'Better than that cripple you been seeing,' he replies. Their row is full of richly vernacular insults and clichéd sayings: for example, 'You chuck your bloody money round like a Scotchman with no arms don't you?'; 'You have to use a spanner to get a thre'penny bit out of his hand, that's why.'; 'Listen what about him you're going with. He's tight as a camel's arse in a sandstorm.' The richness of the language that the characters use during their argument conveys both the ugliness of their animosity and the humorous normality of it.

When mother and son do go out, instead of staying in with Billy the film follows them to the pub, moving away from Billy and presenting the adult society to which Jud and Mrs Casper belong and for which Billy is destined. Throughout the 28 shots that comprise the pub scene, Loach ensures that the extent and kind of relations among this adult society remain unclear; there is, for example, never a firm sense of a welcoming communal space. The scene opens with a cut from Billy reading his book to a band on stage. A shot of Jud and a friend follows: Jud eyes up a young woman, says something to his companion and sidles up to the woman, who smiles at his approaching line. A brief shot of two patrons comes after this.

Pop music plays loudly during these opening shots, all of which are taken from a distance. The next shot returns to the band, with couples dancing in the foreground. As the singer introduces the next song, 'a Tremolos number', he takes a handkerchief

Figure 10: *Kes*

from the pocket of his cardigan and wipes his forehead (figure 10). With the loose quiff, the knitted cream cardigan and the handkerchief, the singer's appearance and gestures – part proud, part nervous – contribute to the momentary exposure of a 'whole sort of world', as Stephen Frears puts it, which is such a feature of Loach's style.[13] The following shot shows us Mrs Casper and Reg, who are disagreeing about when is the best time 'to settle down' (figure 11). One medium close shot reveals them, and their comments lack a more elaborate conversational context. Instead, the film gives as a context the preceding shot of the singer and the following long shot of the band's young drummer, playing enthusiastically. This young man's endeavours, like the singer and his handkerchief, help to quickly evoke a place and time, a Barnsley pub in 1968.

We move from the drummer to Jud, who, in a close shot, surmises: 'I just like to come home, get me meal, get a bath. Not a care in t' world.' The context for Jud's summary of the small pleasures he requires is not his listening companions, but a return to Mrs Casper, who comments: 'Y'see when you've been married once and you marry a wrong 'un it makes you a bit apprehensive towards...' She pauses, looking left to someone off-screen: 'Well, you know, don't you, 'cause he were never good. It makes you a bit wary about getting married again.' She looks to her friend for confirmation, but Mrs Casper directs her reservations towards Reg. After this, the film cuts – perhaps to the other side of the pub – to another close-up of Jud, who grumbles: 'She wants to go with a different bloke, well it's not for me to tell her what to do. I mean she's old enough to know her own mind, in't she?' From there we go to a shot of Mrs Casper and Reg's companion listening to Mrs Casper, who, just off-screen, continues: 'You can't ever tell wi' Billy. I sit and wonder sometimes what he will do.'

When we return, in the next shot, a frontal close shot, to Reg and Mrs Casper, it is the first time in the sequence that Loach adheres to a conventional shot/reverse-shot pattern. Mrs Casper continues: 'Perhaps if he had been brought up in a different environment and had a better education he probably would have made more than what he has done. At the moment, he's just, he's hopeless, he's a hopeless case, in't he?' From her, the film cuts to the singer. The alternation continues between Jud and Mrs Casper, before finally uniting the two spaces in the pub when, after Reg tries to kiss Mrs Casper, Loach cuts to Jud, who mocks Reg. A singer (Joey Kaye) then begins a lewd song about a marrow. Four shots of other patrons laughing at the bawdy song are interspersed with two more shots of the singer. A shot of Mrs Casper and Reg laughing ends the scene.

The pub scene works on several levels. Many of its shots appear to illustrate the pub randomly. Such is the refusal of conventional spatial geography that the scene initially seems to comprise a series of observational shots of the patrons. With its

Figure 11: *Kes*

rapid editing, it moves quickly through spaces within the bar; and it might look as if Loach celebrates, as he observes, and as the camera reveals, an authentic working-class culture; yet, although the scene places people within this culture, it has a dramatic and thematic purpose that emerges when Mrs Casper expresses uncertainty about Billy's future. She states the themes of *Kes* – the problems of environment and education; yet her statements do not constitute a keynote speech. She worries about her son casually, without reflection; her concern draws our attention through the contrast it makes with the previous scene, in which she was noticeably unaffectionate with Billy. The Casper family's hostility resurfaces amongst the crowd, yet the scene does not immediately establish the nature of relationships between people in this communal space. This facilitates the gradual revelation of the continuing familial hostility, while the sharp evocation of other patrons and the comedy of the song about the marrow give relief to the thematic focus on Billy and his family.

When Jud returns home drunk from this night, in the early hours of Sunday morning, Billy goes to the kestrel's nest and takes the fledgling. The film fades to black as he pockets the bird and then cuts to Billy walking through his back garden to the shed in daylight. The middle part of the film begins. Some time has passed; the hawk has grown to an adult. As Billy approaches the shed, his voice-over describes the rearing and training of the kestrel:

> Three good meals a day I'll give her for about a fortnight. If a little piece of meat, held between the finger and thumb of the gloved hand, is offered to the hawk, it'll probably bend and pull at the meat with its beak.

Billy enters the shed and begins feeding the hawk. There is a fade to black, then a fade in on Billy with the bird in a field. As the film depicts the enactment of his self-education, Billy's voice-over recounts:

> As soon as the hawk will come a leash length indoors, she may be tried off a fence or a post out of doors. It's quite likely that although she was coming to the first fist promptly indoors, she will now refuse to come at all. She will stand looking fearfully around her and ignoring the meat and the fist thrust in front of her. When she will come a leash length out of doors she can be called greater distances by means of creons, a long cord that is attached to the hawk to prevent her escaping. With luck she will not attempt to fly away.

Billy's voice-over anticipates his speech in class, but its narrational status is ambiguous. It begins with a personal account of his progress, as if the voice-over represents an interior monologue; yet his careful enunciation of the multi-clause sentences that follow and the detailed descriptions themselves suggest that he reads from the stolen book. The voice-over explains the progression of the bird's training, and it fulfils this role by incorporating Billy's own perspective on these events. After he has flown Kes the length of a field with a creon, the film fades to black and the games lesson sequence commences.

Together with the caning scene, the games lesson offers one of the best examples of a sequence that has sad 'total implications' about education and society, while at the same time containing 'immensely funny' details. Christopher Ricks distinguishes between using clichés and being used by them; he writes, 'a great deal of daily conversation finds wit and humour and penetration in a conscious play with clichés' (Ricks 1984: 356). It is in this sense of daily conversation, of the combination of pointed humour and realism that *Kes* uses clichés to probe school life, emphasising a schoolboy's perspective. The games lesson scene begins with Sugden, the PE teacher, running onto a misty football pitch. A tight-fitting red tracksuit, emblazoned with badges, encases Brian Glover's stocky physique, the physique of a semi-professional wrestler. On his chest a silver whistle bangs up and down as he practises headers and jerks his knees into the air, a football gripped under his left arm (figure 12). Loach accompanies Sugden's entry into the film – the moment that opens up a 'whole sort of a world' – with a vigorous brass band marching song; yet, even in his exaggerated gestures and actions, Glover encapsulates a clichéd sense of self-importance in a PE teacher.

Figure 12: *Kes*

Inside the changing rooms, Sugden strides amongst the boys, dispensing witticisms that clumsily inveigle and rudely scold. He shouts at boys standing on the benches: 'You three, get down, before I come and put you down.' The threat is a cliché, but one that contributes to rather than detracts from the realism of Sugden's bullying authority; it produces a sense of the teacher performing for the boys. Sugden's performance is matched by Billy's performance. When he finds Billy skulking by the showers, trying to avoid games, saying he has no kit, Sugden orders him into a pair of oversize shorts. The teacher shouts at Billy to 'Pull them up'. Billy obeys, pulling the waistband up to his neck, an action that infuriates Sugden: 'Roll them down, Casper.' Billy does so, then asks: 'Like that sir?' The business with the shorts is funny because Billy obeys his teacher's orders, yet mocks him. The other boys laugh and jeer at Billy's appearance and at the challenging mockery that Billy makes of the interaction. Everyone recognises the humour: Billy is aware enough to know how far he can challenge this adult's authority, and there is a sense of him showing off for his class. It is part of Bradley's achievement, in consideration of tone of voice and timing, that he is able to suggest such awareness. Sugden recognises the absurdity of Billy's appearance, and, although he shouts at him, he takes no further action.

While the boys finish changing, Sugden promises: 'I'll give you a sample of my footballing skills – a rare delight.' He pauses for effect, and again one feels the teacher striving to impress. The boys groan loudly. Sugden tries to be jokey with them, but he fails; this failure, as we shall see, prompts frustration and aggression in him. Once outside on the football pitch, Sugden nominates himself and Tibbut as captains and they begin picking teams. As the shivering boys stand on the halfway line waiting to be picked, Billy stands in the middle of the class, the smallest of all the boys. Obviously – and many of the funny details in *Kes* derive from its use of a sense of obviousness – the two captains pick the best players first. Billy, shivering with his hands stuffed into his yanked-up shorts, is apparently left to last. Sugden sighs: 'Casper, I've got to have you, don't I? Come on, put 'em round your waist.' Billy joins his teacher's team, but Loach then cuts to an overweight boy approaching Tibbut's team. The team captains have not even called his name. It is a fleeting moment in the film, but, like the keen drummer and the lewd singer in the pub, it is a crucially important, humorous detail, of which the film is full.

As the teams prepare, Sugden removes his tracksuit, revealing an immaculate outfit of red football shirt and white shorts. A pupil ventures: 'Who are you today sir? Liverpool?' 'Don't be slack,' Sugden replies, 'don't you know your club colours? Manchester United strip this.' The boy continues:

Pupil:	You playing Dennis Law again sir, striker?
Sugden:	No, Charlton today lad. All over the field. Too cold for striker.
Pupil:	Course, er, Charlton's not as good on turn as Law is he?
Sugden:	You trying to tell me about football?
Pupil:	No sir.

Sugden: Anyway, Dennis Law's in the wash this week.

Sugden's 'You trying to tell me about football?' refuses to acknowledge the boy's friendly attempt at conversation, but the film's perspective on his refusal to be told about football is wry: Sugden may offer the boys the 'rare delight' that is a sample of his 'footballing skills', but his roles as midfield player, team captain *and* referee qualify his boasting. Klevan argues that *Kes* uses typage in its characterisation because many of the characters 'play up to type', and their rigidity, amusing precisely because it is so recognisable, helps produce the injustices that Billy experiences; in this sense, the cliché of a bullying PE teacher contributes to the film's realism and its humour. The games lesson sequence invokes the cliché of a failed professional football player who has displaced his ambitions and become a PE teacher. This was the early career trajectory of Barry Hines, and the scene draws both on his experience and that of Brian Glover to observe the PE teacher's thwarted ambitions and subsequent frustrations, presenting the teacher as a frustrated sportsman indulging his fantasy to be Bobby Charlton.

Once the match starts, Sugden dribbles the ball for the length of the pitch without passing and then shoots. He misses, and Tibbut's team take possession and quickly score: Billy, who is in goal, fails to prevent the goal. A caption declares the score: 'Manchester United 0 Spurs 1'. Like the opening brass band music, the caption tips a wink to the audience about the comic status of the scene. Sensing defeat, Sugden pretends to have been tripped and throws himself onto the ball, immediately blowing his whistle for a penalty. He takes the penalty (twice) and scores.

As the match continues, Sugden shoulders Tibbut violently to the ground during a tackle. Tibbut picks himself up and, before he can stop himself, shouts: 'The fat twat, he wants bleedin' milking.' Sugden sends Tibbut off, admonishing: 'We'll play this game like gentlemen.' The football sequence possesses a piercing mixture of humour and thematic point. It makes a general point about the treatment of a class as Sugden bullies Casper *and* his classmates: the scene illustrates the schoolboys' lack of power, indicating how they are prey to their teacher's whims; but it contains this point within a humorous exaggeration of a PE teacher, for Sugden's hypocrisy in stating that he wants to 'play this game like gentleman' is so transparent that it becomes absurdly funny.

One of Loach's strengths as a film-maker is that he is able to create different moods in a film. In the changing rooms after the football match, he sharply shifts the mood of the scene from broad comedy to sinister aggression. The scene opens as Billy, dressed and walking to the door, encounters Sugden.

Sugden: In a hurry Casper?
Billy: Yes sir, I've to get home sir.
Sugden: Really?
Billy: Yes sir.

The background laughter and shouting of the changing boys dies down here, as if they sense the menacing tone of Sugden's voice. He begins casually, but as he continues, placing his hands on his hips and leaning forward, he grins falsely and begins to play with Billy.

Sugden: Forgotten something.
Billy: No sir.
Sugden: Are you sure?
Billy: Yes sir. [It is now very quiet.]
Sugden: What about the showers?
Billy: I've had one sir.

Sugden slaps Billy on the side of the head. We are only three brief shots from Billy lowering himself down from the goal posts: one minute we are laughing at his tricks; the next Sugden slaps him so hard that one winces at the suddenness and harshness of the teacher's aggression; yet, even after this slap Billy tries to wangle his way out of a shower. Sugden forces him in, turning the showers to cold and preventing Billy from exiting. In the boys' eyes, he has gone too far; they protest loudly, but Sugden silences them. Then, unexpectedly, Billy's naked, skinny little body appears at the top of the high, tiled wall. Throughout this sequence, Loach and his collaborators balance the serious themes of the scene with humour, as they do in the family row and the night out. It is unlikely that any real PE teacher would behave this badly; but it is, nevertheless, this sense of an accurate representation stretched to the point of stereotype that makes the scene at once so memorably incisive and comical.

Judiciously, Loach cuts from Billy escaping from the showers to a long shot of Jud walking to work in the early morning sunlight. This shot begins the last day of the film, its third part. As Jud walks through a wood, Loach introduces the same gentle music that he used to accompany Billy's earlier walk in the woods. Jud arrives at the colliery, and colleagues greet him. The film then cuts to him and his workmates getting into the lift that will take them down into the mine. The lift descends, and while its clanking metallic noise fades out, the sound of a school assembly singing morning hymns fades in. Two close shots of children singing ensue. The juxtaposition of images and the overlapping sounds foretell the connections between school and mine, and the edit and the sound mix make connections between Billy and his brother.

We learn soon that Jud went to the same school as Billy; therefore, the two transitions (from Billy in the showers to Jud on his way to work; then from Jud to school) place significance on the link between Jud's past and Billy's future. Besides the edit, the use of pastoral imagery and lyrical music as Jud walks to work, both of which the film has associated with Billy, prompts the thought of Jud being once like Billy, and of Billy becoming like Jud. Jud maybe once possessed Billy's imagination and intelligence; possibly the same school and the same social and economic system that produces manual workers for the mines and factories crushed from Jud those qualities that Billy reveals. That the film provokes these thoughts without stating them is enough evidence that Loach is working at a higher level of creativity in *Kes* than in *Cathy Come Home*. Compulsory secondary education fails Billy, but the film shows how this failure is a systemic problem without resorting to official voice-overs reading statistics. Despite the focus on Billy, *Kes* questions the capacity of the secondary school system to educate by revealing the individual experiences of Billy as shared by his brother and his classmates. The caning of six boys by Gryce, which follows the school assembly, is an exemplar of *Kes'* implication of shared experiences.

When the singing ceases, a girl reads a parable from Matthew 18: 10–14 about saving a 'little one' of a hundred, rather than the other 99.[14] Following this, the assembled children all begin coughing. Gryce orders them to stop, and they do. At that moment, though, a boy at the back coughs, and an infuriated Gryce orders a teacher, Hesketh, to 'fetch that boy out'. Hesketh picks on MacDowall, even though we can see that he did not cough. This is of little importance: MacDowall's reputation ensures his suitability to be a scapegoat; the teacher acquiesces with his headmaster, who orders MacDowell to wait outside his office. The assembly continues. Gryce declares: 'We will now say the Lord's Prayer.' As the assembled school begins to recite 'Our Father which art in Heaven', a close-up shows Billy's eyes closing, while the voices fade out and traffic noises fade in. Loach cuts to a long shot of Billy crossing a busy road with Kes: he is having a daydream about, or remembering, showing Kes off in town. Suddenly, Gryce is shouting 'Casper, Casper', waking him up. He discovers that everyone but him has sat down. The headmaster asks rhetorically, 'Why were you tired? Why? I know why. Because you were roaming the streets at night, instead of being home in bed.' There is a discrepancy of knowledge here between Gryce and the viewer that continues the film's presentation of its world from Billy's perspective: the headmaster neither knows Billy, nor cares anything about why he may be tired, and he orders him to wait outside his office after assembly.

After assembly, five fifth-form boys wait outside Gryce's office: MacDowall, Billy, and three boys caught smoking. While waiting, Billy comments that Gryce likes to make them wait for their punishment. Another boy remarks: 'Argh, he can keep me till four o'clock. I'm not bothered. I'd rather the cane than do lessons.' It is an offhand comment by a pupil whom the film does not name, yet his comment implies a shared experience of a miserable education. After a moment, a younger boy joins them. He brings a message for the headmaster from his own teacher; but before Gryce returns, the older boys force the messenger to hide their cigarettes, arguing that he will not check the messenger's pockets. Significantly, Billy helps to force the young boy to co-operate by gripping his neck. Once inside, Gryce lectures the boys, refusing to be interrupted, not allowing the messenger any opportunity to declare his reason for visiting the headmaster's office. In his lecture, Gryce complains that he does not understand this generation with 'their music and their gear'. Andrew Klevan argues that the 'pontificating' headmaster is 'replicating the self-conscious pose of a retired war leader': 'All his actions are performed with an awkwardness, his lack of poise resembling an amateur actor going through the declamatory motions' (Klevan 2000: 42). Bob Bowes, who plays Gryce, is of course an amateur actor, and the headmaster of the school in the film. Klevan correctly reasons that the 'melodramatic typage' of the headmaster provides 'pleasurable jolts of recognition', and it is Loach's casting and direction of actors that achieves this typage, although Gryce's speech derives, almost word for word, from Hines' novel.[15]

Gryce delivers his speech about the superficial qualities of today's society as if he is distracted, as if he has lectured boys so many times that years of repetition, rather than considered evaluation of the meaning of his words, or the boys whose lives he claims to want to affect and control, now determine his speech and actions. His distractedness and his determination to administer any kind of discipline render his words worthless. This scene, like the games lesson sequence, exposes Billy's relationship to his social environment; it brings to the fore the relationship between a person and their community, between the individual drama and the dramatic world in which it unfolds. Yet this scene too is very funny. Gryce's delivery is, on the one hand, so typical that it constitutes, as Klevan argues, a cliché of a 'pontificating headmaster'; but the humour of the situation is invented: it comes from Bowes' performance, Hines' dialogue and Loach's direction. For example, the headmaster harangues the boys on differences between pupils past and present:

> Why, in the twenties and thirties I could understand it; they were hard times. But they produced qualities in people that you lot will never have. I can be stopped in the street by someone I taught then and we'll talk about the old days and we'll laugh about the thrashings that I gave him. But what do I get from you lot? A honk from a greasy, pimply-faced youth sitting at the wheel of a big second-hand car. I don't know, I just don't know. No guts, no backbone. Nothing to commend you whatsoever. Mere fodder for the mass media.

As Gryce stares out of the window, the boys try to contain their laughter. Bowes has a convincingly authentic delivery as the pompous headmaster. In the novel, Hines writes 'A honk from a greasy youth behind the wheel of some big second-hand car' (Hines 1969: 56); but in the film, as well as adding 'pimply-faced' and switching from 'some' to the more clipped 'a', Bowes' slow and methodical, over-rehearsed 'amateur' delivery turns Hines' sentence into four evenly stressed phrases ('A honk … from a greasy, pimply faced youth … sitting at the wheel … of a big second-hand car'), the cadences of which amuse because they seem so typical.

Gryce checks all the boys' pockets and, despite repeated protestations of innocence, he denounces the messenger as a 'regular little cigarette factory' and canes all six boys. Because of the distance and alienation felt between pupils and headmaster, the punishment is indiscriminate and futile. 'I hope it's going to be a lesson to you,' he says. But what kind of lesson is this? Still the kind that is preferable to sitting in a classroom. As with the PE teacher's bullying, the caning of the messenger makes Gryce's judgement a cynical one: these injustices promote doubt about the legitimacy of the school system.

> Now I hope it's going to be a lesson to you. I don't suppose for one minute it will be. I don't doubt that before the end of the week you'll be back in here again for exactly the same crime, smoking. Perhaps once in a while, it might sink in.

Loach spells out the messenger's role in the scene by ending it with a close-up of him in tears, whimpering 'Yes sir' in reply to Gryce's lecture. Nevertheless, this shot does not detract from the power of the scene, partly because it is so funny: as with so much of *Kes*, even recognising the point-making elements of scenes, one's imagination still warms to the humour of them.

Kes contrasts the headmaster's distracted speech and his alienated listeners with two of Billy's speeches. The first occurs in the classroom, when Farthing coaxes Billy to speak immediately after the boys' experiences with Sugden and Gryce. The second occurs in the playground, after Billy fights with MacDowall at break time. Farthing breaks up the fight and, after showing and telling MacDowall what it means to be bullied, he asks Billy why the fight started. In both scenes Loach films Billy in close-ups and with long takes, giving him the space and time to speak. In class, after the 'entry of the Gladiators', as Farthing sympathetically – because of the mock heroism in 'Gladiators' and his enquiries about how much it hurt – welcomes back the punished boys, there is a discussion of fact and fiction. The liberal English teacher – sincere, attentive, trusting – is as much a cliché as the hectoring headmaster and the bullying PE teacher; but as do Bowes and Glover, Colin Welland endows Farthing with a convincing authenticity (in accent, appearance, and so on) that compliments the cliché and its manifest contrast with the headmaster and PE teacher. When Farthing discovers Billy's inattentiveness, he reprimands him; but he also forces him to participate by threatening the class with detention if Billy does not tell the class a story. Loach and Menges film much of this scene with shot/reverse-shot patterns, cutting between Farthing and the pupils waiting for Billy to speak. Some of these worried pupils shout to Billy that he should tell Farthing about his pet hawk. Farthing notices these comments and, more encouragingly – Welland softens his voice and manner – begins asking Billy questions about Kes. When Billy mentions the jesses he uses, Farthing asks him to come out to the front of the class and write the word on the board.

The camera pans with Billy; character and action lead it from a long shot of him talking at his desk to a close profile shot of him writing on the blackboard. A shot follows of Billy standing in front of the blackboard, explaining what a jess is. Loach then cuts to two reverse-angle close-ups of two other boys listening, before returning to a medium long shot of Billy leaning against the board and talking. The scene continues in this way, with other class members asking questions. It ends with a long take depicting Billy's exalted and excited description of the first time that he flew Kes free, without a leash. This scene is the first occasion on which Billy reveals to his teacher the creative intelligence that the film has already made apparent. The combination of shot/reverse-shot patterns of Billy talking to the class and the final long take underlines the importance of Billy's speech as being a part of his revealing a 'different face' to the one that the institution perceives. In talking thus, at the end of his school life, Billy makes known to Farthing a potential that defies the pigeon-hole of the lower set, the 'Easter leavers', who are going to reach 16 before Easter and leave school lacking qualifications and destined for manual labour. The scene's import lies in its central relationship to the film's theme: a capitalist society depends upon not acknowledging the creative potential of these 'Easter leavers'. Billy reveals his potential to Farthing, but the film does not present this revelation as a didactic statement about the iniquities of the system.

In the playground scene that follows, Billy delivers the second speech that opposes Gryce's lecture. Billy is profound in what he articulates about his experience of school, his frustrations with the school system and his low expectations of work; but Loach does not allow these articulations to disrupt in the way that Eileen's dialogue with George in *Carla's Song* disrupts. Billy and MacDowall fight after MacDowall insinuates that Jud is not Billy's real brother. As they fight, they push each other onto a coal heap. A long shot pans to follow the rest of the children in the large playground flocking to the 'ringside'. Almost immediately, Farthing runs to the centre of the crowd and, after grabbing Billy and MacDowall, orders the crowd to disperse. He begins by trying to discern why they were fighting and who started the fight; but soon gives this up and instead turns to MacDowall, who is twice the size of Billy, and reprimands him for bullying. A single take moves through three positions. With the return to Billy, Loach cuts to a medium two shot as the teacher asks Billy why the others always seem to pick on him. After Farthing asks, 'Is it because you're a bad 'un?' Loach cuts to a close-up of Billy.

Billy:	Maybe I am sometimes but I'm not that bad sir. I know stacks of other kids that's worse than me, but they seem to get away with it.
Farthing:	Mmm. Why else do you think? They're must be some reason, mustn't there.
Billy:	Well take this morning sir. I just came and just dozed off. I weren't doing nowt wrong sir. Y'see I'd been up since six. I had to do papers, then I had to rush home to have a look at t' bird, and then run to school. I mean to say, you'd be tired wouldn't you sir?
Farthing:	I'd be exhausted.
Billy:	And that's not, you shouldn't be caned for that, should you sir? And you can't tell Mr Gryce that. And this little lad sir, he'd only brought a letter sir, from one of the teachers, and he got caned. [Off-screen Farthing suppresses a chuckle.] It's nowt to laugh at

sir. Afterwards he was as sick as a dog. And teachers, sir: they're not bothered about us sir; if we fall asleep, they think we're numb skulls or owt like that, sir. And when they've time, they're always looking at their watches to see how long there's left of lesson. They're not bothered about us and we're not bothered about them.

When Billy finishes his speech, another teacher blows a whistle off-screen. The whistle signals the end of break time, and Loach cuts to a medium shot of Billy and Farthing, taken from the preceding set up. Pupil and teacher turn to look in the direction of the whistle. The scene has a beautifully subtle construction: the close-up of Billy focuses attention on his speech; Bradley's performance, in the face of the camera's scrutiny, is natural and expressive. He describes the alienation felt between teachers and pupils cynically, but perhaps accurately; the close-up attends to his description, but unobtrusively so. Loach, cutting from the close-up of Billy to the medium shot that reveals his and Farthing's glance towards the whistle-blower, subordinates the editing of the film to the naturalistic depiction of school life. The whistle rhymes with the earlier colliery whistle that ended Billy's moment of private pleasure; here it signals Billy and Farthing's mutual subjection to the rhythms and structures of school. Its rules bind them both. Farthing is a liberal, sensitive teacher, able to gain enough of the boy's trust so that he feels sufficiently safe to criticise his colleagues; but the teacher is unable to escape the strictures of the system. In the end, he can do little for Billy. Even so, after the whistle empties the playground, Farthing continues trying to encourage:

Farthing: Think of it, in a couple of weeks you'll be starting a new job. Have you got a job?
Billy: No sir. I've got to see employment bloke this afternoon.
Farthing: What sort of job do you want?
Billy: I'm not bothered sir, anything'll do me.
Farthing: Yeh, but you want something that you're looking forward to, that you're interested in, don't you?
Billy: I've not much choice sir. I'll take what I've got.
Farthing: I thought you wanted to leave school.
Billy: I'm not bothered.
Farthing: I thought you didn't like school.
Billy: I don't but it don't mean I'll like work does it? Still, I'll get paid for not liking it, that's one thing.

Billy's dry and knowing comment that he will at least be paid for not liking work prompts Farthing to agree; the pessimism and sense of defeat in Billy's comment, even though he speaks with an intelligent and profoundly self-aware wryness, is saddening. The scene prolongs this sense of sadness in the ensuing moment.

The novel has Farthing blow the whistle after he and Billy finish talking; Billy, therefore, walks into the crowd of schoolchildren.[16] The film, though, cuts from a shot of them talking, out of which Billy walks, to a slow pan that follows him as he walks away from Farthing and towards the school buildings, across the wet, concrete playground (figures 13 and 14). The shot lasts about ten seconds and it is movingly suggestive. As Billy exits the frame of the preceding shot, Farthing watches him: the subsequent pan may be an optical point-of-view shot representing Farthing's perspective, but this does not explain the feeling that the shot provokes. It gives us an image of the physical environment in which Billy spends much of his life, and it has a documentary richness equivalent to the shots of the tenement block in *Poor Cow*. Puddles dot the playground; Billy walks straight through them, oblivious. It is important that he walks away from the camera, back towards the school building, for he becomes a diminishing figure. As he walks, his slightly hunched posture, with his head tipped down, conveys a feeling of defeat. This shot, a notable modification of the novel, points to Billy's isolation. The lighting of the shot contributes valuably to this impression. The sky is pale grey and cloudy, and the puddles that Billy walks nonchalantly through reflect this. Drabness suffuses the image; it is drained of colour, but also beguilingly light and reflective. The black scuffmarks of the coal pile, on which he fell during his fight, dirty Billy's grey flannel shirt and trousers, and his appearance merges with the grey concrete of the playground and the red bricks of the school building.

Figure 13: *Kes*

Figure 14: *Kes*

The doubling of the windows in the building in front of Billy adds depth and perspective to the shot. The school buildings immure him, yet the windows permit a view through their glass to a world beyond the school. In class and in the playground he delivers articulate, though contrasting, speeches: in class he is passionate and engaged, but in the playground his cynicism and disconsolateness are depressingly evident. This slow pan continues the mood of depression. The quietness of the shot, after the rowdy fight and after Billy's speeches, offers a moment for us to reflect on what is a turning point of the film. Loach integrates the film's protagonist with his environment not just visually, as in *Cathy Come Home*, but narratively. Photographed this way and placed where it is, the shot documents the location, ambiguously represents Farthing's view and offers a metaphor for Billy's isolation; the school buildings themselves recall the ideological strictures which restrict Billy's life and ensure that Farthing can do little to change the system to which he belongs.

The film concludes by linking Billy's interview with the youth employment officer to Jud's killing of Kes, which it does not show. On returning home at lunchtime, Billy sees the note about Jud's bet as he ties the small bird he has shot to the lure.[17] He then flies Kes with the lure and talks to Farthing. After Farthing leaves, he runs to the bookmakers, but throws away Jud's bet. From then on, he is in trouble; he compounds matters by spending Jud's money at the fish and chip shop. Back in school, during the afternoon, Jud comes looking for Billy. By the time Billy emerges from hiding, he is late for his interview with the youth employment officer. The point that the scene can make about Billy's destination for unskilled manual labour has already emerged in his conversation with Farthing, and Loach concentrates on having Bradley suggest Billy's impatient concern for Kes. When he returns home after his interview and fails to find Kes, a suspicion arises that Jud has done something to the bird. Finally, Billy uncovers the truth from Jud, and retrieves the bird's remains from the dustbin. The burial of Kes forms a coda.

The tone of the film shifts during the story: it moves from hope and resilience – hope *because* of resilience – to uncertainty and ambiguity about Billy's future. With the death and burial of Kes the film provokes doubts about how long Billy can sustain his youthful agility and resilience. The ambiguity at the end of the film revolves around whether one accepts that Billy's experience with Kes has changed him irrevocably: he may harden to his life, as his brother has to his, or he may find fulfilment. The ambiguous end refuses to confirm either possibility. We can take the death of Kes to represent the death of Billy's hope, but this feeling does not dominate. Although we may be tempted to read the burial of Kes symbolically as Billy's own spiritual death – the death of innocence, rather than the death of an innocent – *Kes* discourages this reading. Hines' novel describes Billy 'as though he was a hawk' (Hines 1969: 67); but the film does not name Billy in such a way; it refrains from asserting that the hawk be read as a symbol by concentrating instead on Billy's work with Kes. The film's use of the hawk is crucially suggestive, but Loach never makes it crudely symbolic. The death of Kes is an important event in Billy's life, it affects him deeply; but the idea of the hawk as a symbol never strains to make its presence felt. The distinction of *Kes* in Loach's oeuvre is that it is the first film in which he combines detailed narrative patterns with his developing realist strategies in casting, performances and photography. *Kes* combines social comment with a richly described story about an individual's experiences; it indicts the education system, but it does so by implying, rather than stating, that a class shares Billy's experiences.

The preceding chapter quotes Loach's recollection that although he may have used nominally Brechtian strategies early in his career, he always tried to encourage the actors to perform in a way that was 'authentic'.[18] His interest in Brechtian techniques of distanciation wanes soon after *Poor Cow*. On *Kes*, he develops an observational style that dominates his work until the 1980s, when artistically he undergoes something of a crisis, although politically he becomes more steadfast. This observational style enables him, at times, to achieve in his art an extraordinary sense of sincerity and candour in his filming of actors such as David Bradley. For some, the powerful sense of candour that he achieves does not need emphasizing; it is a commonplace to which critics have often attested with their insistence on discussing his realism or naturalism. Yet even when he fails to achieve the coherence of *Kes*, he almost always endows his work with moments of powerful emotional authenticity in the performances.

The following chapter explores Loach's television work with Jim Allen. That work does not always cohere, but the conviction in the performances offsets the imbalances in *The Big Flame* (1969) and *The Rank and File* (1971). Loach's ability to film performances that make us believe that, like Smith in *After a Lifetime* (1971), the people we see on screen are living these experiences, is one reason his work is distinctive. *Kes* represents a decisive moment in the evolution of his work: at the end of the 1960s, he discovers a way of working that differs from his earlier *Wednesday Play* work. These differences originate in choices about collaborators, subject matter, production companies, casting and filming. Loach discovers on *Kes* that he can integrate protest with personal stories. Working away from the BBC allows him to choose his collaborators and develop artistically: his work with director of photography Chris Menges testifies to the significance of this. The writing of Barry Hines is also important, and Loach works with him again. Loach always works closely with writers, and the subject matter of *Kes* determines decisions about style. His work with Jim Allen differs from his work with Hines; and the concerns of the Hines/Loach projects and the Allen/Loach projects reflect the backgrounds and interests of the two writers.

CHAPTER FOUR

the experience of history

Jim Allen wrote six works for Loach: for television, he wrote *The Big Flame* (1969), *The Rank and File* (1971) and *Days of Hope* (1975); for cinema, he wrote *Hidden Agenda* (1990), *Raining Stones* (1993) and *Land and Freedom* (1995) – their writer as much as their director unites these six works. *Raining Stones* and *Land and Freedom* will be discussed in the final chapter, in the context of a discussion of Loach's films of the 1990s; this examines the works that Loach and Allen made in the late 1960s and early 1970s. However, whereas the preceding three chapters present interpretations of films, this chapter attends to the politics of *The Big Flame*, *The Rank and File* and *Days of Hope* by considering the contemporary political context in which they were made, by summarising Jim Allen's contribution and by discussing the reception of *Days of Hope*, in particular how film critics judged its expression of left-wing politics.

In *The Big Flame*, *The Rank and File* and *Days of Hope*, Loach and Allen attempt to express a political philosophy by dramatising a collective experience. In *The Big Flame* and *The Rank and File*, Loach uses the 'mixed aesthetic' with which he experiments in his 1960s television work; but in *Days of Hope*, he omits the drumbeats, jump cuts, observational shots and unspecified voice-overs characteristic of the earlier work. In his fiction films, *The Rank and File* is the last occasion that he uses unspecified voice-overs, the technique that he began using on *Up the Junction*; subsequent voice-overs in his fiction, such as those in *Ladybird, Ladybird* (1994) or *My Name is Joe* (1998), are instances where an identified character describes past events. Loach's narrational strategies change definitively in the mid-1970s: instead of incorporating unabsorbed documentary elements into his fiction in order to make general points about an event, he finds other ways to dramatise the relationship between the experiences of individuals and the experiences of groups, whether those groups be a social class, a union membership or a generation. While his work continues to exhibit increasingly refined dramatic structures, Loach's collaboration with Allen produces a new political application. *Up the Junction* (1965) and *Cathy Come Home* are (1966) political, but Allen brings to Loach's work a coherent political philosophy of anti-Stalinist socialism, one which, although Loach was already on the Left, is absent from his earlier work. Loach acknowledges Allen's influence:

> A lot of my way of looking at the world I got from Jim. He was very important in the redevelopment of a whole group of people. He was steadfast in his polar position. His understanding of politics was very strong and clear. Most of us were ten years younger than Jim, and most had been to university. Suddenly, here was this man whose writing was very strong and sinewy: it was real life, and the characters burst off the page. (Jones 1998: 93)

Of the research for and writing of *Days of Hope* Loach says: 'It was Jim's work. I mean, Jim lives amongst the books. Of course, I read a lot of it as well, as did Tony Garnett. But it was primarily Jim's work.'[1] *Raining Stones* resembles Loach's work with other writers, such as *Riff-Raff* (1991) with Bill Jesse or *My Name is Joe* with Paul Laverty; but Loach and Allen's five other projects all express a concern with union and party politics or history. Their work articulates themes that reflect Allen's belief in revolutionary socialism and his background in industry, union organisation and grassroots left-wing politics.[2] The distinction of their work is that they use mass media to address political issues from an explicitly left-wing perspective. Because of this perspective, and it is one that Allen, Loach and Tony Garnett share in the early 1970s, we should not be surprised that *The Big Flame*, *The Rank and File* and *Days of Hope* focus on industrial disputes. The BBC commissioned these projects during a time of widespread industrial and political conflict, and intense debate on the left about that conflict.[3]

If Loach becomes disillusioned with Wilson's Labour government in the 1960s, his association with Allen turns his disillusionment into a fully-fledged, class-based Marxism.[4] Their work in the early 1970s reflects and contributes to the debate on the left, a debate which eventually becomes a schism. The background, in which Loach and Allen's first three projects try to intervene, is the radicalisation of the left in the face of Wilson's and Heath's economic and industrial policies, and in particular the unions' refusal to accept the Industrial Relations Act.[5] Furthermore, the political upheavals in France in May 1968 were also still in the minds of left-wingers in Britain; and it is in this context that Loach, Allen and Garnett make television dramas that present socialist perspectives on current political issues and their historical antecedents.[6]

The Big Flame: a heady fantasy of revolution

The Big Flame is the first film that Loach directed which encapsulates a coherent political philosophy. With Jim Allen, Loach was working with someone who was, in contrast to Jeremy Sandford, the writer of *Cathy Come Home*, from the class which he wrote about: Allen forged his ideas through his work as a miner, docker and builder. His style as a writer could not differ more from that of someone like Sandford, or David Mercer, the writer of Loach's *In Two Minds* (1967) and *Family Life* (1971). Virtually self-taught, Allen proved to be an original voice in British film and television writing.[7] Garnett produced Allen's second drama, *The Lump* (tx: BBC1, 1 February 1967), for *The Wednesday Play*, and he introduced Allen to Loach. The three men decided to make a film drawing on Allen's experience on the docks: *The Big Flame*. It was Loach's last *Wednesday Play*: by the time the BBC broadcast it, he and Garnett had left the BBC to set up Kestrel Films. They shot *The Big Flame* on location in Liverpool over 20 days (19 February to 16 March 1968), a few months before they shot *Kes*.[8] John McGlashan, who had shot location footage for *Diary of a Young Man*, photographed *The Big Flame* on 16mm. Roy Watts edited it over seven weeks. Given the post-production period, relatively long for *The Wednesday Play*, *The Big Flame* would have been ready for broadcast by the end of May 1968; yet the BBC did not broadcast it until February 1969. It is tempting to suggest that the film's subject, a workers' takeover of the docks, coincided too closely with contemporaneous events in France for the comfort of BBC managers. Julian Petley (1997a) speculates about the delay in its broadcast, citing a series of articles and letters published in *The Listener* and *Radio Times* as evidence of internal censorship at the BBC.[9]

The Big Flame tells the story of a dock strike for better conditions and pay, after the introduction of mechanisation to accommodate container transportation and a government report that recommends the casualisation of dock labour to establish a 'flexible' labour market. The film concentrates on the work of the unofficial strike committee, which Danny Fowler (Norman Rossington) and Peter Conner (Peter Kerrigan) run. After six weeks on strike and, sensing that they can do no more, Danny and Peter meet an experienced and blacklisted labour organiser, Jack Regan (Godfrey Quigley). In a pivotal scene, Regan persuades them that they must shift the strike from 'the industrial to the political' by seizing control of the docks. As he proposes this, though, Regan predicts that the takeover can only last a few days; the government will throw everything they have at them. Nevertheless, he counsels, a few days of workers' control will be worth experiencing. The dockers take over the port and run it successfully for five days, with all the workers living in and around the port. The government retaliates: after capturing the leaders, the police and the army storm the docks in the middle of the night. At the film's end, a judge sentences Danny, Regan and Peter to three years' imprisonment; but outside the court younger workers organise themselves.

Loach uses a variety of techniques to film Allen's script of *The Big Flame*: experimental techniques that he uses on his earlier *Wednesday Plays*, and other, more observational methods that he was about to explore with Menges on *Kes* and *After a Lifetime* (1971). Some scenes, for example, resemble scenes in *Cathy Come Home*, with unspecified voice-overs and a montage of images. Paul Madden describes *The Big Flame* as 'essentially a realist drama', but one that 'retains Brechtian elements, particularly in its use of voice-overs to comment on the action' (Madden 1981: 45). The voice-overs and observational shots offer a wider perspective on the strike; as in *Up the Junction* and *Cathy Come Home*, these elements of a report supplement the story of individuals.

Loach's films with Nell Dunn and Jeremy Sandford have an investigative, journey structure that reflects the journey that these writers had to make in order to reach their subjects. *The Big Flame*, by contrast, does not need this structure: Allen was already intimate with his subjects. Explaining the way he wrote, Allen said:

> I've got a tape-recorder in my head. The characters speak as I speak. I write about characters that come from my world, mainly. And by writing I can visualize the characters ... I mean when I go in a pub, and I go in every night, everybody in the pub works for me. I'm just clocking it and clocking it.[10]

The Big Flame deals with what socialist politics can mean in practice to a group of working men. Allen's adeptness at writing vernacular dialogue serves the project well. For example, in the canteen on the docks, after the workers have been running them for a few days, the older activist, Jack Regan, talks to Danny about what got him started in politics and about why people criticise socialists. Allen wrote Regan's dialogue as follows:

> Regan: What's happenin' here's just a small part of the big picture. Mean even if the troops moved in tonight, f'instance, even if the lot fell in on us, we'd have come out with summat. (Grins) Someone's got to push that cart up the hill, Danny, otherwise we'll never make the top.
>
> Danny: An' you reckon you'll get there anyway?
>
> Regan: Me personally? ... No ... Not because it's impossible or owt like that. Mean the smart alecks'll tell you real Communism's utopian. That man is born with his hand in somebody elses [sic] pocket. That human nature's basically corrupt an' all tha crap, but to my way of thinkin' man never gets the chance to show how good he is, 'cos he's what Society makes him. Ideas, morals, ethics etc, is all reflections of the world he lives in, which means that if you want to change man, you gotta change Society first, an' to do that you need a sharp axe ... As a matter of fact, I reckon what is Utopian is believin' that this bleedin' mad'ouse can continue goin' the way it is...[11]

I quote from an early draft of the script, called *The Docks*, in order to give an example of the cadences of Allen's vernacular dialogue style, but in the final film Godfrey Quigley and Norman Rossington speak this dialogue almost exactly as it is written.

Within the fictional world of *The Big Flame* the occupation of the docks is intended to be a beacon, to be inspirational; but the film itself is meant to be Loach and Allen's 'big flame'. The scene in which Peter and Danny first meet Regan is the central moment in the film's fusion of a realist project and a political hypothesis; Regan transforms the aims of the dockers by persuading Danny and Peter to alter the objectives of the strike. He convinces them to put workers' control to the men, saying: 'You see we never tumbled to the fact that a strike is political ... I mean your wage packet is made up of politics.' As Jack Regan, the blacklisted docker, Quigley delivers his speeches with experiential authority, playing the part as if he has been a docker all his life. Allen's strong vernacular dialogue, full of the writer's characteristically rich and evocative political metaphors, is a keynote speech, but one which is rooted in the character of Regan. He says, and here I quote from the film:

Now I want to see the big flame, Danny – I want to see one big mass of us that'll point the finger at those raiders and say you failed in your management of society, so pack your traps, think yourselves lucky and go. Things aren't just ripe for a change, they're rotten ripe, and all I've got to do is to shake the tree and rotten fruit will fall to the ground ... if we can hold out for a few days, that'll be fine because the Merseyside docker will have lit a bonfire that'll be seen by the workers around for miles.

Allen's use of the phrase 'you failed in your management of society' echoes a phrase used by the revolutionary Ernest Everhard in Jack London's novel *The Iron Heel*, first published in 1907. In 1947, when he was 21 and in prison, Allen read this; it was the first book he ever read, and an early influence on his work. He recalled:

I'd been steeped in London when I was a young man ... I joined the Labour Party about 1951, thereabouts. I got involved because I was a socialist. I'd read London. I can look back on London, analyse him, criticise him and so forth, but London spoke to my generation.[12]

The Iron Heel tells the story of an unsuccessful socialist revolution in America from the perspective of the future. Ernest Everhard led the revolution, and London tells his story by presenting the main body of *The Iron Heel* as if it is a facsimile of a manuscript written by Everhard's wife, Avis, which scholars discover 400 years later. In one scene, Everhard addresses the amassed members of the upper-class Philomath Club, accusing them:

You are fat with power and possession, drunken with success; and you have no more hope against us than have the drones, clustered about the honey-vats, when the worker-bees spring upon them to end their rotund existence. You have failed in your management of society, and your management is to be taken away from you. A million and a half of the men of the working class say that they are going to get the rest of the working class to join with them and take the management away from you. (London 1957: 75)

Allen's writing echoes London's, and although he denied the similarity was deliberate, he acknowledged London's influence:

It must have been there, because I've read so much of London. But there was no kind of conscious decision to use the Everhard speech in that, great speech as it is. I'd been steeped in London when I was a young man, so possibly.[13]

There are thematic and stylistic connections between Allen's and London's work; and Allen and Loach, as socialist artists, were working in a creative tradition where utopianism is a frequent criticism.

Tony Garnett introduces *The Big Flame* in the *Radio Times* by acknowledging the debate about the mixing of dramatic and documentary conventions that *Cathy Come Home* had initiated: 'If anyone should still doubt that it is fiction, we have set it in the future – as no documentary could ever be' (Garnett 1969: 35). This is disingenuous, as the film does not indicate that it is set in the future; in referring to the future, he indicates that a dock strike leading to a workers' takeover is something that has not yet occurred. Kenith Trodd describes *The Big Flame*'s intentions in Allen's obituary:

A powerful 'what if…' parable about workers' occupation seen by a vast unfragmented audience on Wednesday night could maybe start a walkout around the country on Thursday morning. That was the heady fantasy. (Trodd 1999: 16)

The 'heady fantasy' of *The Big Flame* was to be able to offer on mainstream television a hypothesis for political action; as Regan puts it, 'the Merseyside docker will have lit a bonfire that'll be seen by the workers around for miles'. Regan persuades Danny, and the film seeks to persuade us, that taking over the docks will be a worthwhile enterprise: if it is only for a few days, it makes visible the applicability of ideas regarded as utopian. Garnett describes the team's aims:

The Big Flame was a document and we wanted it to have a moment-to-moment veracity, we wanted it to be true, to have the texture of the world, what the world is really like. And yet it was straightforward propaganda; it had a definite point of view. We had used the fabric of the world in order to arrange it in a way that suited our purpose. (Orbanz 1977: 66)

Unsurprisingly, *The Big Flame* becomes embroiled in a debate among left-wing film critics about transparency, objectivity and realism, and the latter's efficacy in promoting political activism, in being a suitable form for, as Michael Walker suggests of the melo-drama of protest, inciting revolution.

In 1977, Raymond Williams wrote a rejoinder to the debate on realism in which he analyses *The Big Flame* within a context of a historical discussion of what realism and naturalism have meant. He argues that because there are so many historical vari-ations of realism, in theory and in practice, it is unsatisfactory to abstract a method from its relationships with other contemporaneous artistic methods and from the aims and intentions of a particular work (Williams 1977: 63). He proposes, nonetheless, that realist projects generally have three tenets: the setting of actions in the present; an emphasis on secular action; and social extensiveness or inclusiveness – to be realist a drama should extend to and include the experiences of many people. In another article, he criticises the terms of the realist debate of the mid-1970s, which had devel-oped after *Days of Hope*:

> This movement [towards realism in drama in the nineteenth century] was begun by the bourgeoisie, but in these critical respects – contemporaneity, secu-larity, social inclusiveness – was at once shared and taken further by the new opponents of the bourgeoisie in the working-class and socialist movements. At this level the diagnosis of 'realism' as a bourgeois form is cant (Williams 1977–78: 3).

The Big Flame has social inclusiveness as one of its motivating principles; and, as Williams points out, in this it continues the tradition of popular television drama that Sydney Newman produced for ABC's *Armchair Theatre* and the BBC's *The Wednesday Play*, both series that sought to extend the relevancy and appeal of television drama to a majority audience. Yet *The Big Flame* tries to do more than represent the under-repre-sented: besides being a contemporary, secular and inclusive drama, it has a dramatic strategy that is, as Williams writes, 'consciously interpretative in relation to a particular political viewpoint' (Williams 1977: 68).

One example of *The Big Flame*'s expression of its 'particular political viewpoint' concerns the workings of the television medium, and the way that television news tacitly assumes a guise of objectivity when reporting industrial disputes. When Peter, Danny and Joe (Daniel Stephens) walk into a meeting in a civic building in Liver-pool, a small crowd of dockers cheers them. A black car then pulls up, delivering the union representative, Logan (Meredith Edwards). A BBC reporter asks Logan for a comment; he refuses. At this point, as it follows Logan's entrance into the building, the handheld camera moves jerkily. After Logan disappears inside, the reporter turns to some of the striking dockers; he asks them about the effects of being on strike for six weeks, and what they hope to accomplish by striking. The dockers reply that they firmly support the committee's attempts to negotiate for a basic wage and employment security. When the reporter has finished questioning the dockers, he turns around and faces the camera, holding the microphone up and talking to the camera:

Well, there we are, six weeks of the dock strike and although the militants are still sticking out for the demands made by the unofficial strike committee, there does seem to be an element amongst the striking dockers which would like to go back to work as soon as possible.

As he finishes, the crowd jeer him off-screen, shouting abuse at the BBC. By having the reporter speak to the camera, the film shifts the status of the camera's viewpoint from an 'objective' presentation of the story to a 'subjective' reporting of events. The moment draws attention to the methods of television news reportage, and how these affect the perception of events. Against the evidence of unity, the reporter divides the dockers into two groups: the militants who lead and the striking dockers who are led. They protest about his misrepresentation of their solidarity.[14] Williams argues that this scene foregrounds the way that meaning depends on viewpoint; it reveals the methods of media production and exposes the fundamental conservatism of mainstream media.[15] However, judging *The Big Flame*'s realist project, he finds that the scene with the reporter creates 'a certain unresolved tension, even a contradiction' (Williams 1977: 70); though the transition in the mode of narration in *The Big Flame* is thematically relevant to and stylistically consistent with other elements of the film.

Williams also considers the way that Loach and Allen introduce 'a wider consciousness of the working-class movement' (Williams 1977: 72) through a song about an American labour organiser. When Freddie and Peter are talking on the last night of the occupation of the docks, after Danny and Regan have left, an American sailor accompanies himself on guitar as he sings 'The Ballad of Joe Hill'. Alec explains that Joe Hill was 'the poet laureate of the Wobblies', a group of labour organisers, otherwise known as the Industrial Workers of the World, who travelled around America drumming up support for the unions. Joe Hill was caught by the authorities and killed in prison; his epitaph, Alec explains, was 'Don't mourn, organise'. Williams argues that the introduction of 'The Ballad of Joe Hill', which refers to the history of working-class movements, fails to match the realism of the rest of the film. His interpretation of the use of the ballad does not fully convince; but if we agree, for the sake of argument, that his reading is convincing we can return to an issue central to criticism of Loach's work. Primarily, the criticism turns upon the idea that by evoking a consciousness of the historical movements that underlie reality, a film risks becoming too didactic in its handling of theme to maintain a surface realism. Williams' criticism of 'The Ballad of Joe Hill' and my criticism of Eileen's conversation with George in *Carla's Song* conclude that these are moments which reveal the authors' intentions, instead of the characters' intentions: in doing so, they break the coherence of the fictional world. However, although the song introduces a 'wider consciousness of the working-class movement', the use of it undermines Williams' interpretation of the moment: it does not disrupt the scene in the way that the Doctor's voice-over in *Up the Junction* does; only one person, Alec, can explain the relevance of the song, and a union member on a strike committee might know something of the history of labour movements.

For Williams, though, the song represents a failure to match the two intentions about which Garnett speaks: the intention to create a realist reproduction of the world, which has 'a moment-to-moment veracity', and the intention to introduce a consciousness of history, 'straightforward propaganda'. Although I disagree about Williams' example, he pinpoints a tension in art that introduces explicitly political issues; where artists propound a political philosophy at odds with hegemonic political forces, the tension can become more apparent.

The Rank and File: fusing the individual and the collective

The tension between producing a realist reproduction of the world and introducing a consciousness of history in order to evoke comparisons between past and present is equally unresolved in *The Rank and File*. The BBC broadcast it as a *Play for Today* on 20 May 1971. Like *The Big Flame*, it is based on a strike, though in this case a real one: it is set not in the future, but in the past, based on a strike at Pilkington's Glass Works at St Helens in Lancashire which took place in 1969. Allen explained its genesis:

> What happened was I got a call. There was a strike on at Pilkington's Glass Works. So I was asked to go down and give them a boost. So I took *The Big Flame* down and I took Peter Kerrigan down and we showed the film and we had a chat, and then we all went for a beer. They were all on strike at this time. So, one old bloke said to me, 'Will you write a film for us?' And I was really up to my neck in work, committed. I said, 'I'm pressed for time'. So this old fella said, 'come to the toilet with me, I'll show you my 'war medals'. We got to the toilet and he whips his shirt off, and his back was lacerated, as if he'd been whipped by glass, and then he put his shirt back on. He said, 'I've worked here all my life, never been on strike and I've been told that unless I scab, they'll take my pension away'. Anyway, this fella refused to scab, and he finished up with no pension and he was sweeping up in a Co-Op shop in St Helens. Well, that was moral blackmail. So, I said, 'yes, of course, I'll write a script'.[16]

Allen describes the way that he and Loach respond artistically to current political events. *The Rank and File* is their first attempt at dramatising a historical event, and, in doing so, they tell the story of the strike by trying to introduce the perspective of the man who lost his pension when he refused to scab.

The film charts the progression of the strike by focusing on the work of the unofficial strike committee and their efforts to represent the rank and file union membership, to whom neither the employers nor the union leaders are sympathetic. In *The Rank and File*, Loach and Allen try, more so than in *The Big Flame*, to depict a collective experience and this concentration on the experiences of groups has conse-quences for the narrative development. Essentially, the narrative comprises a series of scenes that depict the activity of groups of men: mass meetings, picket lines, committee meetings. *The Rank and File* takes as its theme the radicalism of rank and file union members compared with the union leaders, the TUC and most Labour MPs. Loach and Allen develop this theme by filming how the strike affects ordinary people: Johnny (Johnny Gee) gets beaten up and hospitalised by a gang of anti-strike thugs; Les (Tommy Summers) has his window broken after a benefit concert; the police later arrest him on a picket line; Jimmy (Jimmy Coleman) and others, including a young mother and baby, are forced to hide out in some abandoned kilns.

However, although *The Rank and File* presents the day-to-day life of a strike, it focuses mainly on the work of the unofficial strike committee, whose six members meet in rooms above a pub. The committee includes Les, Johnny, Eddie (Peter Kerrigan), Billy (Bill Dean), Bert (Bert King), Mike (Mike Hayden) and Jerry (Neville Smith). After some weeks on strike, they go to London to meet the TUC's General Secretary. He urges them to return to work and they take his advice; but, the film reports, with unspecified voice-overs and observational shots of men at work, similar to those in *The Big Flame*, the employers victimise men who were involved with the strike, especially Eddie, whom they isolate by having two managers follow him around. The committee return to the TUC and accuse it of selling out the rank and file.

Towards the end of the film, Wilkinson's interview a man, Charlie (Charlie Barlow), about giving him his job back. The strike has collapsed; Wilkinson's has sacked and re-employed some of the men involved with the dispute. A voice-over explains that there are two lists: a blacklist of men who will never be employed again, and a white list of men like Charlie who, as the personnel officer explains, is being 'given a chance to mend his ways'. Charlie is in his sixties; he has worked for the company for 43 years, and was due to retire the following month. They offer him re-employment, but not re-instatement: he will lose all his pension rights and will start again on an apprentice's wage. 'Do you understand?' asks the personnel officer. 'Yes, sir,' says Charlie. It is a shocking moment, and the result of Allen and Loach's response to the 'old fella' who had lost his pension and was sweeping up in a Co-Op. The film proposes that the employers do not care about Charlie; they have exploited him all his life and continue to do so, yet he takes his job back. Apart from one shot of the personnel officer, Loach films this scene with a close-up of Charlie: his face is haggard, and he appears worn out; but he can only acquiesce. Throughout the shot, the personnel officer's head is on the left side of the frame, taking up about a quarter of the framed space. In the foreground, and close in, is Charlie's gloomy face: cracked glasses perched on his nose, eyes tired, greying hair greased back. 'Right, thank you sir,' he says. The scene ends with a freeze-frame on his face: he is one of the casualties of the strike.

After the freeze-frame close-up of Charlie, the film ends with a montage of stills of children playing and Eddie's voice-over talking about the Industrial Relations Bill, which will, he says, prevent rank and file actions of the kind depicted in the film. This voice-over refers to the Industrial Relations Bill, which Edward Heath's Conservative government passed and which provoked fierce debate on the left. But the dropped-in reference to the Bill is too abrupt: with this ending of still photographs and a voice-over, Loach and Allen address their audience didactically, trying to make their fiction relevant. Allen expressed reservations about how successful the film was:

> Having written plays like *The Rank and File* about collective action, the Pilkington Glass Strike, I think that if you don't take an individual you lose the thread. *The Lump* is expressed in individuals. It's strong men hustling, fighting. *The Rank and File* was written in three weeks, and had to be done the way it was. The trouble was the imagination limps behind the reality behind Pilkington … If you get too didactic, politically or otherwise, as I probably did in *The Rank and File*, it can be a lantern lecture. To express political ideas you need to fuse the individual and the collective … You should allow objective reality to filter through the subjective (Madden 1976: no page numbers).[17]

Allen worries about fusing the individual and the collective, and his concern illustrates how he and Loach deliberate about how to depict a collective experience and invoke a 'wider consciousness of history'. Viewing *The Rank and File* confirms Allen's reservations about the lack of dramatic focus; yet although the narrative structure fails 'to fuse the individual and the collective', it has clarity as focused polemic. Eddie's final comment over a still photograph of children playing on a building site is, 'I go along with Trotsky, that life is beautiful, that the future generation cleanses all the oppression, violence and evil.' The ending overstates the theme. One can see the purpose behind it, the desire to address contemporary issues; but the film is not as fully realised as its makers hoped. While Loach and Allen learnt that it was important for them to be politically clear, they also came to understand that it was important to focus the drama on individuals.

Days of Hope: a tendency towards personalisation

In contrast to the rushed development of *The Rank and File*, *Days of Hope* had a much longer gestation. Loach, Allen and Garnett developed it from a single script about the 1921 Durham miners' lockout. In 1971, they had planned this as a feature film; when they failed to secure financial backing, they took it to the BBC, who developed it as four feature-length episodes.[18] BBC1 screened the four-part serial in September and October 1975. *Days of Hope* takes place in the past, but it treats issues relevant to contemporary industrial and political conflict with a charged immediacy. As Stuart Laing writes:

> The concerns of all these plays were then fused in Loach's major work of the 1970s, *Days of Hope*, which, although his first fully historical piece, was very clearly created out of the contemporary situation (unimaginable a decade

earlier) of the early 1970s, in which the parallels were easily drawn between the political and industrial struggles of the early 1920s and those of the early 1970s. (Laing 1997: 19)

Allen evokes this parallel with a revolutionary purpose:

The General Strike offered the opportunity for the creation of a workers' state in Britain. This opportunity was lost by the sell-out of the TUC, the Labour Party and the Communist Party. The message is 'don't let it happen again'. (Lyndon 1975: 69)

Similarly direct is Loach, who declares:

We want anybody who feels themselves to be suffering from crises today, people caught by price rises, inflation and wage restraint, to watch the films and realise that all this has happened before. And we hope they will learn some lessons from the opportunities that were lost in 1926 and the defeats inflicted on the working class at the time. (Lyndon 1975: 69)

They use a popular medium, television drama, to address people who were concerned with the labour movement. Like *The Big Flame* and *The Rank and File*, *Days of Hope* aims to provoke debate on the left about how to achieve social and political change.

Days of Hope combines a sweep through ten years of history with an exposition of a left-wing political philosophy; it conveys these via a chronological, linear narrative structure that balances a historical drama about a class-based movement with a focus on individuals. It depicts events in British history between 1916 and 1926 from the perspective of its three protagonists: Philip Hargreaves (Nikolas Simmonds), a Yorkshire Methodist, socialist and conscientious objector during World War One; Sarah Hargreaves (Pamela Brighton), Philip's wife and supporter; and Ben Matthews (Paul Copley), Sarah's younger brother, who is 16 when the first episode begins. In this episode, the army conscript Philip and take him to France: he is a conscientious objector, but they court-martial him as a deserter, and only a last minute decree saves him from execution at the frontline. By 1924, in the third episode, Philip has become a Labour MP in the first Labour government. In contrast to Philip's journey from near-execution to Parliament, Philip's brother-in-law, Ben, progresses from lying about his age to join the army to desertion and communism.

In Episode One, he sees action in Ireland in 1919; when Episode Two opens in 1921, the government have sent him to Durham to quell the miners' strike. En route, Ben deserts, and befriends a striking miner, Joel Barrett (Gary Roberts). Joel explains that the local mine owner has locked them out, hoping to force the miners to accept a reduction in wages. A national agreement existed for the miners during the war; now the situation has reverted to competition amongst local owners. Sensing trouble, the government has passed the Emergency Powers Act of 1921 and sent in the army. Ben's desertion and support of the miners leads to three years imprisonment; when he leaves prison in 1924, he has become a communist. He goes to stay at Philip and Sarah's home. As a Labour MP, Philip has moved to London with Sarah. When Ben joins a local branch of the Communist Party, led by Peter (Peter Kerrigan), a radical split emerges between Philip and Ben.

The split between a 'soft' left and a 'hard' left in *Days of Hope* reflects the schism that was felt to exist on the left in the mid-1970s; and to understand *Days of Hope* we need to recall the context of a widening gulf between left and right factions of the Labour movement. Each of the four episodes opens with a written title that gives dates and introduces the contemporary situation. The opening title of the third episode explains that in 1924, for the first time, Britain elects the Labour Party into office, albeit as a minority government: 'Many feel that the task of legislating Socialism into existence can now begin.' Most of this episode concerns a set of strikebreaking plans which, Philip discovers, have been drawn up under Lloyd George and secretly passed from an outgoing Conservative minister, J. C. C. Davidson, to an incoming Labour minister, Josiah Wedgwood (John Phillips).

The final and longest episode of *Days of Hope* covers the twelve-day period from 29 April to 12 May 1926 that includes the lead-up to the General Strike and the nine days of the strike itself. This episode returns to Philip, Sarah and Ben less frequently than other episodes do, although they play significant roles in articulating responses to the strike. Mostly, it shows the meetings between the leaders of the Miners' Federation, Arthur J. Cook (Dai C. Davies) and Herbert Smith (George Wilkinson); the members of the Special Industrial Committee of the General Council of the TUC, J. H. Thomas (Russell Waters), Arthur Pugh (Neil Seiler), Walter Citrine (Richard Butler), Alfred Purcell (Brian Harrison) and Ernest Bevin (Melvin Thomas); and members of the Conservative government's cabinet, including the Prime Minister, Stanley Baldwin (Brian Hayes), the Chancellor of the Exchequer, Winston Churchill (Leo Britt), the Minister of Labour, Sir Arthur Steel-Maitland (Noel Coleman), the Home Secretary, Sir William Joynson-Hicks (Philip Lennard), the Secretary for India, Lord Birkenhead (Alan Judd), and the Deputy Cabinet Secretary, Thomas Jones (Emrys Jones).

The dispute that led to the General Strike began in the mining industry. Coal mining was Britain's largest industry in the 1920s, supplying the fuel upon which other industries depended.[19] The miners, represented by the Miners Federation, were well organised and influential in the Labour movement; the mine owners, on the other hand, represented by the Mining Association, were close to the Conservatives: then, as in the 1970s and 1980s, key economic and political battles were fought over the mining industry.[20] In April 1926, following the Baldwin government's rejection of the Samuel Report's recommendation of a minimum wage, local mines began to lock miners out and post notices of wage cuts.[21] In response, the TUC organised a special conference on 1 May 1926, where Thomas, Pugh, MacDonald and Henderson addressed nearly a thousand members of union Executive Committees. They voted to strike in support of the miners, whom the owners had already locked out of the mines. The fourth episode of *Days of Hope* begins with this episode.

To show the potential power of collective action, Loach, Allen and Garnett wanted *Days of Hope* to illustrate the strength of rank and file enthusiasm for the strike and the support for the miners, who worked in intolerable conditions and were being forced to accept pay cuts. The General Strike only lasted from 3 May to 12 May 1926; but the miners remained locked out until the end of November, when the owners forced the Miners' Federation to capitulate. By revealing the support that the General Strike received, *Days of Hope* aimed to promote debate about how to achieve political change. Here is Jim Allen on that purpose:

> It was populist. It was an attempt to tell the people, the working class, this is our history; and all history is contemporary; and to galvanise them, and to understand the traitors and the treacheries of the Labour movement. It was, if you like, a people's history of that period. Again, I was steeped in it. I was a Labour organiser long before I became a writer. So strapped to my back when I came into television, was a hardened, well-structured political philosophy. I knew where I was.[22]

Loach, like Allen, finds the historical continuities remain evident; he is quoted here at length because his political analysis informs all his work since his collaborations with Allen in the 1970s:

> It had the possibility to expand. I think it's the story of the century: you know, you see it in the General Strike; you see it in Spain; whenever there's a big dispute. This vast engine that takes a long time to start, but once it starts you feel it could drive anything anywhere and, constantly, the people who are supposed to be behind the wheel keep turning off into a blind alley. And it was absolutely the story of the General Strike. The details of how they did it are just interesting … And apart from just the narrative being interesting, it reveals their [left-wing leaders'] politics; it reveals that they act in the name of the working class, but they don't understand the interests of the working class. So there's this constant dysfunction between people who have leaders who act in your name but actually not in your interests. Blair is the most obvious current example of somebody who comes to power on the back of a working-class vote and on the back of a huge Labour movement that reaches back into the last century and he is absolutely failing; he's acting in the interests of the opposite class. The way that's happened at a critical moment, the mechanism of how that's happened, is very revealing. I mean not to know the story of the General Strike and of what those trade union leaders did; you can't understand twentieth-century British history without knowing that.[23]

1976 was the fiftieth anniversary of the General Strike. In 1972 and in 1974 there had been miners' strikes, and historian Margaret Morris argues that public support for the miners in the early 1970s owed much to the memory of how they were treated in the 1920s.[24] For Loach and Allen, the General Strike offered a paradigmatic example of the defeat of a working-class mass movement, from which it emerges having to fight again to improve pay and conditions.

The debate that they wanted *Days of Hope* to provoke concerns an argument which, because of social and economic changes in the UK since 1979, can seem anachronistic: a debate about reform or revolution, and how best to achieve change. For students of film and television, the ideological division that *Days of Hope* depicts is uncannily refracted through the split that occurs after the broadcast of *Days of Hope*: the split between Loach and Allen's position on politics and the position exemplified by Colin MacCabe's work in *Screen*, as discussed in Chapter 1. The ideological rift between film-makers and theorists seems to parallel the division between the union rank and file and the leaders of the Labour movement in the 1970s, and the division represented by Ben and Philip in *Days of Hope*. Within film and television studies, *Days of Hope* becomes a work that belongs quintessentially to the 1970s as *Cathy Come Home* does to the 1960s. In an extraordinarily direct, almost guileless way, Loach and Allen use a mainstream medium to galvanise political discussion in the Labour movement, to explore, using historical drama, the background and antecedents to contemporary industrial disputes. Reading criticism of it now, one senses that *Days of Hope* was a television landmark in the 1970s, a television drama that sharply divided opinion; as with *Cathy Come Home*, it is necessary to summarise the debates it provoked.

Colin MacCabe criticises *Days of Hope* because it resembles other costume dramas: 'the film [sic] falls within a bourgeois conception of history in which the past is understood as having a fixed and immutable existence rather than being the site of a constant struggle in the present' (MacCabe 1976a: 100).[25] MacCabe's formula generalises; less excusable, because *Days of Hope* unmistakably presents itself as a drama about events that remain controversial, is his implicit assumption that Loach and Allen do not understand that the past is historiographically variable and flexible, that, in Allen's words, 'all history is contemporary'. In 1980, Caughie endorses the classic realist text model when he discusses *Days of Hope* as 'progressive documentary drama' (Caughie 1980: 30). He distinguishes between the classic realist text and documentary drama; but, like MacCabe, he supports a loosely Brechtian or modernist aesthetic, and criticises the apparent illusion of transparency in films and television drama:

If the classic realist film depends on a certain invisibility of form, and on a spectator who forgets the camera, the documentary look takes its appearance of objectivity from its place within the conventions of documentary: thus, the hand-held camera, the cramped shot, natural lighting, inaudible sound. (Caughie 1980: 30)

Caughie expresses a reservation about the tendency to formal generalisation inherent in the concept of the classic realist text – it is incapable of distinguishing between *Days of Hope* and *Upstairs, Downstairs*; yet his reservation only expands Colin McArthur's earlier reservation (McArthur 1975–76). Caughie applies the classic realist text model in three ways: to critique the personalisation of social, political and historical issues; to express a preference for the quasi-Brechtian idea of interrupting emotional identification of spectators with characters through a 'separation-out' of the elements of a film; and to criticise *Days of Hope* for only giving an experience of history, as opposed to an analysis (Caughie 1980: 30). Caughie echoes MacCabe's call for a more Brechtian kind of television drama, where the constitutive elements of documentary and drama would be revealed to the viewer; but he concludes cautiously, arguing that we cannot easily assess the political efficacy of television drama. Twenty years later, Caughie modifies his claims about the personal drama: 'I argued that the family drama compromised the politics of the series; in retrospect, I would want to acknowledge that it may also complicate them' (Caughie 2000: 110).[26]

Looking back, the division between left-wing film theorists and film-makers seems surprising, until one remembers that it follows from divisions within the Labour movement. Theorists and film-makers share, for example, a concern with hegemonic media practices: both address the way that news on television, although it presents itself as neutral, objective and transparent, is constructed by organisations with ideological allegiances. On the representation of the police, for example, Loach says:

> On those rare occasions when people write about us, they write as if we were the only ones producing material of political significance. On the contrary, there are innumerable programmes on TV that have political influence, such as all those police series. Those programmes try to give people the idea that the police are only there to see that people cross the road OK. Actually, they are attempting to reassure viewers that traditional virtues should be adhered to. (Mills 1975: 337)

His comments about television epitomise an analytical stance towards hegemonic media practices which resembles the ideological analyses being produced in the burgeoning field of media and cultural studies. For example, when discussing *Days of Hope*, McArthur refers to the then editor of the *Daily Telegraph*, William Deedes, who, when he appeared on *Tonight* with Jim Allen, argued that audiences were likely to be confused as to whether *Days of Hope* was art or history.[27] McArthur, using a similar argument to that often rehearsed by Loach, points out that no such argument was advanced against a television biopic like *Edward the Seventh*: 'The lesson to be learned, of course, is that programmes which support the dominant ideology are regarded as natural and the few which do not are regarded as political' (McArthur 1981: 297).

Given the industrial and political unrest in Britain in the mid-1970s, it was inevitable that *Days of Hope* divided opinion; and the press responded to it at length.[28]

Two days after the broadcast of the third episode an editorial in the *Daily Telegraph* accused the BBC of being too left wing.[29] The BBC has objectivity enshrined in its charters, but the editorial writer forgets that at times of crisis it has revealed its close alignment with the state. *Days of Hope* points out the biased role of the BBC during the General Strike in Episode Four, when the strike is taking place. Baldwin, Jones and Steel-Maitland discuss the control of the *British Gazette* by Churchill and Davidson. Churchill wants to commandeer the BBC. Jones says, slightly contemptuously, 'Doesn't he realise that we already have control of the BBC?' They agree to preserve an image of impartiality. In fact, Reith was a friend of Baldwin's, and the BBC's support for the government during the General Strike is well documented.[30]

The concern with media representation occurs again when the General Council of the TUC give a press conference. A reporter asks whether 'communist agitators' have been shipped in from Russia to stir up trouble. As in *The Big Flame* and *The Rank and File*, Loach and Allen use the scene to highlight the way that sections of the media discredit mass movements by blaming a 'few militants'. *The Times* ran a fierce anti-strike campaign in May 1926, encouraging people to support the government and volunteer for the Organisation of Maintenance of Supplies (OMS).[31] An editorial states:

> There is abundant evidence that large numbers of those who have yielded to the pressure exercised by the Trade Union despots have done so against their own inclinations, and that their unwillingness to obey the call is by no means solely due to the losses which their attitude of passive obedience must bring upon them ... The government, as Lord Buckmaster pointed out in the House of Lords, are confronted with one of the most wanton and reckless exercises of tyrannical power that the country has been called upon to meet for centuries, and everyone who values ordered progress will support them in their difficult position. (Anon 1926: 3)

Readers in 1975 might have recognised this rhetoric of 'Trade Union despots' leading passively obedient workers 'against their own inclinations'. Its argument, that union leaders dictate to workers, is exactly what *Days of Hope* aims to refute: Loach and Allen's purpose is to draw the attention of 1970s viewers to the historical continuities, to enable viewers 'to understand the traitors and the treacheries of the Labour movement'.

The third episode of *Days of Hope* dramatises what they consider to be such a treachery. Ernest Bevin sends Philip to Liverpool to address a mass meeting of the Transport and General Workers Union. Bevin instructs Philip 'to put the communists in their place'. Under a banner that declares 'Unity is strength', Philip argues that division within the ranks of the Labour movement would be fatal at this crucial moment: 'We must, as it were, hold the fort until we can contain a big enough majority to carry through a socialist programme, which will transform society along more equitable lines.' After the meeting, a reporter (Stephen Rea) interviews Philip in a pub. Philip talks about legislating capitalism out of existence within institutional frameworks – nationalising land, banks, docks, insurance companies, factories and so on; but the reporter argues that the ruling class would never permit this. He alleges that some Labour leaders have already colluded with the Tories to preserve capitalist institutions. The reporter explains to Philip how Lloyd George initiated plans for a Supply and Transport Committee in 1919, which Baldwin revised with Davidson and John Anderson: if ever a strike got out of control and threatened private ownership, the government would implement these plans. In January 1924, when Labour gained office, Davidson passed the plans to a Labour minister, Josiah Wedgwood, who now harbours these plans for a strikebreaking force. 'The fight is fixed,' the reporter declares.

These allusions proved contentious: the *Daily Telegraph* printed its editorial after this episode, and writers have labelled this element of *Days of Hope* as conspiracy theory. As was noted in Chapter 1, John Hill argues that *Days of Hope*'s reliance on the form of classic realism 'inevitably led towards conspiracy theory' (Hill 1986: 60). He levels a similar criticism at Allen and Loach's *Hidden Agenda* (1990), part of which concerns the smearing of Wilson during the mid-1970s by members of the British security services.

> In this respect, conspiracy theory has the virtue of neatness, but its cost is the loss of genuine social and political complexity. The tendency towards personalisation which is encouraged by the conventions of narrative realism is reinforced by the specific properties of the crime thriller, especially when it is structured around the investigation of an individual detective and his quest to reveal or make visible, the truth behind a crime or enigma. (Hill 1997a: 133)

Hill acknowledges the convictions of Loach and Allen and the 'shoot-to-kill' case to be answered; yet he insists:

> Conspiracy, nevertheless, provides a singularly problematic basis for political analysis and explanation, and is certainly of little value in helping us to understand the crisis of social democracy and labourism which occurred during the 1970s, and the subsequent rise to power of the New Right. (Hill 1997a: 132–33)

Hill uses *Days of Hope* as the archetype for his argument about Loach and realism when he writes: 'Loach and Allen presented the failure of the British 1926 General Strike as simply the result of individual treachery on the part of Labour and trade union leaders' (Hill 1997a: 132).

Hill accurately describes the narrative strategies that Loach and Allen use; but his argument does not acknowledge the degree to which they thought about how to express political ideas in a mainstream medium. Hill may disagree with the interpretation of events that the dramatisation expresses; yet it is hard to accept his argument that a focus on individuals when depicting historical events *inevitably* leads to conspiracy theory. The 'conventions of narrative realism' do not straightforwardly encourage a 'tendency towards personalisation', as Hill assumes. In theory, it appears self-evident that because a film concentrates on individuals it cannot invoke a general understanding of the dramas depicted. In practice, however, as Andrew Britton points out, people have created narratives that centre on individuals since 'the dawn of time' (Britton 1988–89: 52). How we understand individual characters' actions in films varies with the context for those actions. If we wish to distinguish between the varying ways in which films evoke relationships between individuals and larger, perhaps more abstract forces, such as ideology, then we need refer to the actions and their contexts.

The example of the strikebreaking force allows us to uncover how Allen and Loach researched the project. When Philip returns home from Liverpool, he is drawn into a political argument with Sarah, Ben and Joel. Ben argues that the ruling class will never give up private ownership and socialism cannot be legislated into existence. Philip defends the Labour Party's 'Clause 4' commitments to nationalise industries and utilities. Later, he tells Sarah of his conversation with the reporter. The deviousness of a Labour minister shocks her; Philip promises to talk to Wedgwood. The film then cuts to this meeting. Wedgwood refuses to deny or confirm Philip's suspicions and the episode ends with a written title:

> Wedgwood did not tell the PM or his Cabinet colleagues of these plans. They were intact when the Conservatives resumed office a few months later. Both Parliament and the people had been kept in ignorance throughout. The plans were used as the basis of the strikebreaking force of 1926.

In the script, Allen writes a note after Philip's meeting with the reporter: 'N.B. This is where the real meaning of this for ordinary people must be clearly spelled out. Why it is all so important.'[32]

Allen wrote the scripts using published accounts of the period as his sources: memoirs and diaries by Thomas Jones and J. C. C. Davidson; autobiographies by Walter Citrine and J. H. Thomas; and histories, like that by David Boulton.[33] He researched the events, aiming to be accurate.[34] Occasionally, his scripts for *Days of Hope* include notes in brackets; for example, he writes after a Vicar's (Bernard Atha) pro-war speech: 'See *Rippon Gazette* February 11 1915, p. 6.'[35] When the army tie a conscientious objector to a post in no-man's land, he writes, 'See D. Boulton, p.168'. Much of Allen's writing quotes source material that is close to records of conversations and meetings; and Loach emphasises that 'a lot of it was verbatim'.[36] The penultimate scene, for example, when the General Council tell Baldwin that they are calling off the strike, features dialogue virtually identical to published minutes of the meeting.[37]

In Loach and Allen's interpretation, the interests of the labour forces and the interests of those who control capital are fundamentally at odds: Hill accuses *Days of Hope* of conspiracy theory, but for its makers, the government's plans illustrate how the state protects capital investment. A written title at the beginning of Episode Four declares that the Conservative government used the nine-month subsidy period, until 30 April 1926, to finalise its plans; the TUC, meanwhile, made no plans for conducting a strike.[38] Morris confirms this interpretation, and she describes how the plans for maintaining services and supplies during strikes, established by the post-war Lloyd George coalition government in October 1919, formed the basis for the Cabinet Supply and Transport Committee.[39] Davidson improved arrangements in 1923, with the help of Anderson. In January 1924, he gave the plans to Josiah Wedgwood, the new Labour Chancellor of the Duchy of Lancaster and an old friend of his. Davidson wrote in his memoirs:

> I told him that, whoever was in power, it was his duty to protect the constitution ... I begged him not to destroy all I had done and not to inform his Cabinet of it. This did not concern party but was a national matter. (James 1969: 180)

For Loach and Allen, though, protecting the constitution *is* a party political matter. In their analysis, Wedgwood typifies Labour leaders. Wedgwood handed the plans back to Davidson after the fall of the Labour government at the end of 1924. By August 1925, the government was prepared to deal with food, fuel, transport, communications, finance, publicity and protection. By October 1925, unofficial organisations like the OMS and various fascist groups had begun to enrol volunteers, although the government was yet to call for volunteers.[40] We can only uphold Hill's charge of conspiracy theory if we ignore the fact that, although *Days of Hope* selects and interprets events, Loach and Allen researched it thoroughly.

The exposure of the collusion of Labour leaders with the ruling class constitutes the heart of *Days of Hope*: its central theme is that members of the Special Industrial Committee of the General Council of the TUC failed to represent union members properly, and, by extension, failed to represent the working class. They compromise their support of the miners when they go behind the backs of Cook and Smith to arrange for the end of the General Strike without getting any concessions from the government or the mine owners.[41] In particular, *Days of Hope* exposes the behaviour of the leader of the National Union of Railwaymen, and General Council member, J. H. Thomas.[42] Thomas is friendly with Lord Reading (Hilary Wontner) and *Days of Hope* shows him passing on information regarding the TUC's unwillingness to support the miners. However, it does not show him deciding, individually, to end the General Strike. At dinner at the house of Lord Wimborne (Derek Farr), a Liberal politician and mine owner, Thomas confesses that the miners are ready to accept the Samuels Report; something we know to be untrue, having seen Cook and Smith reject it.[43] Later, he meets Selwyn Davies (Jeremy Child), personal assistant to Lord Wimborne and a friend of Thomas Jones, the Deputy Cabinet Secretary and Baldwin's confidant. In the middle of a meeting at the TUC Headquarters between the General Council and the Miners' Federation, during which Cook and Smith again reject the Samuels proposals, Thomas tells Davies to inform the Prime Minister that by two o'clock it will be all over. When Thomas returns to the meeting, Jones telephones the TUC meeting and asks Citrine whether or not they have any news for him, as the Prime Minister has been waiting up to hear from them.[44] Jones records this call in his diaries;[45] Allen and Loach incorporate it into *Days of Hope* to demonstrate the close association between Labour leaders and members of the Conservative government; although Thomas does no more than forewarn Baldwin of the General Council's intentions to end the strike. *Days of Hope* portrays his conniving behaviour, yet it does not assert that the end of the strike was his personal responsibility. It discloses the divergent aims and attitudes of the people involved in the strike; but although it reveals Thomas acting behind the backs of those he claims to support, it does not inevitably follow that *Days of Hope* blames the end of the General Strike on one individual.[46]

All four episodes dramatise the impact of national events on individuals, and we see how the progression of the strike affects Philip, Ben and Sarah. The focus on individuals does not evade social, economic and political issues; it presents a perspective on the historical events depicted: we can agree or disagree with the perspective that the story presents. Allen defended his work: 'our business is to write fiction. We don't make documentaries … I don't think we can be made accountable in the same way that *Panorama* is' (Goodwin, Kerr and MacDonald 1983: 459). Loach argues:

> We felt that if we just showed the event without our private people to put them in some political perspective and draw out some general conclusions, the effect would be just an impression – like good journalism – a blow-by-blow report but with no perspective. (O'Hara 1977: 301)

Writers on the right and left criticised *Days of Hope*, but Allen recalled that 'from the Labour movement, the workers, we got tremendous, tremendous plaudits. I was quite proud of that'.[47] A letter to *The Listener* in 1975 is suggestive. D. A. Wilson was born in 1897, served in World War One for three years and was a trade unionist during the General Strike in 1926. He writes of *Days of Hope*:

> If they had been presented from the point of view, above the battle, of the smug, self-satisfied professor, they would not have been worth a damn. What remains vivid to me, some fifty years afterwards, was the innocent loyalty and faith in which we responded, when we were called out on strike; the staunchness and courage which grew during its course; and the surprise and

consternation, followed by white-hot anger, when those who had led us up the hill crumpled so suddenly, and scurried down again. There was nothing in the play which could have exaggerated those experiences. (D. A. Wilson 1975: 507)

As Caughie argues, *Days of Hope* may offer the experience of history, rather than its analysis; but importantly, it offers the experiences of people like D. A. Wilson.[48] Historical dramas, like written histories, offer emphases according to the viewpoint of the writer: *Days of Hope* describes events by drawing on the same sources that historians use.[49] It places political debates within family situations, making the bitterness and recriminations of historical events tangible. *Days of Hope* presents events by emphasising the experiences of three people with opposing views; it privileges no single view. Despite Allen and Loach's political convictions, it offers no singly convincing answer at the end. Ben's view does not emerge as more persuasive than Philip or Sarah's view. The first two films present him sympathetically; but as he becomes closer to the Communist Party, the narrative distances us from him.

We should not doubt the political purpose of Loach, Allen and Garnett's projects in the late 1960s and 1970s. In 1969, they wanted *The Big Flame* to be a beacon for contemporary trade unionists, such as the striking Pilkington glassworkers whom Allen and Peter Kerrigan met. *The Big Flame* provides a hypothesis for an alternative way for a strike to proceed, which, although it may seem now like a 'heady fantasy', then connected with the aspirations of the Labour movement. One result of this connection was *The Rank and File*, a film concerned with the outcome of a strike, which takes a non-mainstream position. In this work, Loach and Allen tried again to connect with viewers: it ends with Peter Kerrigan warning viewers about the Industrial Relations Bill. The Labour movement rejected this Bill, and in 1974 a miners' strike and Heath's apparent inability to deal with Britain's economic problems contributed to the collapse of the Conservative government.

But the return of a Labour government did not ensure an end to the left's problems: divisions grew between the bulk of Labour MPs and the constituency parties and unions; Margaret Thatcher, Keith Joseph and the right wing of the Conservative Party exploited them. After losing the general election in 1974, the Conservative Party rejected Heath and his policies, and moved firmly to the right, electing Thatcher as its leader. In June 1979, following a winter of more strikes, Thatcher won the general election on a platform that included the promise to curb union activities. She drove through major economic and industrial management changes, and her government passed two Employment Acts, in 1980 and 1982. These Acts made secondary picketing illegal, limited the closed shop, and made unions liable for employers' losses during a strike. Meanwhile, the antagonisms on the left split the Labour party, and in April 1981 most of Labour's right wing decamped to form the Social Democratic Party.

Days of Hope was to offer a warning from history about the perfidy of reformist Labour and union leaders; it was to provide historical background to viewers frustrated with Wilson's government. As Loach says:

> We took those films around quite a lot, and if you showed it to an audience of trade unionists they would talk about their own leadership and how they could organise at branch level, which was a much more concrete and sensible way to discuss the film. That's the kind of discussion you want, rather than discussing the semiotics of it. (Hood 1994: 199–200)

Yet their hopes went awry, despite this reception: in part, printed debate about the form – 'the semiotics of it' – sidetracked the political project; but this was marginal compared with the real political changes. In April 1978, the BBC repeated *Days of Hope*. This was a time when the Labour movement and the union rank and file were dissatisfied with Callaghan's Labour government; there were many strikes and Loach, Allen and Garnett must have been pleased that the BBC was repeating *Days of Hope*. However, the reaction in 1979 to the industrial upheaval of the early and mid-1970s was a political shift to the right, a clamping down on unions and an embracing of the free market and privatisation that went far further than those on the left had feared. The Thatcher years of the 1980s are difficult times for Loach: the experience of Thatcherism confirms and hardens his political outlook, yet it takes him nearly ten years to renew himself and rediscover the artistic balance which characterises his best work of the 1960s and 1970s.

CHAPTER FIVE

significance and objectivity

After *Days of Hope* (1975) and his two-part television drama made for the BBC's *Play for Today* series, *The Price of Coal* (1977), Loach in the late 1970s and early 1980s directed three feature-length fiction films: *Black Jack* (1979), *The Gamekeeper* (1980), and *Looks and Smiles* (1981).[1] He single-handedly adapted Leon Garfield's book *Black Jack* (1971), which is about a young girl whose family place her in an asylum in 1749, the first and last time he attempted this. Following *Poor Cow* (1967), *Kes* (1969) and *Family Life* (1971), *Black Jack* was his fourth cinema film. Loach and Garnett had experienced funding problems on *Kes*, and throughout the 1970s, they found it hard to raise money in Britain. *Family Life* did badly in the UK, but it fared better in Europe, especially in France.[2] Garnett discovered that they could finance a feature film if they made a children's film with co-production money from the National Film Finance Corporation and Europe.[3] However, in November 1978, during *Black Jack*'s post-production, the French co-producers withdrew.[4] After the production difficulties and the poor reception of *Black Jack*,[5] Garnett broke off his 15-year partnership with Loach and left Britain.[6] Loach began a ten-year association with ATV, later to become Central.[7]

ATV's documentary department produced *The Gamekeeper*, and their press release promoted it as a 'ninety-minute dramatised documentary', even though it was based on a novel by Barry Hines. In the UK during the late 1970s, Loach was still mainly known for his television work; and he was increasingly working for ATV's documentary department; for example, ITV broadcast his documentary *Auditions* (1980) only a week after they transmitted *The Gamekeeper*. In Europe, however, *The Gamekeeper* was a cinema film; and there at least critics acknowledged Loach as a director of feature films.[8] In the 1990s, his producers find production money in Europe. In 1980 in the UK, where *The Gamekeeper* is publicised as a dramatised documentary on television, there are indications that, on the cusp of Channel 4, the single play for television is becoming anachronistic; although the influence of *Film on 4* is not felt until later in the 1980s when hybrid television/cinema films replace the single play.[9]

Looks and Smiles was Loach's fifth collaboration with Barry Hines (after *Kes*, *The Price of Coal*, *The Gamekeeper* and *A Question of Leadership*). In July 1978, Black Lion Films commissioned Hines to write an original screenplay for Loach to direct; Hines subsequently published a novel based on his screenplay. Loach completed the film in 1981. Like *The Gamekeeper*, it had an ambiguous status: made for British television and European cinemas.[10] Following these fiction films, Loach turns exclusively to documentaries; and for more than five years after making *Looks and Smiles*, until Channel 4 commissions his first *Film on 4*, *Fatherland* (1986), he makes only documentaries.[11] The style of *The Gamekeeper* and *Looks and Smiles* anticipates his documentaries of the 1980s, all of which respond to political changes in contemporary Britain. Accordingly, this chapter primarily continues the exploration that Chapter 1 began; that is, an analysis of the relationship between fiction and non-fiction in Loach's work. It examines his commitment to reveal the world and to film stories about the world, to document and to create patterns which develop a viewpoint on the material he films. An analysis of *The Gamekeeper* constitutes the major part of the chapter; a consideration of his 1980s documentaries ends it.

V. F. Perkins argues that the skill of directors like Otto Preminger and Vincente Minnelli is in finding methods of direction that allow them 'to annul the distinction between significant organisation and objective recording' (Perkins 1978: 97). As was argued in the first chapter, *Carla's Song* includes moments of documentary-like objective record and moments of significant organisation, as well as some moments which, as Perkins writes, 'call[s] attention to the director at the expense of the events *through* which he set out to convey meaning' (Perkins 1978: 86). The difficulty for Loach of deciding to remain open to whatever comes his way while trying to keep a tight rein on a film's structure is not exclusively his. Perkins points out that:

> In many of the finest films images and sounds are simply the means of presenting the essentials of action as clearly as can be. The picture exists solely for what it shows and we gain nothing by attempting to interpret its structure. Its qualities as an image are submerged by its function as a document. (Perkins 1978: 98)

Loach consistently uses the strategies of a documentary film-maker in his fiction films. His exploitation of the transparency of the film medium originates in his desire to document ordinary people; he is committed, as André Bazin puts it, to an aesthetic 'in which the image is evaluated not according to what it adds to reality but what it reveals of it' (Bazin 1967: 28). One benefit of this approach is the possibility for the powerful momentary evocation of a place and time; one problem, however, is that instead of filming motifs or thematic patterns that have what Perkins calls an 'expressive relevance' (Perkins 1978: 93) within the whole film, there is occasionally a tendency to rely on the 'violently asserted conjunctions of stock-markets and battle-fields, or palaces and slums' (Perkins 1978: 102).

This book excludes a detailed exploration of documentary, but it requires a brief definition. Corner proffers this summary: '"Documentary" is the loose and often contested label given, internationally, to certain kinds of film and television (and sometimes radio programmes) which reflect and report on "the real" through the use of the recorded images and sounds of actuality' (Corner 1996: 2).[12] Before *Auditions*, Loach had made only two documentaries, neither of which has ever been publicly shown: *In Black and White* (1969) is a film about the work of the Save the Children Fund in England and Kenya; *Talk About Work* (1971) is a short film made for the Central Office of Information, in which Peter Kerrigan talks to a group of teenagers about work and their expectations of it. Although these are Loach's only documentaries prior to *Auditions*, his use of documentary conventions in his films for *The Wednesday Play* between 1965 and 1969 generates controversy earlier on in his career; for example, his use of unspecified voice-overs or authoritative commentaries over montage sequences of observational shots. Loach uses these conventions to encourage us to recognise that Rube's experiences in *Up the Junction* or Cathy's in *Cathy Come Home*, the experiences of an illegal abortion and of homelessness, may be typical and widespread.

By the late 1970s and early 1980s, Loach has changed the ways in which he tries to make the experiences of individuals seem social and general. In 1983 he looks back to the changes that occur on *Kes*:

> We rejected that earlier style of editing pieces of narrative with factual information because although it might have been appropriate at the time, in the end it seemed to inhibit the development of characters and their relationships. And it often seemed a crude way of saying things that were better implicit than explicit. (Brown 1983: 11)

The 'factual information' to which Loach refers suggests the example of the doctor's voice-over reading out abortion statistics in *Up the Junction*, yet it also evokes the images of places and people that are linked to the protagonists through association, rather than narrative causality. *Cathy Come Home* documents the inhabitants of a block of flats in Islington not because they are integral to Cathy and Reg's story; but because they exemplify the conditions of life in these flats. People speak over images about their experiences in the flats; on the soundtrack and in the images, Loach edits 'pieces of narrative with factual information', creating a hybrid of drama and documentary or, as Corner describes it, of story and report. He takes this practice to its apotheosis with his interviews with real footballers in *The Golden Vision*, though it does not disappear from his work until after *The Rank and File*.

Loach tells us that one reason he modifies his technique is that he wants to avoid imposing his or his writer's interpretation of a film's action upon the narrative. The modifications do not occur in isolation, though, for while he moves, between the 1960s and the 1980s, away from incorporating into his fiction 'factual information' – what we might think of as raw documentary elements – the conventions of documentaries themselves change. The non-synchronised montage sequences of *Up the Junction* or *Cathy Come Home* draw upon historically specific documentary conventions: in part, they are a legacy of a period before technology made synchronisation easily accessible; similarities exist between Loach's early work and Denis Mitchell's television documentaries or Lindsay Anderson's *Every Day Except Christmas* (1957). When Loach makes documentaries in the 1980s, changes in documentary film-making affect his use of documentary conventions. The biggest change comes from the enormous influence of *cinéma vérité*: work by Jean Rouch, Albert and David Maysles, Fred Wiseman, Richard Leacock and later, on television in Britain, work by Paul Watson and Roger Graef, transforms documentary film-making.

In Loach's documentaries of the 1980s, the non-synchronised montage sequences of observational shots and unspecified voice-overs do not give way to a *cinéma vérité* style, although at times he employs its formal conventions. Instead, his documentaries generally use a format of interviews, discussions, archive footage and explanatory voice-overs. In the three fiction films that he makes before his documentaries, however, he extends his technique of mimicking *cinéma vérité* and television *vérité*: in *The Gamekeeper* and *Looks and Smiles* he maintains a discipline of responsiveness that imitates the responsiveness of *cinéma vérité* documentaries, instead of imitating the essayistic and montage-based conventions of earlier documentaries. In the early 1980s, he rigorously sustains his method of allowing the flow of a conversation to determine the movement of the camera, taking further what Caughie characterises as 'the rhetoric of the "unplanned" or "un-premeditated" shot' (Caughie 1980: 28).

Nevertheless, by 1986 Loach recognises that these experiments have been unsatisfactory. Of *Looks and Smiles* he says:

When we made it [1980/81], the appalling escalation of unemployment was just starting and we thought it would be a cliché to make another angry film about it. But, as a result, I think we missed creating the outrage in the audience that should have been there. It may be self-regarding, or self-aggrandising or something, but for me *Looks and Smiles*, like *Poor Cow*, was sort of the end of an era in my work – the end of a whole way of working, which started with *Kes* and was fresh with *Kes*, but became old and lethargic. Seeing it afterwards, I decided I never wanted to hold a shot for so long again. (Kerr 1986: 148)

His description of *Looks and Smiles* as 'the end of an era' is accurate, for the long shot and the long take are typical of his method in *Black Jack*, *The Gamekeeper* and *Looks and Smiles*. With what he calls 'a slightly narrow' fixed lens, he keeps the camera away from the action, maintaining a long shot and a long take, following the characters' movements. This method brings to mind the one take/one sequence discipline that Jean Rouch develops after *Chronicle of a Summer* (1961);[13] and other documentary film-makers have maintained the discipline of the long take: D. A. Pennebaker exploits it profitably in *Don't Look Back* (1967) and *Monterey Pop* (1968), as do the Maysles Brothers and Charlotte Zwerin in their classic documentary *Salesman* (1969). In 1986, Loach recognises the limitations for him of maintaining this neo-*vérité* discipline, though he is yet to find solutions to the artistic problems he identifies.

Since *Kes*, Loach has exploited the personality and experience of his actors, casting them accordingly. He explains his commitment to revealing people in fiction films when he discusses how a real doctor, Mike Riddal, plays the doctor in *Family Life*:

> Obviously, the family in the film is a fictional family, but Mike was very subtle and clever at exploring the real personalities of the people we brought in to play the other characters. In a way, what emerged was almost a documentary about the people in the film – particularly the mother, who was played by Grace Cave, an extraordinary woman representative of so much of what we now call family values … There was no way that the relationship between Grace and Sandy Ratcliff, who played the daughter in *Family Life*, was going to be anything other than what it was because Sandy was a free spirit, true to the sixties, and yet thoroughly able to understand what it was to be dominated by a woman like Grace … So I didn't need to manipulate them off-screen. The casting took care of the relationships that evolved between the actors in front of the camera. (Fuller 1998: 44–5)

Loach describes his method of finding the right people to film as if he was making a documentary about them. Loach, David Mercer and Tony Garnett want *Family Life* to champion the theories of the psychiatrist R. D. Laing, but *Family Life* is also, as Loach says, 'almost a documentary about the people in the film'. In the 1980s this combination of casting and filming becomes his *raison d'être*: it motivates his style in *The Gamekeeper*, *Looks and Smiles* and in the documentaries he makes, ending with *The View from the Woodpile* (1989). Following this collaboration with a youth drama group in the Midlands, he makes other documentaries, notably *The Flickering Flame* (1996) about a Liverpool dock strike; but that film possesses a visual flair and narrative economy which reflects his successes with cinema films in the 1990s. Loach first works with Barry Ackroyd on *The View from the Woodpile*, after which they collaborate on all of his subsequent films, from *Hidden Agenda* to *The Navigators*.[14] In none of their work together do Loach and Ackroyd hold a shot for as long as he and Menges do on *Looks and Smiles*.

Loach's documentaries (some of them shot by Menges, who worked with Loach until *Fatherland*) are considerable political and cultural interventions, but for Loach they lead to an artistic cul-de-sac. His work with Jim Allen and Tony Garnett between 1969 and 1975 reveals a political philosophy harder than that which his work of the 1960s expresses. Loach sustains his political beliefs through the 1980s, but he extends *Family Life*'s quality of being 'almost a documentary', in preference to the dramatic qualities of *Days of Hope*. Some of his documentaries fail to find an audience, and politics play a major part in this failure; but Loach's pursuit of the real through documentary alone also contributes. He has said that in the early 1980s the onslaught of right-wing politics in the UK compelled him to respond as quickly as possible to the changes that Thatcher inaugurated; for this reason he began making documentaries.[15] As he developed his relationship with the documentary department at ATV and then at Central, he found it easier to secure commissions for television documentaries than for feature films. He may have felt he was responding to the politics of the day, yet in making documentaries he fulfilled only one of the possibilities of his work. Increasingly frustrated politically, perhaps he felt that by maintaining a discipline of documentary revelation he would be able to expose injustices and to express his opposition to the changes that Thatcher was initiating. His steadfast maintenance of his political position in the 1980s grounds him, and a solid core of ideas secures his revival in the 1990s; but until that point his failure to acknowledge the importance of individual drama in his work results in nearly ten years of artistic dormancy. The exception in this period is *The Gamekeeper*.

The Gamekeeper: the documentary look

Following his experiment with writing and directing on *Black Jack*, Loach renews his relationship with Barry Hines. In 1975, Hines had published *The Gamekeeper*, a novel he has since described as his best work.[16] Arguably, the film's qualities derive from Loach's collaboration with Hines, who in his novel stays almost as close to describing the life and environment of a gamekeeper as Loach does in the film. As he did with *A Kestrel for a Knave*, based on his brother's experiences as a falconer, Hines based *The Gamekeeper* on the experiences of a real person, a friend of his who was a gamekeeper. Like *A Kestrel for a Knave*, *The Gamekeeper* is about people whose experiences in South Yorkshire are both urban and rural, people who live and work between town and country. Hines writes of a landscape dotted with pit villages, places that are industrial and yet are often set in idyllic countryside. In *A Kestrel for a Knave* and *Kes*, Billy Casper moves between town centre and open fields: the council estate where he lives, although representative of an expanding conurbation, adjoins woodland and pasture-land; it forms a boundary and a link between urban and rural experiences. In the film of *The Gamekeeper*, for which Hines adapted his novel into a screenplay, Loach shares and explores Hines' interest in the experiences of people who live between town and country in a way that rewards his discipline of documentary responsiveness.

In his novel, Hines describes the changing seasons and the environment, and the determining effect both elements have on the work and life of the gamekeeper, George Purse. The film shares the descriptive impulse and the narrative structure of the novel. Aiming to depict George's work and the environment in which he works as authentically as possible, Loach spent a year filming the seasons in Yorkshire. He describes its making:

> It was the kind of thing you could only do for a large company, because it meant going back to the locations throughout the year to shoot each season. It was one of the films I've enjoyed doing most, and I think that's because the images were so concrete – it's about ownership and who does what for whose benefit, and I think the luminous images of the land that Chris Menges captured helped encapsulate that. In fact, one of the problems with my next film, *Looks and Smiles*, was that we simply didn't have such a strong central image. In *Kes*, we had the bird and in *The Gamekeeper* there was the countryside, but *Looks and Smiles* doesn't have such a clear image at its centre. (Kerr 1986: 148)

The Gamekeeper reunites Loach, Hines and Menges from *Kes*, and, as Loach indicates, there are similarities between the two films. Both the kestrel of *Kes* and the countryside of *The Gamekeeper* are, he feels, 'central images'. We should distinguish between a central image and a symbol in Loach's work. The use of the kestrel in *Kes* tempts us to read it as a symbol; Loach discourages this: 'we never thought of the kestrel as a symbol. I don't think we ever once discussed the symbolic resonance of it – again, tending and training the bird was just what Billy did' (Fuller 1998: 59).

While he does not have a monopoly on interpretations of his films, his comments recommend a useful way of thinking about his work. Billy works with his kestrel; Loach films him doing so. George Purse works in the countryside; and Loach films him doing so. Filming what is expressive in the world of Billy and George creates meaning. He organises his material; but he does not refer symbolically to things outside Billy or George's world: there is no sense of an imposed viewpoint on the action that the films present, as there is in *Up the Junction* and *Cathy Come Home*. His aspiration to document people acting in the world does not preclude a use of symbols, but it modifies them. Hines' writing, in his novel and in his screenplay, aids Loach's commitment to document the world; yet, Loach combines this impulse with an integrated narrative structure, one where elements have expressive relevance.

Hines evokes the distance between the gamekeeper and those whom he serves: the Duke, his family and his guests. In transforming the novel into a film, Loach films the world as Hines describes it, organising the material using principles of juxtaposition. His 1983 documentary, *The Red and the Blue* (1983), cuts between a cocktail party at the 1982 Conservative Party conference, where Peter Lilley and his wife meet delegates, and a pub near the Labour Party conference of the same year, where a group of Labour delegates discuss politics. Loach and editor Jonathan Morris repeatedly cut between the two conferences: the result is a compelling portrait of the contrasts between the two groups of delegates. Patrick Stoddart writes perceptively of *The Red and the Blue* that, 'there were moments when you could hardly believe that the Pimms-sipping Sloane Rangers and the tea-slurping Tribunites were members of the same species, let alone the same nation' (Stoddart 1983: 14). *The Red and the Blue* reveals differences between the two conferences and between the delegates who attend them by juxtaposing situations to make comparisons and contrasts. In this, Loach inherits the concerns of *cinéma vérité*; he reveals people on film, as opposed to asserting anything about them; as William Rothman argues, the commitment to a mode of revelation distinguishes the concerns of *cinéma vérité* from those of earlier documentaries.[17] However, Loach's use of juxtaposition is also a form of assertion, of the palaces and slums kind.

Arguably, though, in *The Red and the Blue* and *The Gamekeeper* Loach finds a thematic structure without inventing contrasts where none exist. By filming George at work on the Duke's estate for a year, he maintains the discipline of recording what a gamekeeper does; he then organises the film so that themes emerge gradually. Loach says of Hines' writing:

> Like all of Barry's work, the essence of it is very neat and simple and precise. The image of the gamekeeper as someone who protects land and the game birds by keeping out people like himself – other ordinary people – and maintaining it as a preserve for aristocrats to visit briefly once or a few times during the year when they destroy the birds he has raised is very powerful. (Fuller 1998: 56)

Phil Askham plays the gamekeeper, George. Askham had had minor roles in *Black Jack* and *The Price of Coal*, and he next plays Mick's father in *Looks and Smiles*. According to Loach:

> Phil wasn't a gamekeeper in reality. He was a former miner who was selling cash registers at the time, but he was very good at performing the gamekeeper's tasks and, in a way, the film is partly a documentary about his skills and his personality. (Fuller 1998: 56)

Loach conveys the themes of George's life and of *The Gamekeeper* by filming the relationships between George and those around him: his employers, his family, poachers, men in the estate village, people on the nearby council estate. The film is about social relations; and its themes emerge in George's work, habits and social life.

A central theme of *The Gamekeeper* is that George's work, rearing and protecting the pheasants for the annual shooting party, dominates his life; attending to the pheasants marks the cycle of his year. To this end, he hunts foxes with his dog. At one

Figure 15: *The Gamekeeper*

point, he shoots a fox, and there is no mistaking the life leaving the fox as it shudders, stretches and dies. He then tosses the carcass into the bushes. Later, he shoots a crow out of a tree: crows, like foxes, threaten pheasants. Afterwards, he turns the dead bird over with his foot. On another occasion, he and another gamekeeper use a ferret to force rabbits out of their holes and into nets. In a medium close-up, George's colleague breaks the neck of a rabbit; we hear the dull crunch of the small bones and we see the struggling rabbit become lifeless (figure 15). Loach films the killing of the fox, the crow and the rabbits, and, in doing so, he documents either George or another keeper performing tasks expertly; yet, although the tasks are routine for them, the film's display of the animals' deaths significantly asserts the realism of the film.

The first shot of *The Gamekeeper* shows George working: we fade in on a pheasant in a small cage in a wood. The bird's destiny is to be shot and eaten; and throughout the film, the differences between George and those he serves emerge through a patterning of scenes that revolve around food. The ending of the film completes a pattern of the difference between what George eats and what the Duke eats. In the penultimate scene, George and a colleague take some dead pheasants to the Duke's pantry. Through the open kitchen door, he sees his wife peeling potatoes, helping to prepare a meal for the guests who made up the shooting party. George returns home to his own meal. The last shot of the film shows a meat pie that George will eat:

taken from the fridge, the pie is unappetisingly wrapped in cellophane, factory-made, like the tinned peas and frozen chips that accompany it. These last scenes prompt thoughts about class and look forward to the contrasts Loach achieves by cutting between the Labour and Tory delegates in *The Red and the Blue*. Isolated like this, the contrast between the opening and closing shots is schematic; yet, because Loach films George's work as an integral part of *The Gamekeeper*, the action of the film absorbs its thematic organisation.

When the gamekeeper takes the pheasant from the cage with one hand, the camera pans up to frame him holding the bird while he checks under its wings, then places it in a sack. The camera records these actions from a distance, with the background wood and foreground branches out of focus, only the gamekeeper in focus. His brown jacket and blond hair blend in with the colours of the wood. The image typifies Loach's work during this period: the camera is held at a distance from characters that perform actions that engross them, and medium close-ups present their actions. As the gamekeeper walks home, the credits continue. There is no music, nor is there any in the whole film. Documentaries often use music; but the lack of music in *The Gamekeeper* is part of Loach's aspiration to achieve a documentary-like style for a fiction film, as if he renounces anything that will distract from the sense that his camera is following the gamekeeper.

When the gamekeeper approaches the house, he calls to John for help with the pheasants. John (Andrew Grubb) and Ian (Peter Steels) come out, but the gamekeeper sends Ian back into the house, walking away with John. We cut to a close-up of the gamekeeper opening the sack, from which he removes the pheasant, and shows his son how to hold the bird. We then cut to an establishing long shot, which reveals that father and son are standing in a walk-in cage. In a close-up, the gamekeeper ties the bird's wings. John sets the cock pheasant, with its wings tied, free in the cage with the hens. Beyond the fact that he uses a close-up, Loach does not signal that we should read either the cage or the tying of the bird's wings as symbols, though both suggest limits on freedom of movement. The gamekeeper's actions express meaning in relation to the whole film; yet they form part of his routine, like Billy Casper's training of the kestrel.

Inside their house, George's wife, Mary (Rita May), cooks breakfast. The gamekeeper frowns as he waits with his son, Ian, at the table. John sits by the fire, taking his shoes off. George asks Mary, 'What's up with him?' After some discussion about a stomach ache, she tells him that their eldest son does not want to attend school because the sons of a poacher that George caught have been bullying him. The poacher has eight children, a lot of mouths to feed – the odd rabbit or pheasant must help; but George is unconcerned with the poacher's children: 'I don't care 'ow many they've got, but they all ought to be gassed in beds, like we do with rabbits.' He orders John to school: 'What's he want me to do? Pack job up like and go back inta steelworks because they're going to thump him at school if I catch 'em down t' wood.' It emerges that the gamekeeper has his wings tied: he and his family are socially isolated. George is isolated from the Duke and the people whom he serves. He is also isolated from those whom he prevents from trespassing. Having left the class of his origin, he is akin to the scholarship boy or the sergeant-major, between classes, alienated from both the upper class, whom he serves and on whose land he lives, and the working class, who would be his peers in other circumstances. His job affects his family's life: when John complains of being bullied, or, later, when Mary complains of being lonely, the film hints at the alienation that his work causes. This social isolation does not hamper George's enjoyment of his work in the countryside, even though, it transpires, his employers exploit him. During the busy season, he can work 14- or 18-hour days; his work, he complains, is never finished.

The isolation of the gamekeeper and his family forms the essential theme of *The Gamekeeper*. The film emphasises the alienation of the gamekeepers when the pheasant beaters threaten to strike on the morning of the annual pheasant shoot. The beaters wait on the lawn for the Duke and his guests to arrive. George joins the other gamekeepers. The head gamekeeper, Henry (Chick Barratt), tells him that the beaters want more money. The Duke (Willoughby Gray) employs them on a casual basis; their relationship to him differs from that of the gamekeepers. George proposes to them that they ask for ten pounds a day, as seven pounds only represents an increase of two pounds. This outrages Henry, who is unsure whether George is joking. The film leaves it uncertain whether George supports the beaters. As head keeper, Henry is closer to the Duke than George is; he negotiates with his employer on behalf of the beaters. The Duke agrees to £6.50; but he tells Henry, 'Make a note of their names and we won't employ them again, will we?' The Duke's 'will we' demands that Henry comply with the blacklist; Henry backs away from the Duke, touching his hat as he does so. George instinctively sides with the beaters: he encourages them, although perhaps only jokingly, to bargain; ultimately, though, he aligns himself with other gamekeepers, not with the landowners or the beaters.

As sympathetic as the portrayal of George is, Loach reveals the aims of workers and of employers to be at odds; the gamekeeper finds himself caught between the two. He can speak to the landowners, to the beaters and to the poachers; but although he serves the landowners, he is loyal to none of these groups. The film does not construct its protagonist as a self-aware tragic hero; but it proposes that George is sometimes conscious of his predicament. For example, when he chats to a tractor driver in a field, they both grumble about the long hours of their jobs and agree that there is a 'little bit too much forelock tugging': they are aware of servitude and class. In another example, the film cuts from George and his colleague catching rabbits to him visiting the village at lunchtime, where he sells the rabbits to the butcher and lunches at the pub. As he enters the village, he strides proprietorially, carrying the rabbits loosely at his side. After handing the carcasses to the butcher, who pays him from the till, he asks if the pork pies in the window are fresh. Of course they are, says the butcher. George will have a piece. The butcher starts to cut a quarter, but George asks for half. He does not pay. 'By God, I don't know what you do with all the perks you get in your job,' the butcher tells him. After he has left the shop, the butcher turns to his colleague: 'I hope he chokes on it, the bugger.' George does not hear this comment; here the film enables us to be more aware than the gamekeeper is of his isolation.

George is friendly, but self-important; he adopts some of the characteristics of his employer, dealing with the butcher as if he is taking his entitlement. In the pub, a customer leaves after George tells him to take his dog out from his car. For this intervention, the publican, Stan (Jackie Shinn), calls him 'a right bugger'. George sits down with a pint and his pork pie; Stan reprimands him for bringing in food when he already sells pies. George ignores him, and offers pie to two acquaintances, Frank (Philip Firth) and Jack (Les Hickin). Surely his fresh pork pie is better than the ones that Stan sells, George argues, the ones that are 'wrapped in bloody cellophane' – like the one he will eat at the end of the film. Stan relents and joins them, cutting the pork pie into four pieces. The three men help themselves, leaving George a sliver of crust and jelly. They laugh; he probably did not pay for it anyway, says Frank.

During their conversation, George comments that a local poacher deserved his year's imprisonment. This annoys Frank, and the conversation drifts to the question of whose land it is and how they came to own it – through royal patronage, gifts or inheritance. Frank says, 'It isn't their land. It wasn't their land in first place, was it? And that's what peeves me about it; it weren't their land in first place.' This line closes the scene. Frank begins speaking in a medium close profile shot of him, with Jack in the background, yet after he says, 'It wasn't their land in first place, was it?' the film cuts to a close-up of George listening to Frank's last sentence. As Frank finishes, George raises his pint to his lips; he looks pensive and uncomfortable. Ending the scene with a close-up of George draws our attention to his isolation and to his aware-ness of that. From this close-up, the film dissolves to a shot of him checking the pheasant chicks; the dissolve brings us to another close-up, in which George's face is reflected in the glass of the incubator. We see George attending to the thing that causes his social isolation and the object of his attention.

The men in the pub resent George's position as gamekeeper. Their resentment echoes that of the poacher's sons who bully John at school. By outlining his relation-ships with others, the film shows how George's job restricts his life and that of his family, even to the extent that Ian cannot keep the kitten he brings home from school because it is a danger to the pheasants. George has left the steelworks and the priva-tions that he endured there, but he encounters other restrictions on the freedom that a job in the countryside represents. As the film progresses, the tying of the wings of the pheasant in the opening scene becomes more expressive. George can come and go as he pleases, but his family feels constrained. Mary complains of this one day when George comes home mid-morning for a cup of tea. He finds her cleaning their house, but he asks for a cup of tea anyway – she serves him always, it seems. As he waits for the tea, he picks up a picture drawn by Ian at school that shows George shooting crows. When Mary tells him that Ian's teacher thought his work was cruel, they start discussing his job. He tells her, 'It's not so bad for you is it? I mean we're rent free, cottage, nicely situated out here in wood and fields. There's some folks'd give a fortune to live here.' His remarks hint that he wants to convince himself as much as his wife, who complains that at least when he worked in the steelworks he earned a reasonable wage. She points out that they have no savings and they would lose the cottage if he lost his job.

> You know I used to think it was romantic when we first moved here, cottage in t' wood an' all that. It's lovely but even that wears off. I mean you get fed up of looking at trees and fields all day – as nice as they are ... You know we've lived here ten years and I hardly know a soul. I'm uncomfortable on council estate because of you and them up in village – honest, some of the old gents still look on me as a day-tripper.

Mary feels trapped in a routine and isolated. The only break from keeping house comes when she cleans at the Duke's house three times a week or shops in the village. George does not respond to her complaints; he simply returns to work.

Only a road and a low stone wall separate the redbrick council estate, to which Mary refers, from the Duke's land; yet the road and the wall are not merely these things; they stand for a boundary between the classes. George prevents people from crossing this boundary; this ensures his and his family's social isolation. When Ian takes the kitten home, Loach carefully films the road, revealing the proximity of the council estate to the Duke's land. Mary complains that she and her family can move between the council estate and the Duke's land; but they feel at home in neither place. George's refusal to allow Ian to rear a kitten, as minor as it is, exemplifies this. For Loach, the environment in which people live can determine their lives; in nearly all his films, the environment is significant. In *Poor Cow*, the long, slow pan across a red-roofed suburban housing estate in Ruislip declares the uniformity of the architecture, the shot embodying the ironic, distancing point of view that Joy takes as she reflects on her past. In *Kes*, the Barnsley estate and the comprehensive school determine Billy's life, no matter how hard he resists. The credit sequence of *Family Life* comprises a series of black and white stills of empty suburban streets; the conformity of the architecture and planning anticipates the narrow-mindedness of Janice's parents. In *Raining Stones* the estate where Bob and Anne live shapes their lives, in good ways, in that it offers them the kind of community that Mary misses, and in threatening ones, in that the poverty leads to violence. In *The Gamekeeper*, the Duke's land and his house, unoccupied, the estate manager tells George, for much of the year, contrast with the council estate just across the road, where Ian and John's school is.

Loach and editor Roger James use a two-frame dissolve from a shot of Ian in school, telling his teacher that he will take a kitten home, to a long shot of the council estate. Between the country and the town lies the boundary between private and

Figure 16: *The Gamekeeper*

public land. The road, the grass verge and the pavement fill the foreground of the shot; redbrick houses and a playing field occupy the middle; rows of houses on the council estate dominate the background. In the foreground, Ian climbs up from the playing field and walks into shot. The camera pans right with him as he approaches the kerb, looking up and down the road and cradling his kitten. Behind him are houses and maisonettes, presumably built during the 1950s and 1960s. As Ian crosses the road, the camera pans with him and shows the estate stretching into the distance (figure 16). The camera pans round, almost 180 degrees away from its original position, following Ian over the wall and into the woods. The length of this take and the slow pan signal an interest in the character's actions and the setting in which he acts – the estate, the Duke's land, and their proximity to each other. The poachers and their bullying sons live on this estate; Billy Casper lives on a similar estate in *Kes*, Gryce's 'fine new estate'.

The Gamekeeper expresses the paradox that to live as a gamekeeper in a country idyll, on property owned by someone else, George and his family must live in an alienated way. Locals resent George; their sons bully his son. To live on the council estate, to work perhaps in the steelworks, would be to live in an environment less enchanting than the wooded glade in which George's cottage nestles; yet to live on the council estate would be to live amongst people who accept you, people who, after some time, might acknowledge you as a neighbour and a friend. Contrast the simmering resentment that George encounters in the pub, with the warm reception that welcomes Bob and Tommy when they sell mutton in a pub in the early scenes of *Raining Stones*. Loach and Hines, sensitive to the paradox at the centre of *The Gamekeeper*, dramatise George's position to draw out its political implications. In the 1980 press release for *The Gamekeeper*, Loach explains his concern with setting:

> The setting of the film is important to us. The people of South Yorkshire must be among the most politically sophisticated in the country with the experiences of the miners' strikes and the steelworkers' strike under their belts. Yet estates like the one shown in the film still exist side by side with the pits and the steelworks. In this area the social implications of the gamekeeper's job are sharply revealed.[18]

The council estate abuts onto the Duke's land. Every day, Ian crosses the boundary between the two places, between public and private land, as does his father – with apparent ease. The ease, though, is superficial: Ian attends primary school, and he is yet to face the bullying that his older brother endures, the resentment that his father finds in the village pub or the isolation his mother feels. Concerned as he is with the impact of the social and physical environment, the long shot of Ian crossing the road is an emblematic shot in Loach's work.

George patrols the boundary that his son crosses and he encounters a range of trespassers. In the summer, he finds two girls picking flowers. He tells them they are trespassing on a private wood, and orders them away. On one occasion, he confronts a poacher (Gary Roberts) and decides to take him to the police. Another time, he sees two boys climbing trees. When he confronts them, he discovers they have been stealing eggs. He threatens them with Borstal, and pretends to note down their names. As when he proposes to the beaters that they ask for ten pounds a day not seven, there is a sense here that by jokingly aligning himself with the beaters and by pretending to report the boys George distances himself from the features of his employment that he finds intolerable. Whatever sense these incidents imply of George having an unconscious strategy for coping with his working conditions, it should not detract from the stronger implication that he takes his work seriously, both the rearing of the pheasants and the apprehending of trespassers. The two trespassing boys live on the council estate, which, it transpires as George talks to them, is called, ironically, 'Woodside': Woodside estate lies alongside a wood, which the Duke prohibits the estate's residents from using.

The gamekeeper carries out the Duke's prohibition, protecting the game that he rears on that land. *The Gamekeeper* expresses its theme of class differences partly through food and partly through a concentration on space and settings. The shooting season is short, but the preparation for it determines George's working life. He rears the pheasants for the shoot, preventing poachers from stealing either pheasants or rabbits; yet, he can catch as many rabbits as he likes. He can sell them or use them as bribes to try to speed up repairs to his window. The pheasants are game for some people; the rabbits are game for others. Loach creates a pattern with food, making it relevant to the themes of the film by allowing links to be made between the pork pie that George demands from the butcher, the pheasant in the cage in the first shot of the film, the cellophane-wrapped meat pie of the last shot, and the lunch provided for the Duke's guests during the grouse shoot, in a cottage on the moors. Through the cottage doorway, we see a fire, and a table laden with food and drink, including a large silver soup tureen. Women pour drinks as the men of the shooting party traipse in. Loach's camera stays outside the cottage though, purposefully adopting the perspective of the gamekeepers, outside with sandwiches and beer.

Loach's direction in *The Gamekeeper* combines objective record and significant organisation; although, as always, he does not annul the distinction between the two. He builds on the thematic and structural elements that Barry Hines provides in his novel and screenplay, choosing what to film and how to film, shaping the film in collaboration, creating patterns and motifs that make up its themes, such as the emphases on work, land and food. Menges and Loach's colour photography on *The Gamekeeper* recalls their work on *Kes* and *After a Lifetime*; they light interior shots from windows and doors, supplementing natural light with single light sources; each frame could exist as a documentary record of a gamekeeper's life. After *Kes* and *After a Lifetime*, Loach and Menges revive their techniques on *Black Jack* and *The Gamekeeper*. Eventually, Loach abandons the technique of long shot, long take and restrained lighting and camera movement; but not before he applies these austere techniques to one more fiction film: *Looks and Smiles*.

Looks and Smiles: hanging about for people to bare their souls

In *Looks and Smiles*, Loach maintains a documentary discipline for a fiction film; unfortunately, the drama of the film is insufficiently worked out. It is a bleak film, with a depressing story to tell of the hopelessness of unemployment amongst teenagers. As is usual for Loach, he shot the film completely on location, but he and Menges chose to shoot in black and white, almost as if they wanted to achieve an appearance of stark photojournalism. *Looks and Smiles* tells the story of two unemployed teenagers, Mick Walsh (Graham Green) and Alan Wright (Tony Pitts). Mick signs on and looks for work, but refuses positions as a junior in a warehouse and looks for an apprenticeship. Alan joins the army. When they celebrate his departure for basic training at a disco, Mick meets a girl called Karen Lodge (Carolyn Nicholson). They embark on a lacklustre relationship, eventually arguing and splitting up. When Alan returns on leave, he steals a car; and he and Mick go drinking. At a club, they get into a fight; Alan has learnt how to fight in the army. The next morning Mick goes for an interview as an apprentice fitter. He has a black eye, and he does not get the job. Following the interview, he steals some cigarettes and gets enough money to fix his motorbike. He and Karen are reconciled, but her mother finds them in bed together, and they ride down to Bristol to see Karen's father (Arthur Davies). He cannot put them up because he lives in a one-bedroom flat with his girlfriend and his six-month-old baby. The film cuts back to a pub in Sheffield. Some time has passed, but Mick is still unemployed and squabbling with Karen. Alan tells them of his experiences in Northern Ireland: beating up suspected terrorists, participating in 'snatch squads', harassing Catholic families. Loach cuts away to Mick standing in a dole queue. The film ends with a freeze-frame of his face.

The film has such a loose, open-ended quality that it could end anywhere. When it does end, Mick has not resolved any of the problems in his life, and the film offers no hope for a resolution. Here, Loach is less interested in thematic contrasts than he was in *The Gamekeeper*; and less interested in dramatising history or political hypothesis than he was in *Days of Hope* or *The Big Flame*. *Looks and Smiles* reveals the depression that people felt in the industrial North of England during the early 1980s; but it is as depressing as Mick's life. Its aimlessness may come from a decision to have the film reproduce the aimlessness of the characters. The film records what people were doing, how they were speaking, and what they were wearing in the early 1980s in Sheffield: watched twenty years later, Loach's characteristic attention to detail renders the film a period piece. Loach and Hines wanted to make a companion film to *Kes*, in that it would focus on a school leaver; but employment in the early 1980s differed from that of the late 1960s: unlike Billy, Mick passes a few examinations, but he cannot find a job with an apprenticeship attached, despite his interest in mechanics.[19]

Graham Green, who plays Mick, was an apprentice fitter in a colliery when Loach hired him for six weeks in the autumn of 1980; Tony Pitts was an apprentice mechanic; Carolyn Nicholson was completing her A-levels at school in Newcastle.[20] None of the three leads were professional performers, let alone actors. For Loach, the most important consideration in casting was that the people in the film be as close as possible to the characters. He did not want to direct his actors; he wanted the people in the films to do and to say things; he would then film them as unobtrusively as possible, keeping the camera away from them. After making *Looks and Smiles* Loach decides that he 'never wanted to hold a shot for so long again'; but in 1980 he remains committed to filming people with long takes and long shots. Such is his casting and direction in *Poor Cow* that a lot of the charm and energy of that film comes from the charm and energies of Carol White or Queenie Watts; in *Looks and Smiles* a lot of the dourness of the film comes from the dourness of the three leads and the gloomy character of depression-hit Sheffield, rendered sharply in black and white. Julian Petley writes perspicaciously of *Looks and Smiles*:

These aren't the 'well-made' characters of Hollywood fiction and West End plays, nor are they 'exemplary' à la Socialist Realism – what they *do* convey, however, is an almost tangible sensation of everyday, lived reality. There are no villains and heroes here, just people. (Petley 1983a: 32)

Looks and Smiles conveys a documentary sense of 'lived reality'; it records the lives of Mick, Karen and Alan; but in doing so it is as humourless and hopeless as they are.

In comparison with the ebullience of *Up the Junction* and *Poor Cow*, or the confidently filmed narratives of *Ladybird, Ladybird* and *Land and Freedom*, *Looks and Smiles* renounces organisation; it embodies Loach's commitment to objective record, but at the expense of anything else. According to him:

> I wanted to find some young people who had the qualities of our characters, who resembled them, who came from the same type of area, who could render the fictional scenes completely credible and who could reveal themselves during the film. They had to be vulnerable, sensitive and to have a sense of humour. In a sense, *Looks and Smiles* is a documentary about the people who are in it. (LaJeunesse 1981: 30)

As he does when he describes *Family Life* as 'almost a documentary about the people in the film', he justifies his work in fiction by invoking the values of non-fiction. In *Looks and Smiles*, his camera imitates the action of a *cinéma vérité* film-maker's camera. The cutting from one long shot and long take to another in *Looks and Smiles* is striking, and the use of long takes and long shots logically develops his earlier transition on *Kes* to a mode of 'sympathetic observation'. He keeps the camera fixed

Figure 17: *Looks and Smiles*

on a tripod or held on a shoulder, while its operator pans or holds it still. An example occurs when two policemen question Mick and a group of boys in a shopping centre (figure 17). The camera has followed Mick as he walks towards the other boys and chats, though we do not hear what they say. The policemen approach the group and talk: again, we do not hear what they discuss. Loach and Menges film this action in a single long shot. The lighting is dim; the concrete shopping centre encloses the group; shoppers persistently criss-cross the space between the camera and the boys: the narrative meaning of the shot/scene is obscure, yet nothing motivates this obscurity except the aspiration to record objectively rather than organise a dramatic structure or involve the audience with the characters.

Talking about work: a response to the 1980s

Just before shooting *Looks and Smiles*, Loach made *A Question of Leadership* (1981). This film documents a discussion between trade unionists that were involved in the 13-week national steel strike from January to March of 1980. ATV produced the documentary for a nationwide broadcast, but delayed its transmission for a year and eventually only showed it in the ATV/Central region of the Midlands, insisting that Loach cut it to make room for a 'balancing' documentary.[21] Despite these problems, Loach directed several more documentaries, including *The Red and the Blue* and the four-part *Questions of Leadership* (1983). He then made *Which Side Are You On?* (1985), about people involved in the 1984 miners' strike; LWT commissioned this for *The South Bank Show*, but they refused to show it and Channel 4 screened it. He followed this with *The End of the Battle ... Not the End of the War* (1985), a short analysis of the collapse of the miners' strike, broadcast as part of Channel 4's documentary strand *Diverse Reports*, on which he was credited as guest editor. He then made *Time to Go* (tx: BBC2, 9 May 1989) and *The View from the Woodpile* (1989).

These documentaries analyse issues concerning strikes, trade unions, political party conferences and Conservative government policy during the early 1980s: they are explicitly about politics. *Questions of Leadership* was never transmitted, but Loach returned to some of its issues and subjects in *The End of the Battle ... Not the End of the War*.[22] In his documentaries, he films people talking about work, its conditions or the lack of it. They take a perspective on work and unemployment that differs from the one taken in *Looks and Smiles*; instead of documenting the effects of unemployment on young people, *Questions of Leadership*, for instance, analyses the political causes of unemployment and examines the role of the trade unions and their leaders during a number of strikes. Loach's commitment to analysing phenomena such as strikes and unemployment underpins his move into documentaries in the early 1980s. He turns to documentaries because he finds the difficulties of producing a feature film frustrating and is disappointed with the distribution of his past three films. It is no accident that he does so at a particular moment in the political history of Britain;

nor is it an accident that his aspirations to present his view of Britain in the 1980s are so challenged.

In *Questions of Leadership* explanatory voice-overs and intertitles provide background information; discussion scenes and interviews take up most of the four 50-minute films. In the discussions, the camera moves from one person to another, following the conversation as union members discuss how their employers have mistreated them and their union leaders neglected them. Groups of men and women sit in rooms; Loach films them talking. They articulate what they feel and know about the industrial disputes with which they have been involved. They talk about politics and industrial disputes in a way that is rare on television. Because the four documentaries revealed these people saying these things, Central TV, who commissioned them, pulled them from the schedules and they have never been publicly broadcast or screened. Yet Loach has filmed scenes like these elsewhere: in *The Rank and File* and *Land and Freedom* the camera follows debates, re-framing and re-focusing as it moves. In *Which Side Are You On?* the camera moves between interviewees and the photographs that they discuss, ranging over a number of positions, while *The Flickering Flame* employs a similar technique during an international conference of the striking Liverpool dockers, with the camera panning rapidly to alight on the people who begin speaking.

All his documentaries present ordinary people describing their experiences in their own voices. The documentaries draw their themes from the lives of people whom Loach chooses to film, although he chooses to film people because he has themes in mind – but in this he is not unique among documentary film-makers. The themes of *Questions of Leadership, Which Side Are You On?* and *The End of the Battle...* emerge from the lives of people involved in industrial disputes. In the analysis of those whom he films (and, we can assume, in his own analysis), the interests of those who control capital exclude the interests of those whose lives are determined by where and how that capital is invested. The people in these documentaries argue that neither those who control capital investment nor those who claim to lead the union and labour movement want independent working-class activity. This view emerges in his collaborations with Jim Allen: their fiction tells stories about union and Labour leaders failing to represent the interests of the working class. Loach's documentaries extend this analysis, presenting people who express this view unscripted.

The principal question of *Questions of Leadership* is whether unions are democratic. The people whom Loach films argue that unions control their members: in *The End of the Battle...* people argue that the miners could have won the 1984-5 miners' strike if they had had the support of other trade union leaders; although what winning might mean is not explored. In *Questions of Leadership*, a number of examples are given of industrial disputes in the late 1970s and early 1980s, before the miners' strike, where union leaders apparently betrayed the interests of the people they were meant to represent: the steel strike; the Lawrence Scott closures in Manchester; a series of British Leyland disputes; NHS pay disputes; rail strikes.[23] Workers involved in these disputes argue that their unions had no plans for helping strikers; they left them to organise themselves. Often workers in other industries supported them, but all too frequently union leaders opposed that kind of support.

In this analysis, a combination of management, government and union leaders splits the unity of the workers. Alan Thornett, a shop steward sacked by British Leyland, argues that in the early 1980s the Conservative government used mass unemployment to force through privatisations and to restructure industry in a more competitive way.[24] At the same time, they broke down the shop steward movement with legislation that weakened the trade unions and supported industry leaders like Michael Edwardes of British Leyland and Ian MacGregor of the National Coal Board. The third part of *Questions of Leadership* examines the campaign against a Longbridge British Leyland shop steward, Derek Robinson, whom the tabloid news-papers smeared as 'Red Robbo' and the campaign against Alan Thornett, smeared as 'The Mole'. In both cases, British Leyland sacked senior shop stewards for minor offences after they had organised opposition to the plans of Michael Edwardes. Their co-workers threatened to strike in support of Robinson and Thornett, but the union leadership failed to defend them. Edwardes issued daily bulletins to all staff members, thousands of car workers, taking his case for restructuring to his employees, circum-venting the unions. According to Thornett and Robinson, the campaigns against them were part of a co-ordinated attack on the role of shop stewards in the workplace.[25]

In *Questions of Leadership* and *The End of the Battle...* Thornett argues that a report written for the Conservatives in May 1978 by Nicholas Ridley provided the foundations for Thatcher's changes in industry and union legislation. As *Days of Hope* concludes of the Samuel Report, Thornett claims of the Ridley Report: the TUC knew about it when it was published, knew about the Tories' plans; but did little to prepare for the onslaught. Thornett summarises:

> I think what the Tory government has set out to do since '79 is carry out a fundamental restructuring of British industry to create a much more profit-able situation. And the way they've gone about that, as we all know, is to create mass unemployment on the one hand by shutting down large sections of industry that they regard as unprofitable; shifting them generally to other parts of the world where they think they can produce things more profitably and using the creation of mass unemployment to attack the trade union movement.

Thornett repeats this idea in his book, arguing that the defeat of workers in conflict with employers was a result of the 'misleadership or downright betrayal of the official leaders of the trade union movement' (Thornett 1987: 76).[26]

Participants in *Questions of Leadership* who present contrasting analyses include John Cure, a senior official of the Amalgamated Union of Engineering Workers (AUEW), and Frank Chapple, General Secretary of the Electrical, Electronics,

Telecommunications and Plumbing Union (EETPU). Chapple led the EETPU for 17 years, he was a signatory of the Limehouse Declaration of January 1981, which split the Labour Party by creating the Social Democrat Party, and he supported the privatisation of British Telecom. Loach clearly regards him as a latter-day J. H. Thomas. In the second part of *Questions of Leadership*, members of the EEPTU argue that there is a lack of democracy in their union and that those who have spoken out against Chapple have been banned from holding office. Loach films an interview with Chapple. When questions are put to him about democracy in his union, he walks out, saying:

> As far as I'm concerned I don't want to deal with any of this at all. It's just a set-up, another one of these deliberate things, aimed at making a monkey of me and the union, and I don't want any part of it. And I don't want any part of this broadcast. So that, as far as I'm concerned, it's off.

In the light of the de facto banning of *Questions of Leadership*, Chapple's use of 'broadcast' – it is heard and can be read as either a noun or a verb – is fascinatingly ambiguous. From today's perspective, Loach's documentaries from the early and mid-1980s can appear anachronistic. The final part of *Questions of Leadership* is devoted to a discussion held at the University of Warwick on 19 June 1982. Participants include John Golding, a Labour MP, Alan Thornett, John Cure and Bernard Connolly from the EETPU. The discussions about whether the interests of the working class are tied to a mixed economy seem to come from another era of politics; but perhaps they seemed anachronistic even in 1983, because, as Loach argues, the media suppress this kind of debate. The fact that the four documentaries have not been transmitted strengthens the argument that they provide a valuable record of an oppositional case to Thatcherism.

In *The Red and the Blue* there is an instructive exchange between Dennis Skinner and Neil Kinnock at the Labour Party conference in autumn 1982. Michael Foot is still the leader of the Labour Party; the 1983 general election is yet to be lost, and Kinnock is yet to be elected leader. Kinnock uses rhetoric that recurs in Tony Blair's 1997 general election campaign. The exchange also calls to mind the scene in *Days of Hope* when Philip addresses a mass meeting in Liverpool in 1924 using similar terminology to Kinnock, encouraging unity and reform, arguing that divisions on the left inhibit the Labour Party's chances of electoral success. Kinnock's speech is not especially warmly received. In contrast, when Skinner speaks his relaxed delivery and the support he finds in the audience suggests that he wins the argument against Kinnock. Loach wants to show the support that Skinner's views have amongst the audience. Yet, the irony of watching this scene now is that soon after this Kinnock and his supporters began a campaign in the Labour Party to expel the Militant Tendency, and to reform and bring unity to the Labour Party, paving the way for Tony Blair and New Labour.

The ideas that people express in Loach's documentaries agree with the themes expressed in his and Allen's work, from *The Big Flame* to *Land and Freedom*. The key idea is that rank and file union members or party members will always be more radical than their leaders. In his 1980s documentaries Loach aspires to reveal this radicalism by filming people as transparently as possible; by the end of that decade he has taken his commitment to transparency as far as he can go. Hindsight reveals an inevitability about his transition from a mode where he tries to reveal the world with a documentary style for fiction films, to a mode where pursuing the revelation of the world, in the face of what he regards as unsupportable political, social and economic changes, becomes his *only* aim. He made the documentaries quickly, aiming to oppose the policies of the Tory government; and the political aspirations of *Questions of Leadership* and the other documentaries are so evident that it is impossible not to imagine the frustrations of their director.

In the 1980s, Loach moves from making fiction films with acknowledged non-fiction elements to making documentaries where he eliminates the fiction in his art altogether. This elimination contributes to his longest fallow period. When he only makes documentaries he loses the balance between non-fiction and fiction that distinguishes his best work. He takes nearly ten years to discover this, but when he emerges from the 1980s he recognises what makes his work of the 1960s so vital:

> The energy in *Riff-Raff* [1991] owed nothing to the documentaries, but rather to the idea of going back to the things that worked well when we were doing things like *Up the Junction*: that sense of vitality and movement and not hanging about for people to bare their souls, but just cutting to the core of what was happening. (Fuller 1998: 88)

It is not enough for Loach to stand at a distance from the people he wants to film: he needs to organise images and sounds to cut to what he feels is the 'core'. He differs from those film-makers who are able to express themselves by minimising their impact on what it is they are filming, those film-makers for whom 'hanging about for people to bare their souls' is their work (John Cassavetes, D. A. Pennebaker, the Maysles Brothers and Paul Watson come to mind). When he concentrates exclusively on what compels him to make films like *Looks and Smiles*, his work loses its vitality. Significantly, as he pursues one element of his work, his association with Jim Allen wanes. Allen represents an influence on Loach's work that does not involve waiting patiently behind the camera for people to reveal themselves. They work together in 1987 on *Perdition*, their play that is withdrawn; but they do not make another film together until *Hidden Agenda* (1990).

Before *Hidden Agenda* though, towards the end of the 1980s, Loach directs television commercials. He has argued that this was for money: his documentaries had a poor record of exhibition and his first *Film on 4*, *Fatherland*, did badly. His work on advertisements Loach now considers 'indefensible' (Fuller 1998: 80). He was, he feels, compromising his art and his political beliefs: identified as a socialist, he concedes a political principle by selling his services to advertisers. Equally, though, directing commercials, fictions among fictions after all, allows him to recover the element of his work that his documentaries abandoned; the significant organisation that he evokes with his phrase 'cutting to the core of what was happening'. He remarks tellingly of his experience directing television commercials:

> It enabled me to be seen as somebody who doesn't always make untransmittable work and who has a bit of basic professional craft alongside whatever daft ideas I also seem to have. (Fuller 1998: 81)

Around the same time as Loach made his commercials he also directed a documentary, *The View from the Woodpile* (1989), for Channels 4's *The Eleventh Hour* series. We can read this apparently straightforward film about a youth drama group as an artistic and philosophical meditation on his working methods.

The View from the Woodpile documents a drama group who research and devise a play about homelessness. It records the group's rehearsal and performance of the play; but it includes dramatic reconstructions based on their own experiences. The film shows Jimmy being 'let go' from a Youth Training Scheme in a canteen kitchen, and Steve being discharged from a community project for old people. It dramatises Paul's introduction to glue sniffing and the outcome of this, two years later in real life, when he spends three months in prison for shoplifting. It also documents Caroline's pregnancy and Roy's artistic endeavours. Loach and the group weave together different kinds of performance: the play about homelessness; the reconstructed scenes; past-tense voice-overs about scenes that are present on screen; and scenes that observe them, for example in a pub when they discuss working conditions with a group of ex-factory employees.

What emerges is Loach's concern for thinking about the way that drama can be a means of revealing people on film. He films the same people in similar places performing differently for the camera: he documents these types of performance. The performances are not hidden: the fact of these performances is central to the project. The group devise their play about homelessness after interviewing people in a Birmingham night shelter; and their research and performance connect with Loach's artistic history. *The View from the Woodpile* shows us something about a group of unemployed young people in the West Midlands; yet it uses drama to penetrate their personal experiences. The film concentrates on the way in which these young people use drama in their lives, and we can read it as being about the value of drama generally. At the end of a fallow period and at the start of a period of renewal, Loach seems to reflect on the importance of drama in his work. The film retains the political concerns of earlier documentaries – it is about youth unemployment and how drama stimulates these unemployed young people; yet, equally, it is a film about Loach's own commitment to dramatise, about how he uses documentary and drama.

Towards its end, the film presents a montage of shots of abandoned and derelict steel foundries and factories. In an earlier sequence, the film shows us the 'Woodpile', an empty plot of land where factories used to stand. The title states that there is another viewpoint; one that, like much of Loach's work in the 1980s, offers a view from a place that presents us with a 'strong central image' of the abandonment of industry and the effects of 'market forces' on people's livelihoods.

cutting to the core of what's happening

Hidden Agenda (1990) reunited Loach with Jim Allen, and initiated a sustained series of cinema successes.[1] Rebecca O'Brien co-produced it, and she and Sally Hibbin became his regular producers.[2] Loach, Hibbin and O'Brien set up Parallax Pictures with producer Sarah Curtis and directors Les Blair and Philip Davis. Parallax has since produced all of Loach's films: with a secure production base, he has directed almost one film a year since 1990. He followed *Hidden Agenda* with three films about contemporary Britain for *Film on 4*, *Riff-Raff* (1991), *Raining Stones* (1993) and *Ladybird Ladybird* (1994), what one might call his post-Thatcher trilogy, although he did not plan them as a trilogy, and three writers wrote original scripts for each film – Bill Jesse, Jim Allen and Rona Munro. Each won prizes at European film festivals, and they consolidated his 1990s success. In 1995, Loach and Allen's film about the Spanish civil war, *Land and Freedom*, was released, confirming Loach's status as a director working in a realist tradition of European film-making. He followed *Land and Freedom* with *Carla's Song* (1996), his first collaboration with Paul Laverty. Their second work was *My Name is Joe* (1998), a powerful melodrama set on an impoverished Glasgow housing estate, and their third *Bread and Roses* (2000). *The Navigators* (2001), written by Rob Dawber, followed this.

Both *Bread and Roses* and *The Navigators* hark back to Loach's earlier concern with unions and labour organisation. Like *The Rank and File* (1971), *Bread and Roses* dramatises the progress and outcome of a strike in recent history – in this case a successful union campaign to improve conditions for the illegal immigrants who comprise the major part of the cleaning workforce in Los Angeles' coporate buildings. *The Navigators*, a feature-length television film about the effects of privatisation on British railways, set in 1995, recalls *The Big Flame*'s (1969) protests against casualisation and de-regulation in the docking industry. However, rather than propose a 'heady fantasy of revolution' led by rank-and-file unionists, *The Navigators* offers a grim warning of the dangers of privatisation. In terms of the relationship between focusing on personal and political dramas, it is one of his most assured films to date, charting the decline of an industry and a skilled workforce, noting the powerlessness of the union to prevent this and integrating this with a skilfully succinct evocation of the personal lives of the beleaguered ex-British Rail employees.

Since 1990, Loach has developed his commitment to working out coherent narrative structures; especially refining his use of traditional genre forms of comedy, suspense and melodrama. This chapter assesses Loach's mature work by analysing *Raining Stones*, *Ladybird Ladybird* and *Land and Freedom*.

Raining Stones: embedding characters in contexts

Unlike *Riff-Raff*, the structure of which Loach describes as a mosaic or collage, *Raining Stones* has a linear, quest narrative; although, as Michael Eaton points out, the protagonist in this quest narrative cannot triumph entirely on his own.[3] In 1994, Loach acknowledges the failure of *Looks and Smiles*, when he explains what he thinks make his latest two films, *Riff-Raff* and *Raining Stones*, successful. Gavin Smith comments that there are fewer moments of humour in *Looks and Smiles* than there are in *Riff-Raff*. Loach replies:

> But that's also a technical problem [as well as a problem of casting in *Looks and Smiles*]. That's actually my fault. It's to do with pacing that I was very aware of when we did *Riff-Raff*. The humour was there in *Looks and Smiles*, but I didn't crystallise it. There's a scene where the kids steal from a social club and it's potentially funny, but it doesn't get a laugh because there isn't a moment to release the humour. It needed a specific funny moment that enables you to laugh. I hadn't got the material. It's got to be in the bones of the script. (G. Smith 1994: 60).

He goes on to give the funeral scene in *Riff-Raff*, where the wind blows the ashes of a character's dead mother over mourners, as an example of what he calls 'a payoff ... an old comedy technique' (G. Smith 1994: 62). By evoking a payoff, Loach emphasises his attention to narrative structure, 'the bones of the script'.

Raining Stones tells a story about Bob (Bruce Jones), an unemployed man living with his family on a large council estate in suburban Manchester. Unemployment and poverty force him to do odd jobs: the film opens with him and a friend, Tommy (Ricky Tomlinson), stealing a sheep and then selling the mutton in a pub. Later, Bob tries drain cleaning and working as a bouncer in a nightclub. His goal is to earn enough money to buy his daughter, Coleen (Gemma Phoenix), a dress for her first Communion. When he fails to earn any money, he takes out a loan from an agency;

but he soon falls behind on the repayments. A loan shark, Tansey (Jonathon James), buys the debt. The day before the Communion, while Bob is out shopping, Tansey threatens Bob's wife Anne (Julie Brown) at home. Angered, Bob pursues Tansey. They fight in an underground car park, but Bob fares badly in the fight, and is left sprawled on the ground, while Tansey, who is drunk, gets into his car. Tansey starts his car, but Bob smashes the windscreen with a spanner as he drives off. Tansey crashes the car into a pillar and dies. Bob takes his pocket book and seeks help from his priest, Father Barry (Tom Hickey). The priest absolves him and disposes of the evidence, advising him not to tell the police.

The basic structure resembles Vittorio de Sica's *Bicycle Thieves* (1948). *Raining Stones* especially recalls *Bicycle Thieves*' episodic linearity and alternation between comedy and melodrama. De Sica and his writer, Cesare Zavattini, focus the comedy and melodrama around Antonio Ricci's (Lamberto Maggiorami) son, Bruno (Enzo Staiola); in *Raining Stones* Loach and Allen focus it on Bob's efforts to earn some money. Christopher Wagstaff describes the structure of *Bicycle Thieves*:

> Comedy, therefore, is one of the genre conventions that gives form to the forty-five episodes (separated by dissolves) that make up the narrative. It has a further virtue. Comedy and melodrama deal with the anxieties of the characters, and offer a position from which the viewer can respond emotionally to those anxieties, either with laughter, or with anxiety followed by relief. (Wagstaff 1996: 261)

A similar structure supports *Raining Stones*: the film alternates between comedy and melodrama or suspense throughout the series of episodes in which Bob tries to earn money, though without maintaining the alternation rigidly. The alternating comedy and melodrama come before the suspense of the final sequences: once Tansey terrorises Anne, and Bob seeks revenge, the film is possessed by what Nigel Andrews – invoking the work of novelist Giovanni Verga, an influence on the Italian neo-realists – calls 'the dark spirit of urban *verismo*' (Andrews 1993: 21).[4] Before this, the more burlesque episodes mostly follow troubling, dramatic scenes, alternating, with the method that Wagstaff attributes to *Bicycle Thieves*, relief and anxiety; for instance, the scene of Tommy drunkenly pulling his trousers down at a police helicopter follows Bob and Anne's argument, then the love scene, after Bob's van is stolen, while Bob and Tommy are stealing turf from the Conservative Club, a scene that is as amusing as the opening sheep episode, follows Bob's nasty fracas at the nightclub.

Two patterns of suspense evolve: the first centres on Bob's quest to raise money, his loan and his pursuit of and fight with Tansey; the second depicts Bob's discovery that Tommy's daughter is dealing drugs. When Bob returns home after his van has been stolen, Anne tells him that there are only six weeks until Coleen's first Communion; the film thus establishes its own temporal limits and launches the quest narrative. The alternating comedy and melodrama cover the six weeks leading up to the day before the Communion, the first hour or so of the film; after the film moves into its 'urban *verismo*', 30 minutes of screen time depict the last 24 hours before the Communion. When Anne gives Bob a shopping list, the last chain of narrative events commences: as Bob leaves the flat he picks up the bailiff's letter and, apart from the scene of Tansey terrorising Anne, Loach restricts the rest of the film to Bob's pursuit of Tansey.

The second pattern of suspense begins when Tommy arrives home after talking to Bob at the Employment Office. He is pleased to find his daughter, Tracey, visiting, and he asks her how she is. 'Fine,' she replies; though he comments that she has black marks under her eyes and looks a bit 'washy'. Their conversation continues: he asks her what she is doing exactly. She answers hesitantly that she is selling cosmetics; she seems slightly evasive: Geraldine Ward delivers the line 'Erm, scent, perfume, make-up' while moving her eyes abruptly. Her performance plants doubts in our minds, if not Tommy's, though he does not push her about whether she is lying. As she and her mother leave to go shopping, Tracey gives her father some money. After she has left, Tommy cries. As well as initiating the subsidiary pattern of suspense, this scene of Tommy and his family extends the film's theme of the difficulty of maintaining pride and self-esteem in the intolerable conditions of unemployment, indicating the lives of people other than the protagonist.

The suspense continues when Bob works as a bouncer at the nightclub for a night and discovers that Tracey's money comes from dealing Ecstasy. Loach constructs this scene on an extended shot/reverse shot axis, creating tension as Bob observes, then pursues Tracey. All but two of its 29 shots alternate between shots of Bob watching Tracey, and shots of her selling Ecstasy. Loach still films people in medium close shots, from a distance and with a long focus lens; but he and Jonathan Morris edit this scene using a classical method to create suspense. This kind of shot/reverse shot editing is largely absent from his earlier work, and he develops it increasingly in the 1990s.

The dominant pattern of suspense begins when he and Tommy meet at the Employment Office, the scene preceding that of Tommy at home with Tracey. Bob comes out after signing on and bumps into Tommy, whom he asks for a favour. Tommy says he will oblige if he can, and goes to sign on, handing Bob his paper and asking him to 'pick a winner' so they can have a bet. The music in *Raining Stones* affects tone and mood: in this scene, it contributes to the nascent pattern of suspense. While Bob signs on, the music continues from the end of the previous scene, when Father Barry offers Bob a Communion dress. It accompanies Bob's wait for Tommy, and extends until they walk along the road. There it builds in volume and tension before stopping as the two men stop on the pavement. The abrupt halt of music and men introduces a significant absence of dialogue. For a moment, the soundtrack includes only the traffic noises. This is a characteristic Loach shot: he films Bob and Tommy from the opposite side of the road, as he filmed the boys in the shopping centre in *Looks and Smiles* (figure 18). Here though, the distance from the characters

Figure 18: *Raining Stones*

combines with the soundtrack to encourage awareness that the film conceals something purposefully; the absence of dialogue intensifies interest; and we do not know what favour Bob requests. The long shot and lack of dialogue hold our knowledge of the moment in abeyance: the film withholds narrative information, and this restriction encourages curiosity. As Tommy writes something on the newspaper an eerie, synthesised wail enhances the tension of the moment.

Stewart Copeland composed the music for *Raining Stones*, his third film with Loach; and his work is crucial to the alternating moods of the film. The musical leitmotif of the ominous synthesiser sound, which is used when Bob and Tommy stop on the pavement is, at other times, expanded with violins: at key moments, this leitmotif adds to the images and adumbrates what the film eventually exposes. We hear it first after Bob discovers his van is missing; but its most striking use occurs during Bob and Tommy's unheard conversation on the pavement. As the suspense develops, the film repeats the leitmotif, sometimes only for a few seconds: it sounds briefly when Bob watches Gilbert getting beaten up by Ted outside the post office; and several times during Bob's pursuit of Tansey, notably in the pub when he first sees the loan shark, the music emphasises the threatening atmosphere. Halfway through *Raining Stones'* 16-week post-production of editing and dubbing, Loach sent two faxes to Copeland in Los Angeles.[5] Both faxes contain instructions for the composer about cues, musical phrasing and thematic motivations for types of music. Here are some examples:

(After dole office) … with pauses for lines. Something slightly ominous is being planned as they walk up the hill.[6]

Possibly: music starts as Bob watches Gilbert being beaten up – it is the alarm in his mind – 'this could be me if I'm not careful!'[7]

As is but in second pub where we should have muzak throughout our music should mark Bob seeing Tansey at 9'27.[8]

Loach's notes to Copeland show him working to shape meaning by applying emphasis with music, using it to suggest anxiety or stress. Bob and Tommy's pavement talk is one such example.

The film moves from this talk to Tommy at home, then to Bob and Anne at the dress shop. It is not until the couple walk home that the film offers a glimpse of another part of this pattern of suspense. Anne asks Bob where he got the money for the dress. He replies that he won it on the horses. He warns her that she should not tell Tommy or he will want to borrow some. Importantly, at this point the film gives no indication about whether Bob is lying to his wife, although it later confirms that he is. While the narrative thread begins after Tommy asked Bob to 'pick a winner', this scene ends with Anne asking 'How much [did Bob win]?' Bob does not answer. Instead, the camera lingers on the fence for a moment after the characters have walked out of shot, leaving Anne's question hanging in the air.

The suspense increases during the scenes at the post office when the musical leit-motif is heard. Then, on the way out of his flat, on the day before the Communion, Bob picks up the letter in his hall and Loach uses the ominous music to hint at the worrying contents of the letter, which is presumably from a bailiff. At the market, Tommy asks him if he wants to lay a bet on – again betting is used as a link; Bob responds by showing Tommy the letter. Significance accrues through repetition, for this scene corresponds with Bob's scene with Anne after the dress shop when it too ends with the question 'How much?' asked by Tommy. Loach cuts from his question to Coleen rolling pastry at home. The questions – Anne's on the way home and Tommy's at the market – are answered in the next scene when Tansey invades their home and tells Anne that Bob owes him £285. When Bob returns home and discovers Tansey's harassment of Anne he sets off in pursuit of Tansey. The remainder of the film follows the same pattern as Bob's pursuit of Tracey in the nightclub: an extended shot/reverse shot sequence grounds the progress of the pursuit across different locations until its violent conclusion.

Loach consistently makes space, location and environment important to his work. In varying ways, he focuses on the environment of the characters to render, realistically and politically, an impression of the pressures that they face. For Loach, environment can determine the quality of life and he describes his aims in film-making:

> The subjects which have drawn me are those which relate personal and
> emotional life to a wider background – a class background and an economic

background. I've tried to show how people's personal lives don't exist in a vacuum from these things. To put it crudely, it's a matter of human interest put in a social framework. (Hearse 1994: 25)

Additionally, he describes his approach to the narratives of *Riff-Raff* and *Raining Stones* as follows:

There's got to be a tension between the sequences, otherwise the thing never has any cumulative effect. And the audience has to be aware of a forward movement throughout. But I think it's also important to allow space for those little asides or jokes that help to describe people, make people funny and idiosyncratic and likeable. So it's a balance really, trying to keep good forward movement yet not to squash the life out of the people. (G. Smith 1994: 59)

The two patterns of dramatic suspense, Tracey's selling of drugs and Bob's pursuit of her, and Bob's borrowing of money and his pursuit of Tansey, operate as the 'bones of the script'; yet they rhyme with each other and with other elements of the film. Loach's direction enables us to read out social and economic factors from the space and the people in that space, but in a way that accommodates his efforts to promote empathy with individuals. In her essay on Loach's methods, Deborah Knight argues that in naturalist fiction characters often act rashly or impudently; the contexts in which the films locate them makes sense of their actions: 'This embedding of characters in contexts forces us to recognise the pressures which lead to – or, in some cases, prevent – certain actions or decisions' (Knight 1997: 76). Loach achieves this embedding of characters in social frameworks through his direction of performers and camera.

The director of photography on *The Rank and File*, Charles Stewart, discusses Loach's method of directing actors: 'They do it time and time again and then from that, from probably fifteen takes he then assembles a reality – a reality from an immense amount of material, where people are working out, finding out what makes sense' (Orbanz 1977: 84). Stewart continues:

He repeats a scene and repeats it and repeats it. I mean we might shoot it ten times that direction and ten times the other direction. And Ken decides where to shoot it from by who's 'coming up'. Because of that you have to have lighting which is good from whatever direction, so that you can move right around the room and the only thing you have to do is move the camera not the lighting. (Orbanz 1977: 84)

According to Barry Ackroyd, Loach's director of photography since *The View from the Woodpile* (1989):

Ken's method of shooting forbids any artificial lighting. But we can reinforce any natural light. And most important is freedom of movement for the actors, which is why the camera can't move – it might get in their way.[9]

As he has done since *Kes*, Loach shoots many takes and in story sequence, only giving the actors the outline of the story and a few pages a day. In 1977, Tony Garnett stresses the importance of this method of Loach's:

I think he's very good with actors. First of all we shoot a lot of stock, we shoot up to 25:1. Secondly there is a relationship between what the actors do and the script, and the script is a full script but the actors are not told to learn the lines and to say them just like parrots. (Orbanz 1977: 71)

The average ratio on *Raining Stones* is 10:1;[10] but, despite this technique, according to producer Sally Hibbin: 'the script that is written is the film that you see'.[11] Ackroyd and Loach may film improvised material, and in the rushes the scripted lines might lie embedded in this material; but Loach and his editor, Jonathan Morris, then strip it away during post-production, until only the scripted dialogue remains.

Nicholas Saada recognises that a strength of *Raining Stones* is its integration of Bob's quest with the problems of a wider community; he highlights the link made between the violence with which Bob becomes involved and the poverty and violence in the community.[12] Bob's quest to find money to buy the Communion dress propels the narrative; but this quest is connected to the problems of family, friends and acquaintances. One example of this is that extras are rarely used as background fillers; instead, minor characters expand themes. For instance, when Tommy puts the mutton in the back of Bob's van in the pub car park, a passer-by, Tony, asks him if has the five pounds he owes him. Tommy blames Bob for not passing it on. The scene amuses us incidentally because, judging from what we have already seen of Tommy and Bob, Tommy probably did not give him the five pounds; yet Tony and Tommy's conversation also points to the poverty of the community.

The film emphasises the perniciousness of everyday violence during Bob's two visits to the post office to cash his dole cheques, the cashing of which also marks time. The first visit ends with Bob bumping into two of Tansey's henchmen, one of whom, Ted, he knows. Ted asks him if he knows someone called Gilbert. He replies no. Despite this denial, on his second visit to the post office, Bob greets Gilbert, before witnessing Ted beat him up. During Bob's first conversation with Ted, the camera does not show their faces: we see the two men from a distance in a medium long shot. As Bob walks away, the camera pans right, shifting attention from the protagonist to a woman and a small child, other members of the community (figure 19).[13] Ted and his colleague block her path and harass her for money she owes Tansey. The film intimates Bob's fate by introducing the spectral figure of the loan shark through his two henchmen; yet, the harassment of the woman and the beating up of Gilbert

Figure 19: *Raining Stones*

develop the sense of a community trapped. Loach further illustrates the ordinariness of harassment and violence by filming an elderly woman walking past Ted beating up Gilbert. She ignores the incident completely; and, according to Loach, this was an unscripted moment – the woman was a real passer-by documented by him and Ackroyd.[14]

Two further examples illustrate the way that *Raining Stones* embeds its narrative structure in a social framework. Both occur during Bob's two visits to the Tenants Association. At first, he goes to ask his father-in-law, Jimmy (Mike Fallon), if he can borrow his cleaning rods. This conversation comes at the start of the sequence of events which leads to the payoff of Bob attempting to clean the church's drains. The scene begins with an establishing long shot of Bob crossing a square on the estate. It then cuts to a medium shot of him walking alongside the Tenants Association window, filmed from inside. He opens the door and leans in. Filming his approach from inside the Tenants Association enables Loach to reveal an off-screen conversation between a tenant and her adviser about the tenant's problems with her council flat: leaking pipes, damaged carpets, no compensation. When Bob asks the adviser if Jimmy is in, they stop talking; only then does Loach reveal the two women, in the next shot. The adviser answers him: 'Yeh he's on the phone love. Do you want to sit down a minute? He shouldn't be long.'

The film establishes the mother's worries – she has two children with her – before Bob enters. It then continues to focus attention on her as she talks while Bob waits. A shot/reverse shot couplet shows him watching the two women, before we hear, and his eyes indicate that he sees, Jimmy and a local Labour councillor leaving the office, arguing about the councillor's responsibilities to the tenants. The direction of this scene characterises Loach's late style. While the film follows its hero, it presents the dialogue between tenant and adviser, and then that between the councillor and Jimmy. It thus links Bob's anxieties with those of the mother; it places his quest to earn some money in a context that suggests his difficulties are typical. Loach creates narrative and thematic complexity over edited shots and mixed sound: the mode engages us with Bob's predicament, even as it presents the action via images and sounds which widen the focus, away from the individual drama.

The second example arises during Bob's second talk with Jimmy at the Tenants Association, when teenagers arguing outside about money for drugs disrupt their conversation. These teenagers are minor additions to Bob's story, but their place in the film expands the theme of disenfranchisement. Bob and Jimmy go outside to see what is going on. Observing the row, Jimmy comments on the inhospitable future that the kids on the estate face. Jimmy introduces explicitly political views – he restates the theme of the conflict between the leaders of the labour movement and those whom they claim to represent; but he is not a mouthpiece. As the Labour councillor leaves, he says to Jimmy, commenting presumably about housing problems such as the mother's, 'I'll see to it'. Jimmy's sceptical response – he threatens a rent strike – implies an expectation that the councillor will not fulfil his promise.

Raining Stones differs from Loach and Allen's earlier work because it introduces this political theme via a character whose views are at odds, philosophically and pragmatically, with the hero. The film alludes, via the character of Jimmy, to what its authors see as the historical failures of the leadership of the labour movement; yet it contrasts Bob's two visits to Father Barry with his two visits to Jimmy. Allen's lapsed Catholicism and the history of Loach's work (the use of the General Strike broadcast by Cardinal Bourne in *After a Lifetime*, for example) are relevant;[15] but the film hints that the value of religion and party politics in ordinary people's lives can be measured only by their practical usefulness. Father Barry gives sermons, but his crucial intervention is to throw Tansey's debt book away. Jimmy gives Bob political lectures, but Bob rejects these, telling his father-in-law, 'Look, Jimmy the last thing I need right now is a lecture.' To which Jimmy replies pointedly: 'Or a sermon.' His important role is to lend Bob the rods and give him a tip about where to buy a new van. The ambiguity about Jimmy's role signifies a change in Loach's responses to the challenges that his politics present, a move away from the certainties of earlier projects. Unemployed Bob replaces the politically articulate strikers of *The Big Flame* and *The Rank and File*, those men who were well versed in the history of the 'Wobblies' and Trotsky. By giving Jimmy only a minor role, he and Allen reflect upon the minor impact that his kind of politics has on the life of people like Bob or Tommy.

Raining Stones is digressive, like his earlier work; but the digressions are integrated with a central storyline. Embedding Bob's quest in an environment maintains a balance between a 'forward movement' and not 'squashing the life out of people'.

This process of embedding has three consequences. First, the combination of a fully worked-through narrative and a thematically rich yet realistically depicted environment facilitates performances of expansive depth and realism; even minor characters or scenes have a humorous vitality and relevance that belies the strength of thematic and narrative development. Second, the film connects Bob's problems to other characters' problems, and thus more general situations, so that the film encourages us to adduce that their experiences are shared, yet allows us to remain involved with the individual. Lastly, the arrangement of episodes enables the comedy and suspense to appear to develop organically from the characters' own experiences, even though both depend on precise structural payoffs.

Ladybird Ladybird: a melodrama of protest

Raining Stones combines strong narrative patterns, drawing on the genre conventions of comedy and suspense, with filming techniques that embed those narrative patterns in a social context. Loach's next film, *Ladybird Ladybird*, a film about a wronged woman, combines a less specific environment with a narrative structure that draws on melodrama. It features photography and types of location similar to those in *Raining Stones*, but the two films differ otherwise. Unlike the alternating, episodic narrative and modulated tone of comedy and drama in *Raining Stones*, *Ladybird Ladybird* presents us with a series of emotional highs and lows, orchestrated towards a steadily increasing anxiety and a climactic finale and coda.

The film opens with the title '*Ladybird Ladybird* – Based on a True Story'. That story begins when Maggie (Crissy Rock) meets a man called Jorge (Vladimir Vega) in a pub. As she tells him about herself, it emerges that her four children are in care: an extended sequence of flashbacks depicts her memory of the circumstances of their removal. The flashbacks clarify Maggie's story; they also align us with her. There are nine, and they unfold chronologically as Maggie and Jorge spend their first night together, talking and making love. The flashbacks illustrate Maggie's memory of events; but although her voice-over introduces most of them to Jorge, she cannot completely control her memories and some of the more unpleasant ones commence without an introduction.

The first flashback is interpolated into the shot/reverse shot sequence of her and Jorge in the pub. Having just met, they talk about themselves. Maggie explains that she is from Liverpool, although, she says, she has not been back there for years. Jorge tells her, 'You must have been a pretty little girl.' To which she replies, 'God, that was a long time ago wasn't it, when I was little.' As she says this, the film cuts to shots of the young Maggie (Kim Hartley) and her sister playing in the park with their father (Scottie Moore). As this flashback ends, Maggie's voice-over says: 'I don't remember much about being little. I don't remember much till I was about five.' To contrast the warm memory Maggie has of playing with her father and sister, Loach sharpens the transition to the next flashback by cutting from the bright sunlight of the park to the dark blue blur of Maggie's father hitting and kicking her mother in their kitchen. This scene of brutal domestic violence shocks and prefigures what is to come. In the background, the young Maggie cries as she witnesses her father attack her mother.

After this, Maggie tells Jorge, 'Anyway, I'd really not like to talk about it, to be honest.' As the evening turns to night, they go for a meal. Following this, they return to his flat for a coffee. He asks her why her four children are not with her and the remaining flashbacks explain why: they depict and she explains how she met Simon (Ray Winstone), her ex-partner, and how Simon assaulted her (her children witness this abuse). Following this upsetting memory, she says to Jorge:

> I was in hospital about two or three days. And then I came back. And that's when they started interfering more then. They started coming round making stupid accusations, like, if he'd hit me like that, what's he done to the kids. I mean for all that, he never touched the kids, you got to give him that.

Importantly, she rejects the accusation that her children were at risk from Simon. The flashbacks continue to explain Maggie's story: she moves into a women's refuge; there is a fire at the refuge; her children are hurt; and the police interrogate her about why she locked the children in their room while she went out. In the present, Maggie tells Jorge that her eldest son, who was badly burnt, was placed in temporary foster care. The eighth flashback shows her visiting him, and then alone at night. After she and Jorge have made love, the last flashback shows Maggie reluctantly going to a family centre with her three youngest children. A social worker shows her around the family centre. When she leaves Maggie for a moment, to intervene in another resident's argument, Maggie flees, and returns to Simon. The next morning she, Simon and her children run from social workers and police. The flashback ends with Maggie telling Jorge that she never saw her four children again.

The flashbacks establish that the loss of her children understandably affects her deeply: she hesitates to trust people and is often obstreperous. These tendencies bring her into conflict with figures of authority, even those who attempt to help her. In spite of her emotional wounds, though, she slowly unburdens herself with Jorge; she starts to trust him, and they fall in love. After some time, they move in together and have a baby. Maggie fears that social services will assume that because she is with a man she is going to be with a violent man: she evades a health visitor's questions about her relationship, and, initially, hides Jorge. Eventually, though, social services discover that she lives with the father of her baby. Partly because of her case history and her refusal to co-operate, and partly because of the lies of a malicious neighbour, Mrs Higgs (Pamela Hunt), social services decide that their baby, Zoë, is at risk.

They make Zoë a temporary ward of court, telling Maggie that after 72 hours she can contest the order in court. They take the baby forcibly, with the help of the police, and remove it to a place of safety. Social services then begin to assess the couple. For a while things go reasonably well: Jorge is a calming influence on Maggie and social services seem to recognise this. Still, when they contest the removal in court, they lose, again partly because of their neighbour's false testimony. Soon they have another baby. This time social workers and police act hours after its birth. While Maggie and Jorge are still at hospital, social workers remove the baby. The film ends with them at home; grief, anger and incomprehension overwhelm them; they struggle to reconcile themselves to each other and to the trauma that has befallen them. An end title reads: 'Maggie and Jorge have had three more children whom they have been allowed to keep. They have been given no more access to their first two daughters … Maggie says she thinks everyday of all her lost children.' This end title completes the film's opening declaration that this is a fiction based on a true story.

Perhaps because of this declaration, *Ladybird Ladybird* provoked some enmity in the British press, reprising the debates about *Cathy Come Home* and drama documentary in the 1960s, and *Days of Hope* and realism in the 1970s. On 14 September 1994, six weeks before UIP released it in the UK, *Ladybird Ladybird* premiered at the Edinburgh Film Festival. On the same day, *The Sunday Times Magazine* ran a hostile feature on the film. The writer, Carol Sarler, claimed that the film omits events from the story on which it claims to be based: it is, therefore, untrue.[16] In response Loach, producer Sally Hibbin and Peter Smith, the film's legal advisor, rebutted her criticisms.[17] After its release, the social worker who had originally written to Loach about the real 'Maggie' wrote an article in *The Guardian* describing her involvement with the case. She explained that the real Maggie and Jorge's first child was born eighteen months after they met; it was only six months later that social workers interviewed the couple. Eight months after this, social services placed their baby for adoption.

In the film, these events follow each other rapidly. In addition, Maggie's second pregnancy with Jorge comes soon after the removal of Zoë.[18] Producer Sally Hibbin said that the film was set in the 1980s, and an early treatment confirms that the main body of the film, not including the flashbacks, is based on events that took place over five years in the late 1980s.[19] The film does not indicate that it is based on events which took place over five years, and it compresses the chronological time of the true story for the fiction, perhaps without sufficient indication for those who questioned its veracity.[20] Film melodramas often cover a long period, and the rapid succession of traumatic events can enhance the implausibility of reversals of fortune. Usually in film melodrama, the transformation of long novels into two-hour movies brings disasters and tragedies close together;[21] in the case of *Ladybird Ladybird*, the compression of real events from a long period of time brings events close together.

Ladybird Ladybird is based on a true story, but it employs the 'excessive strategies' that Christine Gledhill describes as characteristic of melodrama; in particular, it dramatises what she refers to as the 'misrecognition of the innocence of a central protagonist' (Gledhill 1987: 30). Loach and Rona Munro compress time, elide events and align the film's point of view with the perspective, knowledge and experience of Maggie, thus shaping our understanding of the misrecognised innocent and encouraging a sense of injustice. As Steve Neale argues, a key convention of melodrama is the use of narrative disproportion,[22] and *Ladybird Ladybird* grounds its use of narrative disproportion in the flashbacks, which connect Maggie's past and present. This presentation of past events via her involuntary and voluntary recall of memory informs our reaction to her. The flashbacks encourage an alignment with Maggie, allowing us to see social services' actions as disproportionate. The flashbacks provide information about the reasons social services made her first four children wards of court: the (unproved) threat of Simon abusing the children; the fire at the refuge; her refusal to enter the family centre; her return to Simon – these things remain on file. The flashbacks and their placement also make apparent that, despite their best intentions, these social services fail to meet their client's needs. Maggie makes matters worse by leaving the family centre, but it should have been as obvious to the social workers as it is to us that she was in no condition to avail herself of the rehabilitation and assessment facilities of a family centre.

After the court confirms the adoption of her four children, and following her distraught conversation with Jorge outside the court, the film increasingly restricts its presentation of its protagonist to a view of Maggie that the authorities do not take. Caughie writes of this restricted view: 'In *Ladybird Ladybird* the individual drama drowns out other voices. This gives it an intensity and a unity which is extremely moving, but, in a way which *Cathy* does not, it substitutes emotional impact for social analysis' (Caughie 2000: 197). Loach always considers the place of 'social analysis' in his films, and, he consistently experiments with ways of embedding 'individual drama' in contexts which suggest 'social analysis'. In *Ladybird Ladybird*, he and Munro choose to uncover Maggie in intimate situations, and they do this to create a melodrama of protest; yet although the film has an emotional impact, the fact that it does not use the same strategies as *Cathy Come Home* (there are no 'official' voice-overs recounting statistics, for example) does not mean that it fails to be provocative about issues such as motherhood, class, the family and the role of the state.

Michael Walker describes the world of the melodrama of protest as polarised, one in which 'our sympathies are enlisted unequivocally with a group of people – defined by race, nationality, class or political creed – who are "innocents", victims of persecution, exploitation or oppression' (Walker 1982: 14). The narrative preparation that the film offers for the removal of Maggie and Jorge's two babies appears insufficient because the film has already enlisted our sympathies for her. If one agreed with Caughie's dichotomy between emotional impact and social analysis, it would be a legitimate criticism to argue that the film fails to analyse the procedures of social work; for instance, before a family centre of the kind shown in the film might accept Maggie, it is likely that there would be a number of meetings and case conferences, with and without her – one of the topics for discussion would be whether or not she was able to avail herself of this kind of support. One counters this criticism with the argument that Loach, Munro and Hibbin never intended to make a procedural movie; they wanted to stay as close as possible to Maggie.

Nevertheless, by using the structure of the melodrama of protest, *Ladybird Lady-bird* prompts thoughts about society. Neither the malicious neighbour nor a single professional are wholly responsible for Maggie's fate: although one social worker acts unprofessionally and unsympathetically, it is the system of rules and codes of practice which fail Maggie. The network of old case files, inter-office communications and court judgements provides the background to the decisions taken against her. Franco Moretti argues that although transgression and punishment recur commonly in literature, disproportion creates emotional impact. He distinguishes between transgression, punishment and disproportion by arguing that while the first two are always human and communal, the third can take many forms: a person transgresses or administers punishment, but disease, war or what Moretti calls 'the enemy' can bring about disproportion (Moretti 1983: 161). *Ladybird Ladybird* establishes the institutional features of the enemy so that it becomes difficult to blame an individual social worker, care assistant, solicitor or judge. The decisions taken against Maggie may appear implausible, untrue or biased; but, considered as part of a melodrama of protest, they are actions by an enemy against an innocent.

Writing of eighteenth-century stage melodrama, Simon Sheperd argues that there was, then, a 'structure of feeling' in which it was felt that emotion was paramount to a benevolent society; privileging feeling was felt to democratically locate 'truth in deeply felt emotions rather than in the discourses of dominant institutions' (Sheperd 1994: 30). One of these dominant institutions was the law. Sheperd argues that there was 'a structure of feeling about the individual in relation to law, where the conflict is produced as nature versus institution. Law is the crucial institution because it is seen to address individuals from outside them, to turn subjects into objects by inventing narratives about them' (Sheperd 1994: 30). This topos of early melodrama corresponds to Maggie's position in *Ladybird Ladybird*. The law does not treat her as an individual subject, but as a fixed object on file: social services judge her past, not her present. The film allows us to witness the truth about her and Jorge's relationship. Maggie, the natural mother, fights the state and the law. The film organises this melodrama so that the disproportion we adjudge in the authorities' actions turns on their belated acknowledgment of the strength and stability of Maggie and Jorge's relationship. As Moretti points out in his section on the 'Rhetoric of the Too Late', the longer the delayed coincidence of a character's knowledge and a reader's knowledge, the more belated the acknowledgment, and the more likely that tears will flow (Moretti 1988: 159–62). In *Ladybird Ladybird*, the authorities do not acknowledge that Maggie and Jorge could be good parents until the end of the film, when the title reveals that their wish to have a family has been fulfilled. At the same time, the end title maintains a sense of irreversibility by revealing that Maggie has not been re-united with any of her six previous children.

The polarised emotions of *Ladybird Ladybird* revolve around Maggie's joy at giving birth, and her despair at losing her children. E. Ann Kaplan argues that 'the women's melodrama articulates women's deepest unconscious fears and fantasies about their lives in patriarchy' (Kaplan 1987: 117).[23] *Ladybird Ladybird* articulates these fears and fantasies by provoking thoughts about who controls a woman's right to be a mother. Some of the most memorable film melodramas have a mother and child relationship at their centre; for example, *Stella Dallas* (1937) and *Imitation of Life* (1959). Traditionally in melodrama, ideological forces connected to class, gender or race frustrate the desire for restoration of a child to its mother; belated or delayed acknowledgment on the part of one or more characters may follow this frustration. Douglas Sirk's masterly *Imitation of Life* offers a powerful example of this belated acknowledgement. Famously, at the end of that film, a daughter delays acknowledgment of her mother until her mother's funeral. One of the strengths of Sirk's film is the way it exposes ideological forces, yet impacts emotionally. Loach's film similarly frustrates the desire for the realisation and development of the mother and child relationship in *Ladybird Ladybird*, intertwining social analysis with emotional impact.

Loach and Munro considered these issues when they developed *Ladybird Ladybird*. Asked by Geoffrey Macnab about whether there was a danger of 'aestheticising suffering', Loach responds:

> I hope not, in that I tried to express what are very powerful experiences, very elemental emotions, in as direct a way as possible. And not to hold back on them. Apart from observing the people sympathetically, apart from trying to make the film with a sense of rhythm and all the other things that film-making is about, I wouldn't try to make it gratuitously pleasing aesthetically if that meant taking away from the power of what was happening. The priorities were always the authenticity of the experience. Obviously you cut to a certain rhythm, and light in a certain way, but that shouldn't be distracting. (Macnab 1994: 13)

As he acknowledges, *Ladybird Ladybird* concerns and provokes powerful emotions, and it achieves these things by concentrating on Maggie's experiences. Munro explains that she felt her task had been twofold:

> To represent as closely as I could the emotional truth of 'Maggie', whose story it tells; and to structure the film so that real events worked as a dramatic narrative. (Munro 1994: 10)

In *Raining Stones*, Loach reveals Bob's world as much as his story: spreading the film's themes allows us to see that Anne, Tommy and other acquaintances share the privations that he experiences. In *Ladybird Ladybird*, instead of spreading the themes, Loach maintains a tight focus on Maggie. The first draft of the script describes Maggie from several viewpoints; in collaboration with Loach, Munro altered it to concentrate on Maggie's story. To the question of whether this film tells the whole truth about the real Maggie, and of its depiction of social workers, she replies:

It is fair to social services – we made a decision to go for one viewpoint, only one story. There is a concentration on telling Maggie's truth. It is only unfair in the context from which they're beleaguered from all sides.[24]

Loach confirms that to keep Maggie at the centre of the story they cut a third principal character, a social worker, from the first draft of the script, hoping to avoid the cliché of an articulate third character acting as a mediator.[25] Of the emotions in the film, he explains:

It's a film about grief, really, and how unresolved grief can turn to anger. It's not a shock-horror about social conditions; it's about two people and how they try to deal with loss. How anger that can't be put anywhere turns inward in the end and just destroys you. (Combs 1994: 6–7)

He emphasises that the dramatic focus is on Maggie, differentiating between *Cathy Come Home* and *Ladybird Ladybird*:

There are obvious similarities, but the stories are very different. *Ladybird Ladybird* is a study of a person and the relationship she's in. *Cathy Come Home* was a much more diagrammatic description of how a family becomes homeless. (Fuller 1998: 98)

The process of his decision to make *Ladybird Ladybird* the story of an individual is revealed by the way he and Munro developed the narrative structure.

Loach wrote comments on an early draft of the script, in which Munro tries out the idea of seeing Maggie from varying viewpoints, later abandoning this, as she says, 'to concentrate on seeing the world through her [Maggie's] eyes' (Munro 1994: 10). In his notes, Loach stresses the necessity of focusing the drama and action of each scene. For example, in a flashback scene that was cut, three social workers discuss Maggie's case in a case conference. Loach notes in red:

This uneasy – breaks connection of Maggie's memory – poss. put it later, when not flashbacks.

In a later flashback, after the fire, when Maggie runs from the rehabilitation centre back to Simon, he writes:

We're missing the dramatic development – suggest we go from the fire to the Rehab centre, – see it, see why M. runs off – how she does it – turns up to Mairead's, then on the street, then to Mullin's [Simon's].

In the court scene, Munro has written lines for two elderly spectators; Loach comments that including their viewpoint is a 'bit indulgent'. Similarly, in hospital, where Munro has written lines for other mothers in the antenatal ward, Loach comments, 'We should stay with M. and J. – otherwise tension goes.' In this draft, the film ends with repeats of earlier flashbacks; Loach writes: 'I don't think we need the f'backs. They will break the emotional impact of the scene.'[26] These comments contribute to the process of focusing the film on Maggie; they work towards refining the narrative so that it reflects indirectly her subjectivity.

Ladybird Ladybird concentrates on Maggie, but it makes evident the social services' reasons for making Maggie's children wards of court. Partly, we can attribute our understanding of their actions to the revelation of Maggie's abrasiveness: her short fuse consistently makes situations worse. The film establishes that social services fail to help her though because the system does not have the resources to help her, either by providing a consistent service with appropriate key workers, or by offering her suitable placements. The scenes in the refuge support this reading. The first contains visual and verbal links to the fire and the police's questioning of Maggie. While showing her the room, Jill mentions the 'dodgy wiring'. After other children run in, she warns her to watch out for rowdy kids in the refuge. Nobody says anything about a cause after the fire, but Jill's 'dodgy wiring' plausibly explains it. Maggie later explains to the police that she locked the door in order to keep rowdy children out, not to lock her own children in. The women's refuge provides her with a temporary escape from Simon, but this proves to be unsuitable as long-term accommodation: the rundown and overcrowded conditions at the refuge indicate the under-funded state of this non-local authority social service, a service which Maggie is, nonetheless, willing to use. Similarly, the family centre, from which she runs after witnessing an argument, appears understaffed. The welcoming social worker leaves her to intervene in the argument. Maggie, made anxious by this stressful encounter, flees with her children, thus foregoing an opportunity to receive help. She then has nowhere else to go but back to Simon and this precipitates the loss of her children. The film proposes that she and her family need their own home; her barrister argues this in court in her defence. He observes that Maggie's environment – the lack of a home and her own family history – has been the major factor in bringing her to a position where she appears, from the law's perspective, incapable of caring for her children.

The film contrasts the law's perspective on Maggie with the perspective it takes on her. Loach and Munro underscore this contrast between perspectives by juxtaposing significant events, emphasising the opposition of Maggie and the law, of innocent and enemy. For example, the morning after they spend their first night together, Jorge tells Maggie, 'We can be close you and I, and understand each other'. Maggie looks pretty, calm and relaxed. The film cuts from this scene to the tribunal where the judge confirms the wardship of her children. A witness (a doctor or a social worker) speaks condemningly about her, ending with: 'Miss Conlon seems likely to continue her pattern of abusive relationships.' The placing together of the loving scene and the court scene highlights the discrepancy between our knowledge of Maggie and the

Figure 20: *Ladybird Ladybird*

law's knowledge of her; it also recalls the cut to the judge in *Poor Cow*. In the second court scene, Maggie and Jorge contest the temporary wardship of court under which Zoë has been placed. The magistrate's summing up demeans Maggie, and his speech, when he declares that 'The evidence suggests a woman of low intellect and little self-control, suggests she is in fact beyond help', exemplifies the power that he wields. The discrepancy between how we see Maggie and how the court sees her creates a sense of outrage.

The concentration on Maggie's point of view renders an epistemic structure that is especially forceful in the scene where a social worker knocks on Maggie and Jorge's door, before talking to their neighbour, Mrs Higgs. The film powerfully articulates relations between character knowledge and spectator knowledge by using a subjective point-of-view shot and eyeline matching when the young social worker looks through Maggie's letterbox. The scene opens by continuing the pattern established in two preceding scenes when the health visitor, Moira Denning (Christine Ellerbeck), visited Maggie. On the first visit, the health visitor uses the wrong family name for her, referring to her ex-husband; on the second visit, Maggie admits Moria to the flat, but is hostile to her.

In the following scene, when the young social worker knocks on the door, Loach uses the same camera set-up that he uses to film the health visitor's approach. Maggie does not answer the door. When the social worker hears a baby crying, he kneels

Figure 21: *Ladybird Ladybird*

down to look through the letterbox. The film cuts to a masked point-of-view shot from the social worker's optical perspective: we see Maggie pick up the baby in the flat and hide (figure 20). We then return to a shot of the social worker peering in. Loach uses a point-of-view shot to offer a precise visual alignment between what the social worker sees and what we see. This shot is significant, though, because it introduces a tension between what Douglas Pye calls the spatial axis of point of view, which the social worker and the film share, and the cognitive axis of point of view.[27] There is a discrepancy between the social worker's knowledge of Maggie and our knowledge of her; this discrepancy emphasises and contributes to the distance between the law's perception of Maggie and the film's presentation of her. The film shows her avoiding the social worker, yet it has established her resentment of the authorities; it has made clear that she has nothing to hide from the social worker. What she inadvertently hides is the revelation that might prevent the intervention of social services – the revelation of the quality of her and Jorge's relationship and of their parenting skills, those things that could influence the situation in her favour.

The social worker knocks again, then leaves. The film cuts to the interior of Maggie's flat; Loach now changes the relationship between the spatial and the cognitive axes of point of view, between visual and epistemic relationships between audience and character. Checking to see that the unwanted visitor has gone, Maggie enters the kitchen, still holding the baby. She looks out of the window. In response to what she sees, she exclaims, 'Oh no, oh no'. Only then, after the film has allowed a moment for curiosity to develop about her anxieties, does Loach cut to a reverse shot from Maggie's position. In a long shot through some railings, looking down onto the courtyard of the flats, Maggie sees the hostile neighbour, Mrs Higgs, talking to the social worker (figure 21). She exclaims: 'The nosey old bag.' As Loach bracketed the social worker's view through the letterbox with two shots of him looking, here he completes the bracketing of the shot taking Maggie's point of view with a close-up of her looking down.

The social worker spies on Maggie through the letterbox but, despite the spatial alignment, our knowledge exceeds his and that of the institutions he represents; in sharp contrast, the long shot from Maggie's point of view aligns us spatially and epistemically with her, and the film uses these alignments to promote empathy for her; in an important way the action of the film is here presented *through* Maggie. The film has already made known what the social worker does not know, and what Maggie reiterates when she whispers 'the nosey old bag': the neighbour harbours grudges against her and Jorge, and is prejudiced, racially and regionally, and generally mean-spirited. Importantly, though, Loach does not reveal Mrs Higgs' conversation with the social worker; instead he withholds narrative information, although because of the film's prior establishment of Mrs Higgs and Maggie's relationship, we may guess its incriminating content.[28] As in *Raining Stones*, when Loach withholds the content of Bob and Tommy's conversation on the pavement, here he delays confirming suspicions until the second courtroom scene. Moreover, as in *Raining Stones*, he uses music to replace the dialogue and add an ominous quality to the moment.

In *Poor Cow* the juxtaposition of Joy's perspective on Dave and the law's perspective on Dave, with a similar emphasis on environment and background, is more disruptive than the juxtaposition of varying perspectives in *Ladybird Ladybird*. This is because *Ladybird Ladybird* opposes Maggie's consciousness and point of view to that of the law more systematically than *Poor Cow* does. In *Land and Freedom* Loach further develops this method of allowing the story to emerge through a character's experiences.

Land and Freedom: seeing with your own eyes

Land and Freedom depicts the journey of its central character, David Carr (Ian Hart). David's journey is one of moral growth; his progression to clear-sightedness is the schema that dramatises his moral education. While in *Ladybird Ladybird* Loach and Munro create a dramatic narrative from the range of possibilities in a person's life, turning a 'true story' into a melodrama of protest; in *Land and Freedom*, Loach and Allen create a dramatic narrative from competing versions of history, as they had done with *Days of Hope*. Caughie argues that *Ladybird Ladybird* offers 'individual drama', but not, unlike *Cathy Come Home*, 'social analysis' (Caughie 2000: 197). Caughie's criticism of *Ladybird Ladybird* restates criticism of *Days of Hope*'s 'tendency to personalisation'; it also echoes his 1980 article, in which he writes:

It [*Days of Hope*] is therefore vulnerable to the critique of Lukács that it is a 'subjective protest', or to the critique of Brecht that it fails to expose the spectator to the contradictions which have to be worked out. Thus *Days of Hope* offers the experience of history – memory – rather than its analysis; *The Spongers* or *Cathy Come Home* offers the experience of social injustice – bad conscience. (Caughie 1980: 30)

In this earlier piece, Caughie categorises *Cathy Come Home* with *Days of Hope*: both offer the 'experience' of either social injustice or history. Twenty years later, though, Caughie holds *Cathy Come Home* up as an exemplar of his ideal 'text' that offers 'social analysis'.[29] The separation of 'experience' and 'analysis' in 1980 seems close enough to the separation of 'emotional impact' and 'social analysis' in 2000 to warrant the assumption that Caughie has the same issues in mind.

Land and Freedom takes place in Spain during the Spanish Civil War. In August 1936, David Carr, a member of the British Communist Party, makes his way to Spain in order to fight for the Second Republic. All winter he and his comrades are entrenched along a stagnant front. In the scene discussed below, it is now early spring 1937; the militia group to which David belongs have raided a village at dawn and taken it from the Nationalists. The fighting has subsided, and the men have begun to gather in the church square. As they do so, a sniper begins to shoot at them from the bell tower. People run for cover. David and a comrade, Coogan (Eoin McCarthy), watch from the roof of a house as two fascist soldiers emerge from the church using two local women as shields. At first the militia refrain from firing at the soldiers, but when one of the soldiers shoots another woman, they fire on them. Loach intercuts this action with Coogan and David on the roof. When Coogan realises he is out of ammunition, he turns and asks David for ammunition. David refuses and as they argue about whether or not Coogan can safely shoot the soldiers from their position, the sniper shoots Coogan in the back. After the battle is over, the soldiers and one woman are dead, the other woman is wounded and militiamen have gone to look for the sniper, who is soon revealed as the village priest. Coogan's lover, Blanca (Rosana Pastor), then discovers his body. David witnesses her discovery, and the film shows us that her grief touches him.

That David cries after seeing Blanca cry when she discovers that Coogan is dead suggests that her expression of grief triggers his own feelings of remorse and moves him to tears: he responds, it would seem, to Blanca's heartfelt cries. As with Carla on top of the bus in *Carla's Song*, *Land and Freedom* here evokes a sustained moment of emotional authenticity. Loach and his collaborators carefully shape the presentation of Blanca's discovery and David's response to it in order to draw out the melodramatic potential, and create an acutely poignant moment, one that has an emotional impact. Central to Loach's shaping is the shot that follows Blanca as she runs up the street. As Rosana Pastor seems to discover an event in the film's world, an inquisitive, hand-held camera seems to find positions from where it can film her discovery.

Figure 22: *Land And Freedom*

It begins in long shot with Blanca and one of her comrades, Maite (Iciar Bollain), standing at the end of the street in shadow (figure 22). Behind them, villagers and militiamen move about the square; to their right, several villagers carry away the body of the young woman whom the nationalist soldiers have shot. Maite speaks to Blanca; but something catches Blanca's eye and she ignores her. She turns, looks up the street and begins moving towards the camera. As she does so, the camera pans slightly right and then left, a little unsteadily, almost as if the cameraman, Barry Ackroyd, though alert to Pastor's potential for movement, remains unsure about how she is going to move. We have seen Coogan being shot, so we can guess what Blanca is about to discover. She has seen Coogan on the ground; but her facial expression, the way she ignores Maite and her gradual increase of speed all imply that, although she has seen something awful, she does not yet know, and surely dreads finding confirmation, that Coogan is dead. As Blanca approaches him, becoming progressively aware of the gravity of the situation, she starts to run up the street (figure 23). Having found her in the distance the camera follows her: from a position at the side of the narrow street, it films her short run, panning quickly from left to right as she runs past it, so that her blurred head overspills the frame at one point.

As Blanca kneels down, in the same take, the camera moves towards her, around to her right, finding a place near Coogan's feet, from where it can reveal her crouching near his head. While it finds this spot a woman and a man who have been attending to Coogan move away from him, passing the camera close enough to obscure, momentarily, our vision of Blanca. Instead of using a shot in which the camera anticipates the action and presents it in an unobstructed way, Loach favours a shot that gives a

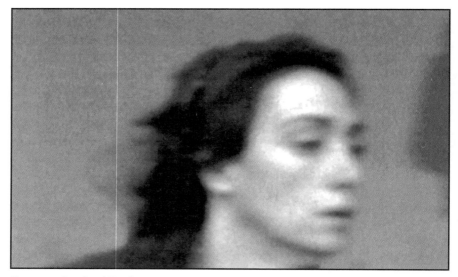

Figure 23: *Land and Freedom*

sense of the camera responding to the action, moving as if there were no plan. Blanca tries to cradle Coogan's head. As she does so, she begins to whimper. She looks up and down his body, all the time trying to grasp him to her chest: Eoin McCarthy is a big man and he allows his heavy head to loll lifelessly in her arms; Pastor has to grab him firmly (figure 24). Her struggle to hold his physical weight seems to facilitate her performance, for as she grapples with his head and upper-body she increases the frequency and volume of her whimpers.

While she does this, the film cuts to a shot of Jimmy (Paul Laverty) and David, the latter of whom stepped away from Coogan as Blanca approached. He and Jimmy now stand in a doorway near Coogan's head. Jimmy looks away, but David looks down, stunned and silent, shocked by what he sees and feels. As Blanca's sobs get louder, David turns slowly round. The film cuts back to a close shot of Blanca. She gasps deeply for breath and then cries out loudly, with her head moving back as she grips Coogan's chin with her right hand. The proximity of Blanca's dark hair and tanned, olive skin to Coogan's fair hair and bloodless, blue-grey skin and lips strikes a dramatic contrast between the living and the dead. As she pulls his face towards her, Loach again cuts to David looking on. He walks out of the doorway and down the street, away from the camera. He moves lethargically, dragging the rifle along. With his back to us, he sniffs. As he does so, Bernard (Frederic Pierrot) puts his arm around David's shoulders and holds David's head against his own. Hart rocks his shoulders slightly and starts to sob. As the two men walk away from the camera, the serious and sympathetic faces of their militia comrades come slowly into focus.

Besides the visual presentation, the sound mix, including the music by George Fenton, contributes to the shaping of this scene. Pastor increases the intensity of her cries as if she is wrenching the expression of emotion out from within herself. Yet in the lead up to her loudest cries, other sounds provide a context for her performance. Just before kneeling down, for example, Blanca's rifle clatters on the stone street when she drops it, her concern for Coogan overriding her concern for her weapon. At the same time, music from the previous sequence continues to play during the shot of her running, although it changes substantially: the timpani subside and in their place the lower strings, using only two or three sustained notes, play a rising motif that builds to a crescendo before fading out. This new theme possesses a tempo slower than that which accompanies the preceding sequence; it signals a change of sentiment and anticipates Blanca's discovery of this individual tragedy; its sombreness guides us to her loss. The music fades out just before she emits her loudest cry, focusing attention on Blanca's pain. Before this, its sombreness isolates her initial quietness and the quietness of those people standing near Coogan's body. Yet, the film gives relief to her quietness and her cries with the background hustle of the villagers in the square. The immediate onlookers remain silent as Blanca approaches Coogan, but off-screen villagers in the square shout as they attend to people wounded. While the music evokes a mournful sentiment and isolates her individual experience, preparing us to respond to this moment of melodrama, the off-screen shouting, the clattering rifle and the rough scuffing of Blanca's boots as she kneels down affirm her connection to a world beyond her pain.

Four important scenes in the village follow this one: the execution of the priest, David's comforting of Blanca, Coogan's funeral and the debate on collectivisation. When the POUM (Partido Obrero Unificación Marxista) militia march away from this village, which they have liberated from Franco's troops, they leave behind them

Figure 24: *Land and Freedom*

revolutionary conditions, in which the majority of the villagers have voted to collectivise all the nearby farms, both the large estates and the smallholdings. As they march, David speaks in a voice-over that recurs throughout the film as a framing device. His voice-over presents the text of letters that he wrote from Spain in 1936 and 1937 to Kitty (Angela Clark), his fiancée at home in Liverpool. Kitty does not read them in the film though; her and David's granddaughter, Kim (Suzanne Maddock), discovers and reads the letters soon after David's death, which the film depicts in the opening scenes as happening in 1994. As David marches away from the village, he reflects on his experiences: 'What I'm saying Kit is that I'm not the man I was. I feel like I'm standing on higher ground if you see what I mean. I can see further and I notice things I hadn't even thought of before. Like I left Liverpool with a daft, romantic idea; but in war people get killed. Fellas like Coogan and the women and kids who died in this village.'

David refers to the emotional impact that seeing people killed has had on him; and throughout *Land and Freedom* his experiences in Spain affect and inform him. The more he experiences, the more the film reveals his initial understanding of the Spanish Civil War to have been restricted. Nothing in *Land and Freedom* suggests that its makers assumed its viewers would possess an understanding of the Spanish Civil War that was superior to David's own understanding. Loach and Allen made it to draw attention to political differences that they believed were becoming obscure, differences between Stalinism and socialism. They began developing it in the early 1990s, following the collapse of communism in Eastern Europe, when there were pronouncements of the end of socialism, both as a practice and as an ideal. Within this context, they were committed to making a film that would have a wider audience than the audience we see at the beginning of *Land and Freedom* watching the film about Spain. As someone who often uses the structure of the melodrama of protest, Loach has an ambivalent relationship to the form of propaganda film shown at the beginning of *Land and Freedom*. The audience for that film comprises members of the British Communist Party, including David and Kitty; they watch a film in August 1936 that aims to rouse them to go and fight for the Republican cause in Spain. Loach and Allen made *Land and Freedom* to inform audiences as the film within it informs David, but they aimed to reach a large audience. To reach this audience, they tried to balance a sense of events, institutions and policies with a story about individuals whose emotions and experiences are engaging.

As David's voice-over describes his increased perception, the film cuts from the militia marching in early spring 1937 to David's flat in 1994. Kim reads her grandfather's letters and clippings from the Communist Party newspaper, the *Daily Worker*, with articles by the Communist reporter Claude Cockburn, known as Frank Pitcairn, and Harry Pollitt, then general secretary of the British Communist Party. She also studies photographs of David and his comrades. Kim cannot experience what her grandfather did; she can only look at these documents as a historian might, trying to imagine why David recorded his thoughts about the events in which he was involved.

After his emotional experiences in the village, David feels that he has enlarged his perception – he can see further, and his attitude has changed from one where he held a 'daft, romantic idea' to one where he understands that 'in war people get killed'. His experiences of the violence of the raid on the village, of Coogan's death and of the execution of the priest have apparently enabled his increased vision, facilitated his political education. When he cries in the street, it is Coogan's death, his own feelings about that and about Blanca's response to it that overwhelm him; his letter implies that the experience of powerful emotions allows him to understand war. However, what is crucial to Loach and Allen's project and what prevents their film from being a generic anti-war or anti-fascist film, is that although David feels that his perception is now more penetrating he is yet to achieve the understanding that marks the end of the film. In the debate about collectivisation, for example, David's preference for winning the war against Franco before engaging in social revolution indicates that he, like the American, Gene Lawrence (Tom Gilroy), remains loyal to the Communist Party and supportive of the policies of the Comintern, despite the fact that both men are fighting with the anti-Stalinist POUM.

Land and Freedom refracts the hostility and conflict between the POUM, the powerful anarchist union, the CNT (Confederación Nacional del Trabajo), the Moscow-directed Spanish Communists, the PCE (Partido Communista de España) and the Catalan Socialist Party, the PSUC (Partido Socialista Unificat de Catalunya) through the characters of David, Blanca, Lawrence and Pepe (Pep Molina), the smallholding farmer who resists collectivisation. These fictional characters operate as ciphers in that their value in the film derives from the degree to which they articulate political ideas. Each character represents part of a larger whole, and the film uses David's interaction with Lawrence and with Blanca to show his moral growth in Spain. Until the sequences in the village, the film presents the events in Spain as a story of republicans versus fascists.

The scenes in the village display the collusion between the Church, the army and the owners of large, landed estates, the *latifundistas* – those elements that made up the nexus of elites which the Second Republic challenged; yet the village scenes also include the first indication of the political differences amongst those challenging these elites. David's voice-over describes his experiences, but his comments during the village debate (e.g. 'Unless we win the war there's no point in having the ideology') confirm that he has not yet acknowledged either the scale of these differences or their potential to turn violent.

David describes his ability to 'see further', but he has not yet 'seen with his own eyes', as he says later, the implementation in Spain of Stalin's policy of suppressing the POUM. Eventually, the film undermines his declaration of increased perception. Some months after the village raid, an old rifle explodes in his grip, and the militia send him to Barcelona to recuperate. Before he leaves the front, he becomes close to Blanca and, after he is released from hospital, she surprises him in Barcelona. They stay in a pension together and become lovers. On the morning after they have made love, she discovers that he has joined the Communist-led International Brigades. They argue, and Blanca tries to alert him to Stalin's policy; she argues that the Stalinists are using torture chambers. David replies: 'I'll wait till I see it with my own eyes.' Blanca retorts: 'But you don't see it; you don't want to see.' After Blanca storms out, the film returns to Kim, who unfolds a newspaper clipping about the bombing of Guernica, with the date of its destruction – 27 April 1937 – visible. So, Blanca and David are arguing in Barcelona just before the conflict between the factions on the left comes to a head, before the eruption of what Paul Preston calls 'a small-scale civil war within the civil war' (Preston 1996a: 185). Kim looks at a photograph of Blanca, which has 'Con Amore' written on the back. She uncovers, apparently, a romance from her grandfather's youth, while she learns about his experiences of the Spanish revolution, although it is a moot point whether or not the film wants us to imagine that David told Kitty about his love affair with Blanca.

More than a dozen drafts of the script exist, together with many extra pages, inserts and revisions. Draft scripts of *Land and Freedom* carry two earlier titles: *May Days* and *The Earth is Red*. Early drafts contain scenes with characters based on real people, who interact with wholly invented characters; these scenes resemble similar scenes in *Days of Hope*. More scenes take place in Barcelona in May 1937; they describe, for example, the crowds at the funeral for the CNT leader, Durruti, speeches made by the leader of the POUM, Andreu Nin, at the POUM headquarters and those of the welcoming committee for the Soviet Consul, Vladimir Antonov-Ovseenko. Allen's first eight-page treatment describes how Nin and 40 members of his executive were arrested on 16 June 1937. It mentions that the arrest warrants for the POUM leaders were signed by Colonel Ortega, the Communist Director General of Security, under pressure from Orlov, the NKVD chief. It describes how Nin was tortured and then killed when he refused to sign a confession. On this typescript, Loach comments at one point, 'We must keep the narrative going.'[30] In a later note to Allen, dated 9 January 1992, Loach comments on a draft script, and on the comments by its initial producer, John Daly:

> It is too long. This is, I think, true, but it *seems* long because we lose our focus halfway through. We lose contact with David, cease to see it through his eyes, and the impression is that the film is rambling. This makes it seem long ... The emotional life of the film is not sharply drawn enough.[31]

Loach later tells Allen: 'The present structure has some great scenes but the thrust of the story is not very strong. As you read it – or watch it – you don't really know where you're going.'[32] Loach is concerned with the dramatic structure of the film and with keeping the focus on the relationships; he wants to ensure our involvement with the story; primarily, he wants to enlarge the degree to which the film presents its events through a central character's point of view, so that we can 'see it through his eyes'.

Loach proposes to Allen during the process of revision that they edit in interviews with survivors of the Spanish conflict. In a note to his collaborator, Loach asks: 'What about intercutting interviews with survivors? I think it would be good, add to the complexity and give it more dimensions. Also it would resolve the pressure on the narrative to tell everything.'[33] They did not do this, and gradually, under Loach's direction and, in the late stages of revision, with Roger Smith's contributions as Script Editor, Allen dropped the scenes that recreated documented events, choosing instead to allude to historical facts, arranging narrative events so that they embodied their interpretation of those facts. The final film integrates these allusions with a story about individuals who can embody ideological and social forces, but who can also act out and allow us to see and to respond to experiences that David's granddaughter Kim, in sifting through the documents, cannot see, but can only imagine. Blanca is a character whose experiences – of grief and of love – are created for us to respond to; but she also symbolises the revolution. When the Popular Front soldiers shoot her at the end of the film, her death may move us, yet it represents the violent crushing of the revolutionary project, the hint of which first emerged in the village debate. For David, her death constitutes the last thing to be 'seen with his own eyes'.

In the early 1990s, after directing *Riff-Raff* for Channel 4's *Film on 4*, Loach and Allen decide to make *Raining Stones*. Loach sends a fax to his collaborator, in which he writes: 'As you know, I think this is *very important*. After *Riff-Raff*, we must capitalise on the opening we've made. We *can* make it this year without a lot of hassle.'[34] Within the context of changes in British cinema and changes in British politics, and acutely aware of his own lack of success in the 1980s, Loach is keen to 'capitalise' on the rising value of his work, eager to re-establish himself as a commercially viable film-maker. He realises that, after the problems getting his documentaries shown and then having to shoot television commercials in the late 1980s, he needs to adapt to a newly market-orientated British cinema or he will not be making films at all. The success of *Riff-Raff*, *Raining Stones* and *Ladybird Ladybird* in Europe enables Sally Hibbin and Rebecca O'Brien to finance future work by pre-selling rights in Europe. These production set-ups facilitate the development of *Land and Freedom*. Despite various exhibition problems over the years, Loach secures a place as a European film-maker with a deservedly strong international reputation. In the 1990s, he hones his methods of film-making, working closely with a scriptwriter to refine the narrative, and combining his previously developed realist techniques, the casting of 'natural actors' and 'the rhetoric of the "unplanned" shot or "unpremeditated" shot' (Caughie 1980: 28), with traditional genre and narrative conventions. *Land and Freedom* provides evidence of Loach's ability to renew himself while retaining a link with his past work: it expresses the same political concerns as his earlier work with Allen, but it differs in its integration and in its European dimension, both in theme and in influence.

CONCLUSION

A further consideration of *Land and Freedom* and of its achievements and limitations will permit me to conclude and to summarise the achievements and limitations of Ken Loach's work. *Land and Freedom* uses deaths and responses to deaths to generate emotional impact: David's death at the start of the film; Kim's response in the ambulance; Coogan's death and funeral midway through the film, after which David speaks of his new knowledge of war; Blanca's death and funeral, which mark the final betrayal of the POUM and CNT by Stalinists; and, lastly, David's funeral. This strategy of using sudden deaths connects *Land and Freedom* to the melodrama of protest. As was quoted in Chapter 1, Michael Walker argues that in the divided world of melodrama, where misrecognised innocents confront impersonal, institutional or ideological forces, the death of such an innocent is a device used to rouse people in the film and in the audience.[1] In *Land and Freedom*, Loach and Allen use the death of an innocent, Blanca, in their dramatic interpretation of history. It functions as a trigger for 'emotional impact'; yet, their film is not simply an anti-war or pacifist film.

Blanca's death is part of a symbolic drama about ideological conflicts on the left. In order to fuse the unique and the general Loach and Allen invent things, basing them on real events, but dramatising them without asserting the time of events as they did in *Days of Hope*. Loach's proposal to Allen that they use interviews with survivors of the Spanish conflict offered the potential to incorporate a technique recalled from his 1960s work; in particular, it brings to mind *The Golden Vision*, with its interviews of Everton players; 'factual information' edited into a fictional narrative. The proposal indicates the continuing thought that Loach applies to the question of how best to ensure that narrative fiction films involve audiences emotionally, so that we see a story through a character's eyes, *and* point to social and ideological forces. Individuals are part of social processes and I do not want to imply a false opposition between personal and impersonal narrative causality, but Loach has struggled to make films which dramatise how social processes envelop individuals. He has incorporated his belief in socialism into his work using different strategies throughout his career.

Earlier works, such as *Up the Junction* and *Cathy Come Home*, show us details of individuals' lives; they then tell us that these individuals' experiences relate to the experiences of larger social groups, using authoritative voice-overs and statistics to tell viewers what their claims are about abortion or homelessness. One reason why I judge the scene in *Carla's Song* where Eileen tells George about Nicaragua didactic is that Loach and Laverty fail to make their film absorb this 'wider consciousness of history', as Raymond Williams writes of *The Big Flame*, other than to use a character as a mouthpiece for the director and writer's views. Some might want to make a case for the importance of being jolted out of our involvement with the characters, but I judge it to be a momentary lapse. In the 1970s, in *The Big Flame*, *The Rank and File* and *Days of Hope*, Loach and Allen try to express a political philosophy by dramatising a collective experience. In *The Big Flame* and *The Rank and File*, they use the more overtly self-conscious 'mixed aesthetic' with which he experiments in his 1960s television work. However, in *Days of Hope*, working with producer Tony Garnett, instead of incorporating unabsorbed documentary elements into his fiction in order to make general points about an event, Loach and Allen find other ways to dramatise the relationship between the experiences of individuals and the experiences of groups.

In collaboration with his writers, Loach consistently devises means for introducing historical processes into his films; he considers E. H. Carr's question: 'Is the object of the historian's inquiry the behaviour of individuals or the action of social forces?' (Carr 1985: 44). *Land and Freedom* contains an argument about social and ideological forces, and yet it attempts to balance this with individual drama. It wants to involve us with a hero and his experiences, and to evoke emotions by depicting details from a fictional hero's life, such as his feelings when seeing Blanca discover Coogan's death, or subsequently when seeing Blanca's death. While Loach wants us to see events through David's eyes, he also wants to present an argument about controversial historical events without resorting to anonymous voice-overs.

Land and Freedom aims to show that the anti-fascists could have defeated Franco if the republican government had used the initial popular support that erupted in the summer of 1936; the widespread support for the Spanish revolution legitimised it. For this reason the debate about collectivisation, held in the village after Coogan's funeral, assumes great significance: it outlines arguments for and against revolution and shows that the majority of the villagers and peasants support the revolution. During the debate, Pepe, the smallholding tenant farmer, invites the militia to speak; the American Communist, Lawrence, mentions the republican government's Land Decree of 7 October 1936. This decree sanctioned the division of estates that belonged to known supporters of the insurrection led by General Franco, but it allowed other landowners to keep their land.[2] After the militia speak, the majority of the villagers vote to collectivise the land. Their vote exemplifies the way that *Land and Freedom* indicates support for the revolution; it proposes an imaginative extension – what happens in this village could happen all over Spain.

The Spanish Civil War historian Paul Preston summarises both sides of the argument:

> The two diametrically opposed positions are based on a partial view of the war. In denouncing the revolutionaries as wreckers and the objective enemies of the popular cause, the Communists ignore the fact that the one great and unique weapon which the Republic possessed was popular enthusiasm. That weapon was destroyed when revolutionary structures were dismantled by ruthless methods. The revolutionary position tends to ignore both the international situation and the scale of conventional military might confronting the Republic. (Preston 1996a: 172)

Preston reviewed *Land and Freedom* on its release and he argues that the crushing of the POUM is a 'minor episode' that is 'allowed to dwarf the wider issues of the war' (Preston 1996b: 21). Preston concludes that 'the problem [with *Land and Freedom*] lies in the fact that Loach's position is virtually identical to that of George Orwell' (Preston 1996b: 21). Allen and Loach did use Orwell's *Homage to Catalonia* (1989) as a source for *Land and Freedom*. They also used Felix Morrow's *Revolution and Counter-Revolution in Spain* (1974); Burnett Bolloten's *The Spanish Civil War* (1991), Mary Low and Juan Brea's *Red Spanish Notebook* (1937), Victor Alba and Stephen Schwartz's *Spanish Marxism versus Soviet Communism: A History of the P.O.U.M.* (1988) and Abel Paz's biography of Durruti, *The People Armed* (1976). The main historical advisor was Andy Durgan, and the film credits several Spaniards, presumably survivors of the conflict. As with Allen's scripts for *Days of Hope*, the *Land and Freedom* scripts refer to these sources.

Historians like Hugh Thomas and Paul Preston may argue that the crushing of the POUM is a 'minor episode' but other historians, like Burnett Bolloten, George Esenwein and Adrian Shubert argue differently. *Land and Freedom* may appear too narrow in its focus, yet one story can only tell a fraction of what happened in Spain during this period. Loach and Allen aimed to present a view that counteracted what historian George Esenwein, co-author of *Spain at War*, calls the 'idealized' view of the Spanish Civil War.[3] As they did in *Days of Hope*, Loach and Allen dramatise events that will illustrate their viewpoint. A significant marker of this viewpoint emerges after David's involvement in the Barcelona May Days. In the café in Barcelona, the waiter, having broken up a fight between David and some PSUC soldiers, shouts at the soldiers: 'If the leaders of the POUM and the CNT get together we're fucked.' Here *Land and Freedom* hints at a criticism of the leaders of the POUM and the CNT for not calling for a united front in the aftermath of the May Days. This view corresponds to the criticism of union and Labour leaders in *The Big Flame*, *The Rank and File*, *Days of Hope* and *Questions of Leadership*; additionally, it represents the Trotskyist analysis found in Felix Morrow's *Revolution and Counter-Revolution*.

As quoted in Chapter 4, Loach says of the political analysis behind *Days of Hope* and *Land and Freedom* that he finds the historical continuities evident, but as persuasive and convincing as Loach's analysis is, and as correct as he is about injustices perpetrated, a doubt remains. Evaluating Loach's work involves considering economic and political values about which people are sensitive. It is one thing deciding whether or not *Land and Freedom* is a good or a bad film (although that may be no easy task); it is another deciding whether one agrees with the film's and, by extension, with Loach and Allen's interpretation of history. Hindsight aids condemnation of the Communist Party's repression of the POUM. Equally though, a retrospective glance could judge the revolutionaries in Catalonia as going too far in wanting to collectivise all the land.

In 1987, when Loach was having difficulty finding a subject and a budget for a feature film, Allen wrote and Loach directed *Perdition* for the Royal Court Theatre. *Perdition* is a courtroom drama based on a real libel trial that took place in Israel in 1953. A Hungarian Jew, Rudolph Kasztner, a member of the Zionist Relief and Rescue Council of Budapest during World War Two, took to court a journalist who had accused him of collaborating with Adolf Eichmann, thus allowing the deportation of hundreds of thousands of Jews to Auschwitz within a short space of time at the end of the war. Loach summarises:

> The essence of the story is that Zionist leaders in Hungary did a deal with the Nazis that allowed for certain people selected by the Zionists to go free and leave the country provided instructions were given to the vast majority of Jews to board the trains going to the camps. That deal was actually struck and accepted. It's a matter of record and it all came out in the trial in Israel after the war. (Fuller 1998: 73)

Allen fictionalised the case and created a new character, but pre-publicity caused so much controversy, including an allegation that Loach and Allen were anti-Semitic, that the director of the Royal Court Theatre, Max Stafford Clark, cancelled the play days before its scheduled opening. Just before Jim Allen died on 24 June 1999, Elliot Levey staged a fine production of the play at the Gate Theatre. Whatever we conclude about *Perdition*, we need to acknowledge the sensitivity of the historical events that it interprets; Kasztner's negotiations with Eichmann in Budapest in 1944 have long been controversial. In the early 1960s, Hannah Arendt, in her book on the Eichmann trial, *Eichmann in Jerusalem: A Report on the Banality of Evil*, writes that 'the Jewish Establishment is bitterly divided on this issue' (Arendt 1994: 284); more recently, historians have concluded that Kasztner did not collaborate with the Nazis.[4] While we cannot dismiss the play's proposition as fantasy, the divided scholarly debate surrounding Kasztner's role restricts assurance for someone who is not a scholar of this period and who lacks Loach or Allen's ideological faith.

In the early 1990s Allen and Loach attempted, with producer John Daly, to make a film of *Perdition*. The film was to present the story of the putting on of the play through the point of view of a young Israeli actor who feels the pressure from Zionist pickets. They never managed to get the film made; instead, they began work on *Land and Freedom*, initially with John Daly, then with Rebecca O'Brien. In addition, Allen quickly wrote *Raining Stones* in 1992. Evaluating *Land and Freedom* is as difficult as evaluating *Perdition*, and indeed much of Loach's work: it brings up questions, for example, about why the Spanish Civil War has acquired a reputation as an exclusively anti-fascist struggle. In answer to this Allen explained why he chose the POUM, in preference to the CNT, who were a far bigger organisation in Catalonia:

> Because CNT had tremendous courage and so forth, but we wanted to show a more politicised reaction to the Communist Party. The only man in the CNT it would have been worth writing about was Durruti: the rest, no. POUM was a highly politicised organisation. They had the theoretical tools to oppose and destroy the Communist Party. Andreu Nin, who directed POUM, an old pal of Lenin's, he was tortured and killed. Now I wrote scenes about that. That had to go out. I went more into the political differences between them. That had to go. I mean Trotsky hated the POUM: Trotsky said, these aren't Trotskyists. I couldn't go into any of that. Had I gone forward with every particular argument it would have been so dense, people would have walked out. I had to simplify it a lot.[5]

Like most of their work, *Land and Freedom* tries to bring Allen and Loach's ideas about history and politics to a large audience; Allen felt that in order to keep an audience in their seats he 'had to simplify it a lot'. One of these simplifications includes the fact that the English-speaking squad of the POUM militia is fictitious. Out of 600 POUM and 15,000 CNT in the Lenin Column there were 200 internationals, including 30 Britons – amongst them were George Orwell and John Cornford; but there was no English-speaking squad.[6] The invention of the English-speaking squad is excusable perhaps as a necessary convenience for getting the film made and for enabling the key themes to be debated in English, but the changes in chronology are a more troubling matter.

Land and Freedom fuses a depiction of what we imagine to be an accurate historical chronology and David's moral growth as an individual involved in national and international events. Unfortunately, in creating this fusion, Allen and Loach veer away from complete accuracy, bending chronology for their political project. The raid on the village, during which the Priest shoots Coogan from the bell tower, takes place at the wrong time. The POUM militia did seize villages (the battalion commander, Vidal, lists them at the end of the film when the Popular Army arrest the militia and shoot Blanca), but they did so between July and September 1936, not in early spring 1937. The Huesca front, on which the POUM militia were fighting, stagnated after October 1936 until the offensive in June 1937, which *Land and Freedom* depicts towards the end, when the militia take a position but are unable to hold it.

Andrew Britton warns against one possible response to this kind of simplification:

> Inaccuracies and simplifications of historical fact in a work of scholarship are very seriously culpable, but they are not in themselves valid criteria for impugning works of art which represent historical events ... It follows, therefore, that an Elizabethan history play or a western is to be judged, not by its reliability, justice or accuracy as *history* but by its use of the conventions – which pertain, in any case, not to the past as such, but to an ideological construction of the past sanctioned by the dominant culture in which the artist is working. (Britton 1988/89: 53)

If a film proffers a fact that is not in fact a fact, does this affect the film? That depends on the type and genre of film and on what claims the film makes on our attention. Loach's work purports to be accurate in its relation to the world; therefore, if we accept *Land and Freedom*'s changing of the dates, then, hypothetically, at what point would we stop accepting changes? Christopher Ricks provides a useful way of resolving this issue. He writes that 'it will always be critically relevant to consider accuracy and inaccuracy', and that one should not decide in advance that inaccuracy is irrelevant or immaterial (Ricks 1998: 283). Ricks argues:

> A writer's responsibility might be put like this: you can't both lean upon historical or other fact (this being not only permissible but indispensable to many kinds of literary achievement) and at the same time kick it away from under you. You can't get mileage from the matter of fact and then refuse to pay the fare. (Ricks 1998: 298–9)

In fact, the re-shaping of chronology may be irrelevant to evaluations of *Land and Freedom*.

If we consider how difficult it would be, as Ricks phrases it, 'to put the matter of fact right' then we can appreciate the importance or irrelevance of Loach and Allen's re-shaping of chronology. The correction of the inaccuracy about the timing of the raid on the village would not necessarily entail a complete restructuring of the film. David Carr would need to have arrived in Spain in the summer of 1936, immediately after the insurrection by Franco. Yet, if he had arrived in Catalonia between July and September 1936, when the POUM militia did seize villages from the fascists, this might have had important ramifications for his character, perhaps requiring changes in social status or in political alliance. How might David have reached Spain so quickly, for example? Would it have been plausible for a card-carrying Communist Party member to join the POUM so early, as opposed to someone like George Orwell, a member of the British International Labour Party, which was affiliated to the POUM?

These questions do not raise insurmountable problems, but to resolve them may have required changes in David's character and changes in the type of action that the film could plausibly show. Because Loach and Allen wanted to reveal the widespread international support that the Spanish revolution received and fasten this revelation to the schema of an individual's moral growth the change in the chronology remains a problem, although perhaps a minor one.

Throughout this book, I have examined the ways in which Loach has tried to make films that are emotionally engaging and analytical. *Land and Freedom* offers us a central character whose emotions and experiences we are encouraged to empathise with as the film unfolds – we are involved with the individual drama. Yet a crucial part of *Land and Freedom* is the way that the film modulates our involvement with this character moment by moment so that we come to realise that although he declares his increased ability to see further, he remains sympathetic to a position that the film ultimately undermines. I end the book with this discussion because the achievement of the film indicates the limits on success that Loach's work can achieve. *Land and Freedom* presents both individual drama and social analysis without breaking the rhythm of the story; but with its divided world and its undivided hero who learns to see Stalinism, it remains a schematic melodrama of protest.

In Chapter 1, I used John Hill's essay on *My Name is Joe* as a catalyst for describing my own views on melodrama. I elaborated my disagreements with Hill's comments – quoting, for example, 'what separates Loach's work from conventional melodrama is the way it discourages too strong an emotional identification with the characters while insisting on the economic and social underpinnings of their actions' (Hill 1998: 20) – because of the apparent unwillingness to acknowledge the complexities of 'conventional melodrama'. My overall assessment of Loach's work agrees with the reservation about the 'divided world' of melodrama voiced by Michael Walker – too often the 'misrecognised innocent' (Cathy in *Cathy Come Home*, Billy in *Kes*, Janice in *Family Life*, Bob in *Raining Stones* or Maggie in *Ladybird Ladybird*) pitted against an unjust ideology, institution or society produces a narrative structure that does not allow for complexity of character. Therefore, even when the hero is 'divided', as David is in *Land and Freedom*, he follows a straightforward schema of moral growth. However, although Hill correctly argues that Loach's films insist 'on the economic and social underpinnings of their [the characters'] actions', his comments reverse my view, which is that films which may be considered 'conventional melodrama', films such as *Stella Dallas* (1937), *Letter from an Unknown Woman* (1948) or *All I Desire* (1953), are considerably richer and more complex than Loach's films, particularly in their combination of individual drama and social analysis.[7]

Loach's work improves in the 1990s *because* he starts to work more in the mainstream traditions of narrative cinema, in the tradition of European realist film-makers; one can appreciate the influence on his work of the Italian neo-realists, and the Czech and French 'new waves'. Equally, though, his work connects to a tradition in British film-making and broadcasting: the instructive documentary. The sub-title of this book refers to a comment made by Sydney Newman, who described his aim to make television drama that was 'art in the service of the people'. Newman provides a link between the ethos of John Grierson and that of Ken Loach. Newman said he aimed for 'art that had to leave a residue of conscious thinking on the part of the audience, so that the art would stir them into action the following day, the following days'.[8] Although the techniques of Ken Loach's work have changed continually in the course of a 40-year directing career, the dominating aim to make 'art in the service of the people' has remained consistent. Although we might sympathise with that aim, an incident that took place in December 1994, during *Land and Freedom*'s post-production, exemplifies some of the complexities that are involved in it. Loach, Alan Parker and Mike Leigh were lobbying the Heritage Select Committee. Joe Ashton, Labour Member of Parliament for Salford, in an aggressive reply, accused British film-makers of being elitist: '99 per cent of my constituents are Philistines – maybe I represent them – but we do not get reactions from our constituents that we do to other industries – your industry is run at the top, making stuff for each other, quite frankly.'[9] Loach firmly reminded Ashton that his position as a Labour MP was a result of the labour movement, which was largely built upon the principle of increased education for the working classes through working men's libraries and so forth; as such, he should show more respect towards a cultural tradition that dealt with class and British history.

Ashton's comments recall the debate in the 1960s around the *Pilkington Report*, about 'giving the people what they want' or 'giving them what they need'. Loach's career took off at a moment in British cultural history when, for television, 'relevance' had been strongly endorsed over 'triviality'; and one can imagine Ashton being given short shrift by Richard Hoggart and the Pilkington Committee. We might disapprove of or recoil from Ashton's comment, yet he raises important issues about who exactly constitutes the audience for Loach's films. At an early stage in the writing of this book, I decided to put these questions to one side, as it would have been impossible to write properly about both stylistic issues and reception issues in one volume, but the question remains. Instead, I have evaluated Loach's films according to artistic principles. To justify the claims that I make about their meaning, I would argue that although each spectator brings his or her own personal experience to a film, shared cultural values exist; film-makers need to conceptualise what dominant responses their films might provoke in audiences in order to make the film. We can only test an interpretation of a film against the film itself; only then can we judge how accurate and appropriate an interpretation is. In his inspirational essay, 'Must We Say What They Mean?: Film Criticism and Interpretation', V. F. Perkins concludes:

> An interpretation will be adequate or not in relation to the particular purposes for which it is advanced, and in relation to the particular aspects of the film that it claims to cover. Insofar as it hopes to illuminate a whole film or a body of work by drawing attention to overall patterns and representatively eloquent

detail, an important test of its validity and usefulness will be the degree to which we can internalise it and use it to enrich our contact with the film. (Perkins 1990: 6)

We cannot prove an interpretation, as no interpretation offers proof; it only appeals to a reader's memory of the film and a re-viewing of the film. I hope that my interpretations of Ken Loach's films will enrich readers' contact with his films, and help readers to see them in another way.

NOTES

INTRODUCTION

1   Kerr (1986: 145) notes Loach's 'gradual shedding of all non-naturalist devices'. See also Petley (1997a).
2   Interview with the author, 6 August 1998.

CHAPTER ONE

1   Stephen Frears on *The South Bank Show*, tx: ITV, 3 October 1993.
2   *Carla's Song* was lawyer-turned-writer Paul Laverty's first filmed script; his second script, *My Name is Joe*, benefited from the contributions of an experienced writer and script editor, Roger Smith, who had worked with Loach on his *Wednesday Play* films in the mid-1960s and who also edited, at a late stage, Jim Allen's script for *Land and Freedom*. Smith has since been a script consultant on Loach and Lavery's *Bread and Roses* (2000) and, with Barry Hines as Script Editor, on Loach and Bob Drawer's *The Navigators* (2001).
3   Four parts tx: BBC1, 11 September, 18 September, 25 September, 2 October 1975. See Goodwin, Kerr & MacDonald (1983) for a summary of the responses.
4   McArthur (1975–76) and MacCabe (1976a). See also Bennett, Boyd-Bowman, Mercer & Woollacott (1981).
5   MacCabe (1974: 13). He writes of the following as classic realist texts 'in book and film': *Toad of Toad Hall*, dramatised by A. A. Milne in 1929, based on Kenneth Grahame's *Wind in the Willows* and filmed in 1946, starring Kenneth More; John Steinbeck's 1939 novel *The Grapes of Wrath*, filmed in 1940 by John Ford; and Rodgers and Hammerstein's 1959 stage musical *The Sound of Music*, filmed in 1965 by Robert Wise.
6   When he discusses Allen's second play, *The Lump*, MacCabe compares it with the British 1970s police series *The Sweeney*, arguing that 'the mechanisms at work in *The Lump* are the same as those used in *The Sweeney* to elicit sympathy for a copper who bends the rules' (MacCabe 1976b: 27). MacCabe's concept of 'classic realism' is linked to, but should be distinguished from, the ontological and epistemological realism which Cavell identifies when, referring to film's photographic basis in transparency, he writes: 'objects participate in the photographic presence of themselves; they participate in the re-creation of themselves on film; they are essential in the making of their appearances' (Cavell 1979: xvi).
7   For an assessment of the importance of Brecht's work for the left, see Adorno, Benjamin, Bloch, Brecht & Lukacs (1977).
8   For theoretical background to what is sometimes called contemporary film theory see Allen (1995). Key texts in contemporary film theory can be found in Rosen (1986). See also Johnston (1985).

9   On these film-makers see Bazin (1971).

10   See Britton (1988–89) and Pye (1989).

11   See McArthur (1978); Caughie (1980); Hill (1986) and (1997a); Paget (1990).

12   For Hill, *Saturday Night and Sunday Morning* (1960) is as much a classic realist text as *The Sound of Music* (1965). He argues that the British 'kitchen-sink' films of the late 1950s and early 1960s are characterised by an injection of new content (working-class lives, language and sexuality, particularly male), rather than an invention of new dramatic forms: as with MacCabe's arguments about classic realist texts, for Hill the 'kitchen-sink' cycle of films still tends towards personal, rather than socio-political explanations. See Hill (1986: 59–61).

13   Hill (1997a). For a discussion of *Fatherland* see Tulloch (1990).

14   Petley (1997a) provides a comprehensive history and analysis of criticism of Loach's work. He points out that, in the 1970s, the *Screen* left-wingers and the Fleet Street right-wingers shared common ground: 'both construct a convenient ideal type ("classic realist text"; "fictional faction") and then use this as a crude measure by which individual works may be judged and found ideologically wanting and "incorrect"' (Petley 1997a: 51).

15   Ken Loach on *The South Bank Show*, tx: ITV, 3 October 1993.

16   Klevan (2000: 36) demonstrates how 'the pursuit of the "more real", the seeking of styles and scenarios with a more natural resemblance to life (which has taken a variety of forms), has often produced varieties of anomalous melodrama'. He gives as examples *Pather Panchali* (Satyajit Ray, 1955), *My Childhood* (Bill Douglas, 1972), *The Southerner* (Jean Renoir, 1945), *The Wrong Man* (Alfred Hitchcock, 1957), *Kes* (Ken Loach, 1969) and *Paisà* (Roberto Rossellinni, 1946).

17   Thomas' (2000) discussion about Nicholas Ray's *Bigger than Life* (1955) demonstrates very effectively how a domestic melodrama centred on 'interpersonal relations' can evoke ideological forces.

18   Martin (1992) provides an excellent account of the relationship between critics who focus on what a film expresses and critics who focus on what is symptomatically excessive in a film.

19   Klinger (1994) questions Thomas Elsaesser and Paul Willemen's Brechtian readings of Sirk's films. Similarly, Shattuc (1994) questions the defence of formal, stylistic excess as a pre-requisite of progressive readings of melodrama. Shattuc argues that it is a principle derived from European high Modernism and a cultural competency dependent on class and racial privilege.

20   See also Walker (1992), (1993) and (1996).

CHAPTER TWO

1   Loach told me that it was broadcast live, and no copy survives in the National Film and Television Archive; but *Radio Times*, 16 January 1964, bills it as a telerecording. It was possibly recorded as live, but broadcast from a telerecording.

2   Memo from File T5/2,399/1 at the BBC Written Archive Centre, Caversham Park, Reading (henceforth BBC WAC).

3   Contemporary examples of the way that the concept of immediacy, rooted in live broadcasts, continued to dominate thinking about the medium include Maddison (1963) and Bakewell (1966).

4   Having written the first series of *Z Cars*, Troy Kennedy Martin and John McGrath left the series complaining about the imposition of overly schematic plots. Loach's second assignment was directing three episodes of *Z Cars*: 'Profit By Their Example' (tx: BBC, 12 February 1964), 'A Straight Deal' (tx: BBC, 11 March 1964) and 'The Whole Truth' (tx: BBC1, 8 April 1964). On *Z Cars* see: Lewis (1962); Casey (1962); McGrath (1975); and Laing (1991).

5   The six 45-minute episodes were broadcast every Saturday night at 9.30pm from 8 August 1964. Peter Duguid directed episodes two, four and six.

6   Memo from Sydney Newman addressed to James MacTaggart, Troy Kennedy Martin, John McGrath, Ken Loach and Peter Duguid. Memo 5089 T.C. PABX 3798/9, in BBC WAC File T5/63011, 13 August 1964.

7   Besides Loach, the other person who rose to prominence on *The Wednesday Play* was Dennis Potter. Although they were both scholarship boys, and were at Oxford at the same time, they make different aesthetic choices. Loach says of Potter: 'The early thing, the Nigel Barton play, was a big success and I thought that was good, but when it became like the theatre of self-revelation, I found it got less and less interesting ... I mean he would talk a very good script, but actually when it was written down I found it a bit shallow and meretricious. And then, I found him personally quite difficult to deal with. He could be quite a bully, like David Mercer could.' Interview with the author, 6 August 1998. For more on Potter and *The Wednesday Play* see Gilbert (1995).

8   For details of Newman's relationship with Grierson and Grierson's work at the National Film Board of Canada, see: Hardy (1979); The John Grierson Project (1984).

9   At the time he said: 'As our plays reflect the British way of life, I believe only our writers can provide the authentic

background and story.' Sydney Newman in Bird (1958: 9).

10   See Greene (1969) and Tracey (1983). Petley (1992) argues that Greene's liberal reign at the BBC is an important context for Loach's work and *The Wednesday Play*.

11   Before the publication of the *Pilkington Report* in 1962, the BBC had been suffering in its ratings battle with ITV. Gaining the franchise for BBC2 allowed BBC1 to become populist. With this in mind the BBC hired Newman. However, Newman's plans for *The Wednesday Play* met with opposition in the BBC from those who believed that investment in serials and sit-coms, such as *Z Cars* and *Till Death Do Us Part*, was the key to winning the ratings battle with ITV. On Newman's support of *The Wednesday Play* series, in the face of opposition from the Director of Television, Kenneth Adam, and the Chief of Programmes for BBC1, Donald Baverstock, see MacMurraugh-Kavanagh (1997a). On Newman's impact on BBC television drama see: Corner (1991); Sutton (1982). For a description of Newman's appointment at the BBC, see Tracey (1983: 223). For a less sympathetic account of Newman's replacement of the previous Head of Drama, Michael Barry, see D. Taylor (1990: 100–2).

12   See Filmography for a list of Loach's *Wednesday Play* productions. For details on *The Wednesday Play* see Shubik (1975), which includes a list of *Wednesday Play* and *Play for Today* productions between 28 October 1964 and 11 December 1972, including writers, directors and producers. For a list of which of these plays are preserved in the National Film and Television Archive see Baker and Terris (1994).

13   Dunn's preface in *Up the Junction* states that four stories were first published in the *New Statesman*. I found only three: Dunn (1962a), (1962b) and (1963). MacMurraugh-Kavanagh (1997b) points to the strength of the collaboration between writer, story editor and director, correctly emphasising the importance of Tony Garnett's contribution to the script of *Up the Junction*. *Up the Junction*'s credits state 'By Nell Dunn', but a memo sent to James MacTaggart from J. V. Beesley on 23 September 1965 notes that the BBC paid Loach a £150 fee for 'assisting' in the writing of the script. BBC WAC File T5/681. The BBC1's *Programmes as Broadcast* microfilm, held at the British Film Institute library, records: 'Author – Nell Dunn', but 'Adapted by Ken Loach'. To confuse matters, Briggs writes: 'Nell Dunn's novel was adapted by Kenith Trodd' (1995: note 26, 522). Rather frustratingly, Briggs does not give the source for this claim, though it may be Trodd. Nell Dunn remembers: 'Ken Loach had read the book [at the suggestion of Stanley Myers], and wanted to do it for TV. There was very little alteration of the TV version – Ken picked out what to use, I really wrote bits for continuity. Both of us and Tony Garnett worked out a script. A lot of the suggestions came up during shooting.' Dunn interviewed in Madden (1976: no page numbers). Given what Loach has said of the importance of Garnett's contribution as story editor, it seems likely that Dunn's account is the most accurate.

14   Dunn was a wealthy heiress who, in 1957, had a much-publicised marriage to Eton-educated author Jeremy Sandford (later to write *Cathy Come Home* and *Edna, the Inebriate Woman*). Two years later, in 1959, the couple moved from fashionable Cheyne Walk in Chelsea to then unfashionable Battersea.

15   Referring to Dunn's preference for dialogue, reviewer David Lodge notes, '*Up the Junction* might have been called *I am a Tape-Recorder*' (Lodge 1963: 852). Dunn called her second book *Talking to Women*.

16   Loach's first seven films for *The Wednesday Play* all contain various mixtures of telerecorded studio material and filmed location footage. Some, like *Three Clear Sundays* (tx: BBC1, 7 April 1965) and *Up the Junction* (tx: BBC1, 3 November 1965), comprise almost half studio telerecorded material; others, like *Cathy Come Home*, have much less. The amount of telerecorded footage and 'Specially Shot Film' used on each *Wednesday Play* is on the BBC's 'Programmes as Broadcast' microfilm, held at the BFI Library, London. Telerecording (known as kinescope in the US) was a means of recording a live studio performance on film. The studio and camera plan for *The End of Arthur's Marriage* (tx: BBC1, 17 November 1965) reveals that Loach had six sets built in the BBC White City Television Centre, Studio 4, and that he telerecorded the performance with five electronic studio cameras. Television Centre Studio 4 and Camera Plan in BBC WAC File T5/1,313/1. This is the only surviving studio plan I found in any of *The Wednesday Play* files connected with Loach. In a memo to the *Wednesday Play* producer, James MacTaggart, Loach notes the plan to make the whole production on 16mm, rather than the usual 35mm, and advises transmission on a twin-lensed telecine channel, better suited for 16mm telerecorded material. Memo, 9 August 1965 from Ken Loach to James MacTaggart in BBC WAC File T5/313/1. The production file for *Three Clear Sundays* provides an example of a schedule that incorporates telerecording: location shooting on 35mm for two days, 26 February and 1 March 1965; 14 days outside rehearsal, 2–14 March; three days in Television Centre's Studio Four (TC4), 15–17 March, of which two-and-a-half days were on-set camera rehearsal and three hours (7–10pm) were allocated for staff and equipment to telerecord the play. Three days editing and one day dubbing followed, and the play was broadcast less than a month later (Schedule in BBC WAC File T5/659/1). See: Caughie (1991b); Jacobs (2000); Barr (1992b) and (1996).

17   Abortion law was not liberalised in Britain until 1967. The Abortion Act passed on 27 October 1967 made the medical termination of pregnancy legal and free for the first time, on the condition that two doctors agreed '1.1 (a):

that the continuance of the pregnancy would involve risk to the life of the pregnant woman, or of injury to the phyical or mental health of the pregnant woman or any existing children of her family, greater than if the pregnancy were terminated; or (b) that there is a substantial risk that if the child were born it would suffer from such physical or mental abnormalities as to be seriously handicapped.'

18 It was this scene that so incensed Mary Whitehouse. She writes: 'The screaming girl undergoing an illegal abortion was enough to make anyone pick up his or her pen and write to their MP. The sooner those terrible back-street abortionists are put out of business the better! True. But what about a play which would make it clear that any kind of abortion, legal or otherwise, has dangers to mental and bodily health far greater than natural childbirth? How about a programme which would demonstrate that clean living could cut out a great deal of this problem at the root?' (Whitehouse 1967: 167–8). For Booker, the year 1965 is the culmination of several years of English 'revolution', the year that London becomes 'The Swinging City', courtesy of a *Time* magazine 12-page cover story, 13 April 1965. November 1965, the month *Up the Junction* is broadcast and received so controversially, is the climax of the year's 'events': Booker calls it the 'Month of Madness' (Booker 1969: 268–75).

19 Tony Garnett interviewed on the *South Bank Show*, ITV, 3 October 1993. Archival records show that Garnett's doctor was paid a facilities fee for medical advice and a sound recording. Memo, 11 October 1965, in BBC WAC File T5/681.

20 Willett (1967: 213–25) appraises Brecht's impact in England, arguing that Brecht was an 'active influence' in English theatre in the late 1950s. Lovell (1976) discusses how, in the 1960s, critics and artists on the left in Britain developed an interest in Brecht after the visits of the Berliner Ensemble. He suggests that there is a Brechtian influence in work by Lindsay Anderson, Joan Littlewood, John Arden, Troy Kennedy Martin, John McGrath, David Mercer and the magazine *Encore*.

21 Loach interviewed by Jeremy Issacs on *Face to Face*, BBC2, 19 September 1994. Loach also cites the influence of Joan Littlewood's 'Theatre Workshop' projects, in Ryan & Porton (1998).

22 Willett writes of Christopher Logue: 'Mr Christopher Logue in particular so steeped himself in Brecht's style and mannerisms that he carried over whole lines and successions of images into his own work, translating them not only into English but at times into a rather unnatural framework of self-conscious rhetoric and strained pugnacity ... The arrival [in Britain] of *The Threepenny Opera*, however, at once set entirely new standards; in Mr Logue's *The Lily-White Boys* of 1960, for instance, the verse was strictly for singing: an independent element contributing to a different form of play. And this went with a new spontaneous wave of interest in the performance and public delivery of verse – in poetry to jazz accompaniment, in the narrative folk or pseudo-folk ballad that Brecht himself so liked' (Willett 1967: 220–21).

23 Loach interviewed by Jeremy Issacs on *Face to Face*, tx: BBC2, 19 September 1994.

24 Dunn and Loach adapt Barny's dialogue from her book, and his speeches match those of the character in the book almost exactly. See Dunn (1966: 107–20).

25 The studio sets are listed on the Property Requirements Form, requested for 17 September 1965, in BBC WAC File T5/681. There were ten sets built in TC4: Castle Pub and Ladies WC; factory tea-room and WC; smart pub; Tallyman's customer's room; Winnie's room; Rube's house – kitchen and bedroom; transport cafe; pub – saloon bar; cafe; prison visitors hut. I have listed the studio sets in the order they occur in the film. There is one scene filmed without any discernible set and in one shot only: it is a close-up of Dave in court. Unfortunately no studio plan survives; however we can estimate from the plan for the six sets of *The End of Arthur's Marriage* that the ten sets would have been built around the edges of a studio and that Loach would probably have directed his cast on those sets with four or five studio cameras in the three hours allocated for telerecording. Two writers who disagreed with each other about the use of film and telerecording in *Up the Junction* were Taylor (1965–66) and Kennedy Martin (1965–66).

26 Mitchell later made filmed documentary reports for current affairs programmes *World in Action*, *The Wind of Change* and *This England*. See Purser (1961b).

27 Corner's segmentation and analysis of *Cathy Come Home* builds on work by other scholars, notably Fiske & Hartley (1978). Following Roland Barthes and Christian Metz, Fiske & Hartley analyse the overlap of documentary and dramatic conventions, the 'code-mixing' (Fiske & Hartley 1978: 55–8) by singling out the differing tenses of the images and voice-overs.

28 Director Alan Parker credits *Cathy Come Home* as his inspiration: 'That was the fundamental pivotal point. For me to look at it and think you can do that and you can do it that well was the first time I was excited about something that was British and not American.' Alan Parker interviewed on *Typically British*, tx: Channel 4, 2 September 1995.

29 Some press reviewers vilified *all* of Loach's fiction films of the 1960s for looking too much like documentaries of the period; yet it is to *Cathy Come Home* that students and scholars have returned to analyse what is thought of as the

quintessential documentary drama. Some scholars have discussed it within an analytical framework that concentrates on documentary. See: Rosenthal (1971) and Corner (1996).

30   Christopher Ralling offers an early example of the typical criticism of *Cathy Come Home*. He writes: 'It might be said that *Cathy Come Home* has proved its legitimacy once and for all by winning the Italia Prize for drama. It was billed as a drama, and the fact that it did more to stir the conscience of the nation on the subject of homeless families is a comment on the average documentary rather than on *Cathy*. Yet even here it was not always possible even for experienced professionals to know when they were listening to the voices of actors or real people, such was the skill with which the two were blended. There was also a caption at the end which stated that all events in the play had actually happened. In other words, even a perceptive viewer might have been left in a state of confusion about what exactly he had been watching: confusion between dramatic truth and actual truth'. (Ralling 1968: 827)

31   For a discussion of the history of 'docu-dramas', see Petley (1996).

32   Key figures of the period were Head of Drama Michael Barry and producer Robert Barr. For more information on the period, see Barry (1992). Examples of early drama documentaries include: Barr's *I Want to Be an Actor* (6 October 1946) and Barr's *I Want to Be a Doctor* (20 May 1947), such a success that it was broadcast live twice more with different casts (3 November 1947 and 19 January 1950).

33   In the early 1950s current affairs programmes, such as *Foreign Correspondent* and *International Commentary*, were largely preoccupied with overseas issues and world affairs. For an excellent overview of this area see Scannell (1979).

34   See Rotha (1956). Other examples include: *Under her Skilled Hand* (tx: 4 February 1953), directed by Gilchrist Calder, who, like Barry (and Loach) came into television from repertory theatre. Calder also directed George Sara's 'series of true stories from a surgeon's casebook', *They Came by Appointment* (six 30-minute episodes, tx: 5 January 1955–9 February 1955). See: Gilchrist Calder interviewed by Norman Swallow for the ACTT [BECTU] Oral History Project. Copyright held by BECTU.

35   Sandford recounts the development of *Cathy Come Home* in Rosenthal (1971: 164–75).

36   Memo from Tony Garnett to Graeme MacDonald, 2 August 1967 in BBC WAC File T5/695/3.

37   Briggs claims mistakenly of *Cathy Come Home* that it was 'filmed mostly in the studio and not in the streets, where Loach would have preferred to work' (Briggs 1995: 522). The five scenes telerecorded in a studio are very brief: an estate agent's office (with Geoffrey Palmer as the estate agent); a court scene where Reg receives an eviction order; a scene at Reg and Cathy's home where a social worker interviews Cathy; a council meeting about the common land on which Reg and Cathy are living on in a caravan; and a pub where Reg is drinking with men from the caravans. *Cathy Come Home* was filmed on location on sound 16mm film in London and Birmingham on 25–29 April, 2–6 May, and 9–12 May 1966. There were rehearsals on 13 and 14 May and the telerecording of the five studio scenes took place on 15 May between 8–10 pm. Schedule in BBC WAC File T5/965/2. Location work was done in story sequence, a practice Loach later adopts as a tenet of his directing strategy. *Cathy Come Home* is his last production to use any telerecording.

38   As Rothman (1997: 110) points out, towards the end of the 1950s technology became available that made it possible for people in documentaries to speak with their own voices about their own lives. What allowed the filming of ordinary people in documentaries was the development of synchronised sound and lightweight 16mm cameras: specifically the Nagra, a battery-driven portable magnetic tape recorder, and the hand-held Eclair NPR 16mm camera, designed by André Coutant, a prototype of which was used by Raoul Coutard and Michel Brault on Jean Rouch and Edgar Morin's *Chronique d'un été* (1960). (Brault had previously shot documentaries for the National Film Board of Canada.) At the same time, as Rouch and Morin were developing *cinéma-vérité* in France, in America Richard Leacock and Robert Drew were making *cinéma-vérité* documentaries, initially for television, like *Primary* (1960).

39   Carol White's own two sons, Sean and Stephen, then three and two years old, played Cathy's sons, Sean and Stephen in *Cathy Come Home*. See White, with Thurlow (1982).

40   Walker (1982: 2–38).

41   White (1943–1991) came from a family of entertainers: her father was a boxer and subsequently performed in vaudeville; both her sister and her brother were briefly singers and actors. White attended Corona Stage School from the age of nine onwards, and began acting as a teenager. Examples of her early films include: *Circus Friends* (1956, Gerald Thomas), in which she had her first lead role; *Carry On Teacher* (1959, Gerald Thomas); *Never Let Go* (1960, John Guillermin), in which she starred opposite Adam Faith; *The Man in the Back Seat* (1960, Vernon Sewell); *Linda* (1960, Don Sharp); *A Matter of Who* (1961, Don Chaffey); and *The Boys* (1961, Sidney Furie), in which she performed with one of her future producers, Tony Garnett. See White, with Thurlow (1982).

42   Peter Collinson's cinema version of *Up the Junction* would qualify as an example of a typical 'swinging London' film. For discussion of the cycle, see Carson (1998). On the kitchen-sink realist films see Hill (1986).

43 Though not quite the earliest British director to move from television to cinema, Loach is known in Britain for his movement between the two media. An earlier British director to move from television to cinema is Tony Richardson, like Loach, an Oxford alumnus. Ten years older than Loach, Richardson worked consistently for BBC TV throughout 1953 and 1954, before he co-directed (with Karel Reisz) *Momma Don't Allow* (1956) and his first feature film *Look Back in Anger* (1959), a version of which he had already directed for Granada TV's *Play of the Week* series on 28 November 1956. Examples of Richardson's early television work include two *Wednesday Theatre* productions: *Curtain Down* (tx: BBC, 21 January 1953), adapted by Nigel Kneale from a Chekov play, and *Box for One* (tx: BBC, 18 February 1953), written by Peter Brook. In 1968, when the financial backers for Loach's second feature film, *Kes* (1969), pulled out, Richardson, through Woodfall Films, used his relationship with United Artists to persuade them to fund its whole budget.

44 Nat Cohen interviewed in *Daily Cinema*, 1 November 1967: 12.

45 *Poor Cow* opened at the London Pavilion on 7 December 1967 and, despite blizzards, the following week's *Daily Cinema* (13 December 1967: 1) reported a very busy weekend – £5,400 in four days on one screen – under the head-line '*Poor Cow* already a smash hit'.

46 White herself was unhappy with the comparison: she recounts an experience at a press conference in New York, promoting *Poor Cow* in January 1968: "Are you worried about being labelled the 'new' Julie Christie?" someone asked. I replied: "Of course I'm not worried. Julie should be worried about me!" (White, with Thurlow 1982: 30).

47 On the critical reception of *Darling* and its portrayal of a 'good-time girl' see Tarr (1985).

48 See Anon. [J.A.D.] (1968) and Taylor (1967).

49 The letter is taken almost word for word from Dunn (1968: 46–47).

50 The presence of John Bindon connects *Poor Cow* to the 1960s glamorisation of the London criminal underworld that is such a pervasive ingredient of *Performance* (1970), in which Bindon plays Moody, the sidekick of the lead character, Chas (James Fox). Colin MacCabe writes about Loach's casting of Bindon, whom the director heard 'holding forth in a west London pub'. He cites Bindon's earlier career as a violent criminal who had spent a lot of time in prison, and who was convicted of murder towards the end of the 1970s. MacCabe notes Bindon's presence in *Poor Cow* by way of stating that Loach's *Up the Junction* and *Poor Cow* were the only precursors to *Performance*'s 'neo-realist representation of the London working-class'. However, MacCabe unfortunately seems to be referring inadvertently not to Loach's *Up the Junction*, but to Peter Collinson's *Up the Junction*, since he gives the date of Loach's BBC film as 1967 not 1965, and in describing Dunn's original book names the one feature that Loach and Dunn dropped completely from their *Wednesday Play*, the story which 'charted an upper-class Chelsea girl's investigation of the sexual and social possibilities offered by working-class Battersea' (MacCabe 1998: 43).

51 Jean-Luc Godard's *Une Femme Mariée* (1964) uses a similar technique. In the words of Chris Auty, it 'plays off fictional form (a day in the life of an adulterous wife) against documentary moments (face-on interviews in which characters lecture on abstracts like "Memory" and "Childhood")' (Auty 1999: 293).

CHAPTER THREE

1 Having read Barry Hines' first novel, *The Blinder*, Garnett arranged to see his second, *A Kestral for a Knave*, in proofs. In August 1967, he and Loach decided to film it. In spring 1968, after finishing *The Big Flame*, Loach began casting and setting up locations for *Kes* in Barnsley on a seven-week schedule during the school summer holidays in 1968. Loach and Roy Watts finished editing in early 1969, and it premiered at the London Film Festival on 19 and 22 November 1969, just after Loach had finished shooting *After a Lifetime*. It had a staggered release in England throughout 1970. For further details see: Stephenson (1973); Taylor (1970); and Walker (1974).

2 *Kes* was Chris Menges' first feature film as director of photography. Both he and *Kes*' composer, John Cameron, had worked in lesser capacities in the same departments on *Poor Cow*: Menges as camera operator, rather than director of photography, Cameron as musical director, rather than composer.

3 Loach on *Close-Up*, tx: BBC2, 2 November 1995.

4 Menges says of his work with Loach: 'I remember doing a television film for Ken Loach, *After a Lifetime*, where we had a quality control boss from Head Office on location in Liverpool dictating to us that we should use a certain exposure to get the high contrast, etc... Since *After a Lifetime*, made for LWT, Ken Loach has been working for the BBC [*Days of Hope* (1975) and *The Price of Coal* (1977)] and as they won't employ freelance cameramen I have been desperately trying to encourage both Ken Loach and Tony Garnett to work for an ITV company so that we can work together again' (Badder 1978: 75). See also Wyver (1983).

5 Interview with the author, 6 August 1998.

6   Ken Loach on *The South Bank Show*, tx: ITV, 3 October 1993. In 1994, Loach said: 'I try to keep the actors away from the camera as far as possible, not so that it looks like you're looking down a telescope but so that you're not crowding them. Also, I think the images are more sympathetic if you're slightly distanced. ... More observed. Rather than manoeuvring the performances, you sit back and observe what's happening' (Smith 1994: 63).

7   Hines interviewed by Paul Allen on *Kaleidoscope*, Radio 4, 17 July 1997.

8   The producer and director Leslie Woodhead describes the distinctive visual style of Loach's films: 'I suppose for anyone who's interested in that low-key, overheard photography, the person who's shown us all the right direction is Ken Loach. I've always loved the way his films look, and the astonishing visual and aesthetic self-confidence that allows him so boldly to put cameras in positions and stay with them even when it makes images which are, in any conventional terms, the very opposite of engaging. Just the power of the performances he then generates legitimises that ... I've certainly spent years trying to screw up my own courage to the point of that degree of self-effacement' (Leslie Woodhead quoted in Sussex (1988: 119–20).

9   Kestrel Films produced *After a Lifetime* for London Weekend Television (LWT), who transmitted it on network ITV, as an episode of *Sunday Night Theatre* on 18 July 1971 between 10.15pm and 11.30pm, less than two months after the BBC had broadcast *The Rank and File* as a *Play for Today*. Loach actually shot *After a Lifetime* before *The Rank and File*, in twelve days around Merseyside, between 20 and 31 October 1969. LWT and Kestrel disagreed about *After a Life-time*, because in March 1971, 18 months after the film's production, Garnett arranged a screening of the film for national press television critics. Some of these critics praised the film, and three months later it was shown. Production dates are from the script of *After a Lifetime* held at NFTVA; Neville Smith mentions the shooting location in Madden (1976). Smith began work in television as an actor on Loach's *Wear a Very Big Hat*, then in 1968 he co-wrote his first television film, Loach's *The Golden Vision*; he wrote Stephen Frears' first feature film, *Gumshoe* (1971) (also shot by Chris Menges), and collaborated with Stan Hey on Channel Four's series *The Manageress* (1989/1990).

10   Loach interviewed by Jeremy Isaacs on *Face to Face*, tx: BBC2, 19 September 1994.

11   In his autobiography Watt describes how he cast the leading characters in his drama documentary *North Sea* (1938) by casting extroverts, therefore 'potential actors', and people who looked the part (Watt 1974: 115–16).

12   The film's scene is more extended than its original in Hines (1969: 38).

13   Stephen Frears on *The South Bank Show*, tx: ITV, 3 October 1993.

14   This is used in Hines (1969: 48).

15   Hines (1969: 53–8).

16   Hines (1969: 85).

17   In the novel, Mrs Casper asks Billy to place Jud's bet at the start of the day that the novel describes (Hines 1969: 20–1).

18   'There was never an interest in getting actors to behave unnaturally, stylistically, for me; it was – perhaps you might take a series of stills, but you would still try to make the content of the still as realistic as possible, or the performance as authentic as possible.' Loach on *Face to Face*, tx. BBC2, 19 September 1994.

CHAPTER FOUR

1   Interview with the author, 6 August 1998. For an early assessment of Allen's work, including films that Loach did not direct, such as *The Spongers* (tx: BBC1, 24 January 1978), directed by Roland Joffé, see Madden (1981).

2   Allen became active in left-wing politics after he left the Merchant Navy in 1949. After a series of jobs he found work at Bradford Colliery in Manchester. In 1958 he joined the Revolutionary Communist Party, which later became the Socialist Labour League and later still became the Workers Revolutionary Party, led by Gerry Healy. From Bradford, together with two other SLL colleagues, Allen launched a political newspaper, *The Miner*. For this he was blacklisted in the mining industry. He left the SLL in the 1960s, and was expelled from the Labour Party. It was through the SLL that Loach, in the late 1960s, met Alan Thornett, the Cowley British Leyland shop steward who participated in his documentaries in the 1980s. See Slaughter (1999).

3   As Wrigley writes, 'The late 1960s and early 1970s were marked by inflation and by the return of massive mining disputes. In both cases those aggrieved took strike action to pressure the government into easing incomes policies in the public sector or more generally to affect collective bargaining. Alongside this there was substantial politicisation of industrial relations through proposals for legislation (*In Place of Strife*) and legislation (the Industrial Relations Act 1971)' (Wrigley 1997: 26). Laing (1997) provides an overview of the historical contexts for Loach's work, including the early 1970s.

4   Loach comments on Wilson, the 1960s and his first meeting with Allen in Fuller (1998: 10–12).

5   For an analysis of the background to the increasing militancy of the unions during the early 1970s see Hain (1986);

Wrigley (1997); and Cronin (1979).

6　For an account of the impact of the French *événements* on British film culture, see Harvey (1978).

7　Allen began his television career in January 1965 writing for Granada's *Coronation Street* for eighteen months. Kenith Trodd produced his first drama, *The Hard Word* (tx: BBC2, 16 May 1966), for *Thirty Minute Theatre*. *The Hard Word* was the first play directed by Ridley Scott, who like Loach was born in the late 1930s (30 November 1937) and learnt his trade directing for *Z Cars*. Scott directed 'Error of Judgement', written by Alan Plater (tx: BBC1, 9 June 1965). He left the BBC in the late 1960s to set up his own production company making advertisements. He later became famous for *The Duelists* (1977), *Alien* (1979), *Blade Runner* (1982) and others.

8　Rehearsal Script in BBC WAC File T5/695/4. Shooting schedule also referred to by Loach in an interview with Stewart Lane, *Morning Star*, 24 March 1968.

9　A BBC producer, Christopher Ralling, wrote an article (1968) criticising documentary drama. A month, later an anonymous article (1969) was published in the *Radio Times* which signalled management concerns about documentary drama. The following month *Radio Times* printed a collective letter of response from producers, writers and directors who worked for *The Wednesday Play*, including Tony Garnett, Jim Allen, Roy Battersby, Clive Goodwin, Ken Loach, James MacTaggart, Roger Smith and Kenith Trodd (Garnett *et al.* 1969). See also Petley (1997a).

10　Interview with the author, 30 May 1997.

11　*The Docks* held at the BBC WAC. The quotation reproduces all punctuation from the original.

12　Interview with the author, 30 May 1997.

13　Interview with the author, 30 May 1997.

14　Jim Allen said of this scene and of a similar one in *The Rank and File*: 'That came out of very personal experience. That was always happening to us, on strike. I've had that so many times, y'know, involved in strikes. So I thought I should get that dig in, y'know.' Interview with the author, 30 May 1997.

15　Williams points out that viewpoint is crucial to the production of meaning and that it is hypocritical for television news to pretend to be objective or transparent. Television news, Williams argues, shapes public opinion about incidents such as strikes: 'Oppositional elements who are outside the existing structures of representation have to find other ways to present their views: by petition or lobbying, directed towards representatives; or with much more difficulty, by actions and demonstrations directed towards the already 'represented' people. Characteristically, and in direct relation to the mediating nature of current television, many such efforts are governed by the attempt to become real – that is to say, to become present – in television terms' (Williams 1974: 52–3).

16　Jim Allen, interview with the author, 30 May 1997.

17　Allen told me that he wrote the script for *The Rank and File* in three weeks: when shooting commenced he was still writing the following day's scenes in the hotel on location. Kenith Trodd, then at Granada, agreed to produce *The Rank and File*; but halfway into pre-production Granada cancelled it. Graeme McDonald agreed to produce it for the BBC, on the condition that they change the name of the company from Pilkingtons to Wilkinson's, and shot in Stoke not St Helens. Interview with the author, 30 May 1997.

18　See Mills (1975). Loach has said that while Jim Allen did all the research and writing, Tony Garnett and himself were involved in the scripting. Interview with the author, 6 August 1998. Allen subsequently wrote a 'novelization' of *Days of Hope* (1975). He wrote it quickly, and was dissatisfied with it.

19　Glynn & Booth describe the coal industry of the 1920s as the 'cockpit of British industrial relations with a high proportion of disputes and total working days lost through disputes. The struggle for control in the coal industry became symbolic of the clash between labour and capital, supported by government, and coal was seen as by employers and workers in other industries as a test case, especially over wages.' (Glynn & Booth 1996: 104)

20　The Miners' Federation of Great Britain was established in 1889 and affiliated to the Labour Party in 1909. It was not a single union; indeed one was not created until 1945. It was a democratic organisation, whose leaders had to achieve the support of the miners in all key decisions. A belief in socialism only became dominant in miners' leaders after 1912, when the first national mining strike took place. Early Miners Federation leaders were Liberal, not Labour supporters. A demand for nationalisation was their prime aim not because they were socialists, but because the owners seemed incapable of modernising the industry. See Morris (1980: 110).

21　An earlier Royal Commission, headed by Justice Sankey, and including Beatrice and Sidney Webb on the committee, had recommended nationalization (not achieved until 1945). Lloyd George, leading a coalition government, rejected the report, and this prompted the 1921 Durham miners' lockout. By 1925, with many mines running at a loss, Baldwin commissioned another report from a committee led by Sir Herbert Samuel. The government gave a nine-month subsidy, which ended on 30 April 1926 when the owners locked out one million miners and offered new, reduced terms to them. *The Times* printed a letter from the Executive Committee of the Miners Federation, including the President, Herbert Smith, and the General Secretary, A. J. Cook: 'The miners note with regret that, although the Report of the Coal Commission was issued on March 6 1926 [the Samuel Report], the mine owners have only submitted a proposal for a national wage agreement and a national uniform minimum percentage so late as April 30 at 1.15pm, when at least two-thirds of the mine workers in the coalfield are already locked out by the coal owners' (Smith and Cook 1926: 14).

22 Interview with the author, 30 May 1997.

23 Interview with the author, 6 August 1998.

24 Morris 1980: 286.

25 Bennett, Boyd-Bowman, Mercer & Woollacott (1981) anthologises six articles on *Days of Hope* in its chapter on 'History, Politics and Classical Narrative', including McArthur and MacCabe's articles. Goodwin, Kerr & MacDonald (1983) includes substantial sections on the four films.

26 Caughie summarises and extends the 1970s realist debate in his chapter on 'The Rush of the Real: An Aesthetic of Immediacy' (2000: 88–124).

27 Jim Allen, William Deedes, Shaun Sutton, Sue Lawley discussion from *Tonight*, tx: BBC1, 2 October 1975, reprinted in Goodwin, Kerr & MacDonald (1983).

28 The Letters pages of *Radio Times* during the four weeks of broadcast contain examples of comments both for and against the serial, often from ex-soldiers, enlisted men and people involved with the General Strike. The BFI Library's Press Cuttings microfiche on *Days of Hope* contains a selection of differing professional opinions.

29 Anon. (1975b).

30 *After a Lifetime* uses a voice-over by Cardinal Bourne during the funeral of Billy. He states that there is no moral justification for the General Strike: 'It is a sin against the obedience which we owe to God for Catholics to support the strike. All are bound to uphold and assist the government, which is the lawfully constituted authority of the country.' Whether or not this is a genuine archive recording, its use is historically accurate. During the General Strike, Reith allowed the Roman Catholic Archbishop of Westminster, Cardinal Bourne, to broadcast on BBC Radio because he supported the government; yet he did not allow the Archbishop of Canterbury, who was sympathetic to the strikers, to broadcast. On the use of broadcasting during the General Strike, see: Scannell and Cardiff (1991: 32–33 and 108–13) and Briggs (1961: 360–84).

31 The OMS was not the official organisation of the government, although it received tacit support. The official organisation, which grew out of plans by J. C. C. Davidson, was the Cabinet Supply and Transport Committee, which, as Deputy Chief Civil Commisioner, Davidson ran during the General Strike.

32 Jim Allen, *Days of Hope-Episode 3*, Filming Script held by the NFTVA, 32.

33 See Jones (1969); James (1969); Citrine (1964); Thomas (1937); Boulton (1967). Boulton has a credit on *Days of Hope* under 'Additional Research', but according to Loach his contribution ended with his book and all the research was done by Allen. Boulton did, however, write a letter to *The Times*, 13 October 1975, defending the portrayal of the treatment of Conscientious Objectors in the first episode of *Days of Hope*.

34 Tribe (1977–78) continues the debate begun by McArthur and MacCabe. Tribe is wrong about much of *Days of Hope*; in particular, he fails to acknowledge Allen's research and writing, concluding: 'The veracity of the image thus conceals the "ahistorical" nature of the politics that is presented' (Tribe 1977–78: 17–18). Tribe takes a similar tack to McArthur, who also criticises *Days of Hope* for personalising complex historical events. McArthur writes: 'The effect – whether conscious or otherwise – of structuring historical drama round the lives of (usually famous) individual men and women is to suggest that history is made primarily by the individual interventions of men and women acting as free agents, rather than by the complex interplay of *classes, institutions* and *modes of production*' (McArthur 1978: 16).

35 Scripts for the first three episodes are held by the NFTVA.

36 Interview with the author, 6 August 1998.

37 See: 'Downing Street Meeting – Full Official Report', *The Times*, 13 May 1926, p. 2. Morris (1980: 333–7) describes the same meeting and cites the Cabinet Minutes in the Public Record Office, P.R.O. CAB 24/279.CP.195(26) and Bullock (1960).

38 Morris writes: 'Baldwin later said that the government had not been ready to face a strike in 1925. This has led to the subsidy being seen as an attempt to buy time. So it was, but mainly in order to guide public opinion on the issues involved' (Morris 1980: 151).

39 Morris (1980: 152) cites R. H. Desmarais, 'The British Government's Strike-Breaking Organization and Black Friday', *Journal of Contemporary History*, 1971. See also Laybourn (1993: 16-17) on the Supply and Transport Committee.

40 Morris (1980: 153). *Days of Hope* uses the premature printing of a poster that declares a State of Emergency and asks

for volunteers as an example of the government's provocation. During the first meeting between the General Council and Baldwin on the evening of 30 April 1926, before a State of Emergency has officially been called at midnight and before the strike begins on Monday 3 May, J. H. Thomas produces the poster and confronts Baldwin. Citrine (1964: 159) recalls the incident; Laybourn (1993: 41) discusses it. *Days of Hope* uses another similarly well-documented incident. After the TUC conference on Friday 30 April 1926, when all members voted to support the miners, the General Council continue to meet Baldwin over the weekend, without the Miners Federation leaders Smith and Cook. (The hostility between the Miners Federation and the General Council, especially between A. J. Cook and J. H. Thomas, who was widely distrusted by the miners, is documented in both Morris (1980) and Laybourn (1993).) Their efforts are brought to a close late on Sunday night when Baldwin is told that union members at the *Daily Mail* have refused to print Monday's paper because of an inflammatory anti-union editorial. The Cabinet protested about this so-called infringement of free speech and asked him to cease negotiations. Morris speculates that this may have been a plot between Churchill and the right-wing editor of the *Daily Mail*, Thomas Marlowe, a good friend of Churchill's, to bring things to a head. Morris (1980: 228–31). Citrine (1964: 171) records the *Daily Mail* incident and how it interrupted his and the General Council's meeting with Baldwin.

41   Walter Citrine was Acting Secretary of the General Council of the TUC in 1926, and in 1975, at the age of 88, he was one of the few of those involved still alive when *Days of Hope* was transmitted. *The Listener* interviewed him about *Days of Hope*. Perhaps unsurprisingly, his account differs from the contemporary accounts of Davidson and Jones, and the historical accounts of Morris and Laybourn: Citrine insists on calling the General Strike a 'national strike' and he defends Baldwin's government as 'having no power to *compel* the owners'. D. A. N. Jones concludes: 'all the same, none of us is compelled to accept the fictional Ben – always looking for the *exciting* left-wing thing to do – as the film's hero, nor the fictional Phil – the disillusioned idealist, gone stale ... *Days of Hope* is like a historical novel: one need not be Tory to appreciate Walter Scott' (Jones 1975: 459).

42   There was open animosity between the Miners Federation Secretary, Arthur Cook, and the General Council leader, J. H. Thomas. Thomas' role in 'Black Friday' and his actions over the Industrial Alliance were seen as sabotage and he was widely distrusted amongst the union rank and file. When he was President of the TUC in 1921, he refused to support the Durham miners during the lockout. According to Citrine, Cook told him that most miners suspected Thomas would trick them. Citrine (1964: 153) quoted in Morris (1980: 170).

43   On the day after the end of the General Strike, 13 May 1926, A.J. Cook writes in *The Times*: 'In regard to the TUC's decision to call off the general strike, that was decided without consulting the Miners Federation and we were party to it in no shape or form. The decision of the TUC has nothing to do with us, and our men will have to decide what they will do in the light of the present circumstances. Our stoppage may still continue for an indefinite period' (Cook 1926: 4).

44   Morris writes of this event: 'The discussion was interrupted by a phone call from Downing Street. The PM was waiting up, did the Council want to see him that evening? This phone call shows very clearly that someone must have leaked the news that the Council were on the verge of calling off the strike. After a few seconds' consultation, Citrine was instructed to say that the Council would call on Baldwin at noon the next day. As Citrine observed: "our fate was decided in those few seconds"' (Morris 1980: 269).

45   Jones (1969: 44–5).

46   In response to the criticism that *Days of Hope* blames the end of the strike on the betrayal by a TUC leader, Loach says: 'Well, it depends what one means by the word betrayal. It's an emotive word, and those at the top of the trade union movement who took the actions they did, wouldn't see it as a betrayal; they would see it as acting in the best interests of their members and saving them from acting unwisely. The fact remains that the strike was gathering strength; it was gathering momentum and all sorts of new questions were coming on the agenda' (O'Hara 1977: 300). Morris backs up Loach's claim that the strike was holding firm. She cites the government's own reports to the Cabinet. Morris (1980: 94–104 and 268). She writes of the collapse: 'Historians have found it difficult to reconcile the [TUC General] Council's fear of impending collapse with the known facts about the situation on the last two days of the strike. Indeed, the suggestion that strikers were returning to work on any significant scale was labelled a myth by the first academic historian of the strike [W.H. Crook, *The General Strike* (1931)]. Later evidence has confirmed the verdict. The Council's fears are more surprising because its own Intelligence Committee Reports showed that the strike was gaining momentum right up to the day it was called off' (Morris 1980: 94).

47   Interview with the author, 30 May 1997.

48   Caughie 1980: 30.

49   Laybourn (1993) endorses Morris (1980) (which confirms the accuracy of the events in *Days of Hope*). Laybourn agrees that the General Council, especially Thomas and Citrine, was opposed to the strike from the start, and that they

sought an end to the dispute with 'indecent haste' (Laybourn 1993: 78).

CHAPTER FIVE

1   Loach directed *The Price of Coal* from an original script by Barry Hines. Subtitled 'Two films set in South Yorkshire', it was Loach's last work for *Play for Today*. The first part is called 'Meet the People', subtitled 'A film for the Silver Jubilee'. It centres on a colliery that has been chosen for a royal visit by Prince Charles. The second part is called 'Back to Reality'. It follows an accident in the mine and how the community copes.

2   Daney & Oudart's (1973) detailed and appreciative analysis of *Family Life* possibly helped the film in France.

3   See Fuller (1998: 53).

4   Anon (1978: 1). In McAsh (1980) Loach explains that eventually the NFFC gave four-fifths of the £500,000 budget.

5   Wilson argues: '*Black Jack* does have a story to tell, but loses it in a thicket of naturalistic detail' (Wilson 1980: 126). See also Buscombe (1980); Pulleine (1980); Millar (1980); Tremois (1980); and Delmas (1980).

6   Throughout the 1970s Tony Garnett had produced other directors' work; notably, *The Spongers* (1978), written by Jim Allen and directed by Roland Joffé, and *Law and Order* (1978), written by G. F. Newman and directed by Les Blair. Following *Law and Order* and *Black Jack*, Garnett directed *Prostitute* (1980) in the UK. He then moved to America and directed *Handgun* (1982) in Dallas, about a woman who takes revenge on a man who rapes her. In 1990, after producing a handful of films in America, Garnett moved back to Britain. Throughout the 1990s Garnett produced a number of television series for the BBC, including *Between the Lines* (1993), *Cardiac Arrest* (1994), *This Life* (1995/96) and *The Cops* (1998–2001). For an overview of Garnett's career see Saynor (1993) and MacMurraugh-Kavanagh (1998).

7   Loach recounts how ATV Programme Controller Charles Denton first invited him to direct work for them (Fuller 1998: 56). Other key figures in ATV's documentary department, and key figures in Loach's working life throughout the 1980s, were ATV's Head of Documentaries, Richard Creasey, and documentary editor, later producer, Roger James. James produced most of Loach's documentaries during the 1980s.

8   ITC Entertainment production notes held on *The Gamekeeper* Microfiche at the BFI Library, London. See Eyquem (1980) and (1983).

9   In the 1960s and 1970s, when Loach directed work for the BBC, one-off television dramas or single plays could be distinguished from cinema feature films; since the early 1980s, as stronger ties have emerged between British television and cinema, aesthetic distinctions between one-off television dramas and feature films have blurred. Channel 4 took the lead in the 1980s with their *Film on 4* productions; the BBC followed this lead. Sue Summer comments on the efforts of BBC Films to produce theatrical features akin to those produced by *Film on 4*. She quotes the then Head of BBC Films, Mark Shivas, on television films: 'It's impossible to raise money to make them anymore. They are difficult to export and their cost is not hugely different from a modest budget feature. It's more profitable to put money into a feature film, where you can show the film as often as you like and also get a position in the profits, if any' (Summers 1996: 10). For background on Channel 4 see Brandt (1993); Pym (1992); Harvey (1994); Auty & Roddick (1985); Hill & McLoone (1996).

10 The history of the exhibition of *Looks and Smiles* reflects the relationship between cinema films and one-off television dramas in Britain in the early 1980s, before Channel 4's *Film on 4* strand transformed feature film production in Britain. Loach filmed *Looks and Smiles* in Sheffield, Barnsley and Bristol between 23 September 1980 and 6 November 1980. He delivered the edited film to Central (which had taken over ATV's franchise) in May 1981. During the same month, *Looks and Smiles* premiered at the Cannes Film Festival, where it jointly won the Contemporary Cinema Award. A French distribution company, MK2, then released it at cinemas in France in October 1981. In the UK, ITV screened it on Wednesday 19 May 1982 at 9.30pm; Artificial Eye released it at selected cinemas in Britain in December 1982. Production and release dates taken from: 'In Production', *Screen International*, 18 October 1980, 18; Assayas (1981); Preston (1982); and the Production Notes for *Looks and Smiles* held on Microfiche at the BFI Library, London. For an account of Channel 4's impact on UK feature film production, see Hill (1996).

11 Channel 4 helped to resurrect Loach's feature film career when they commissioned him to direct his first *Film on 4*, *Fatherland* (1986). It was a critical and commercial failure: Loach maintains that there was a mismatch between his direction and Trevor Griffiths' writing. He says: 'I'd rather lost touch with the sort of things that I used to do. After not having done any sort of cinema work for a bit, you get more desperate to do a film at all costs, and my judgment wasn't very good about it' (Hill 1997b: 163–4). Tulloch (1990) writes at length on *Fatherland*.

12 There has recently been a growth of interest in documentary. As well as Corner (1996), see Warren (1996); Plantinga (1997); Rothman (1997); Grant (1998). Both Corner and Rothman suggest that the recent growth in interest in documentaries may be a response to a long period of philosophical scepticism in academic film and television studies, during which the supposed ontological claims of documentary film-makers were seen as problematic for theory and historiography.

13 On Loach's camera technique, see Fuller (1998: 40–1). On the work of Jean Rouch, see Rothman (1997: 89–94).

14 As well as working with Loach on some very different looking films (compare, for example *Raining Stones* and *Carla's Song*), Ackroyd has revealed his versatility by photographing Carine Adler's *Under the Skin* (1997) and Rob Rohrer's *Bumping the Odds* (tx: BBC2, 7 December 1997). Appropriately, perhaps, in 1998 he photographed the fourth film directed by Chris Menges, *The Lost Son* (1999), starring Daniel Auteuil and Natassja Kinski. Mike Eley was co-photographer on *The Navigators* (2001).

15 See Kerr (1986: 148).

16 Barry Hines interviewed by Paul Allen, on *Kaleidoscope* Radio 4, 17 July 1997.

17 Rothman writes: 'In *cinéma-vérité* films, no assertions have absolute authority; words are spoken in particular ways by particular people to particular people on particular occasions for particular reasons. "Truth" is to be revealed, not asserted by a narrator whose authority is not to be questioned.' (Rothman 1997: 110)

18 Ken Loach in *The Gamekeeper* Press Release. Birmingham: Press Office, ATV Centre Birmingham, 1980. Held on microfiche at the BFI Library, London.

19 Fuller (1998: 58).

20 Furness (1982).

21 Press releases held on the *Questions of Leadership* microfiche at the BFI Library, London.

22 For a detailed account of *Questions of Leadership* and an account of its censorship see Petley (1984). For an account of all Loach's problems with censorship see Petley (1997b). For an account of the period during which Loach made his documentaries see Laing (1997). For Loach's own account of *Questions of Leadership* see Fuller (1998: 66–72).

23 For a full account see Petley (1997b).

24 Loach met Alan Thornett in the late 1960s at meetings of the Socialist Labour League (formerly the Revolutionary Communist Party, later the Workers' Revolutionary Party), which was then led by Gerry Healy. Thornett was expelled from the SLL (WRP) in 1974. He gives an account of his expulsion in Thornett (1979). Thornett was also President of Oxford and District Trades Union Council and a senior shop steward at British Leyland's Cowley plant, where he worked from 1959 until 1982. Thornett has written a book chronicling his experiences at the Cowley British Leyland plant, for which Loach wrote the foreword (Thornett 1998). Loach's foreword is also available on-line. Available HTTP http://www.internationalen.se/sp/rev5bhtm (7 January 2000).

25 Jones (1986) gives a useful account of how, in the late 1970s and early 1980s, people like Michael Edwardes and Ian MacGregor, as well as union leaders like Arthur Scargill, President of the National Union of Mineworkers, used the media as a central part of their strategy.

26 On the basic programme of the Trotskyist movement – the 'Transitional Programme of the Fourth International' – see Thornett (1987: 76–81).

CHAPTER SIX

1 There was a small, but vocal protest against *Hidden Agenda* from conservative newspaper critics, first at the 1990 Cannes Film Festival, then in Britain. See Petley (1997a).

2 Sally Hibbin produced *Riff-Raff, Raining Stones, Ladybird Ladybird*, and *Carla's Song*. Rebecca O'Brien produced *Land and Freedom, The Flickering Flame, My Name is Joe, Another City, Bread and Roses* and *The Navigators*.

3 G. Smith (1994) and Eaton (1993).

4 See Nowell-Smith (1967: 15) on Luchino Visconti's *Ossessione*.

5 There were five weeks pre-production from mid-August until 20 September 1992, five weeks production from 20 September until 23 October 1992, and 16 weeks post-production from October 1992 until February 1993. It premiered at Cannes in May 1993, and was released in the UK on 7 October 1993. Dates taken from *Raining Stones* production files at Parallax, London.

6 Fax from Ken Loach to composer Stewart Copeland, 'Thoughts on Music Cues', 8 January 1993. Held in *Raining Stones* production files.

7 Fax from Ken Loach to Stewart Copeland, 'Further Thoughts for *Raining Stones*', 13 January 1993. Held in *Raining Stones* production files.

8 Fax from Loach to Copeland, 'Further Thoughts for *Raining Stones*', 13 January 1993.

9 Barry Ackroyd, 1993, *Raining Stones* production notes, held on *Raining Stones* microfiche at BFI Library, London. On *Raining Stones*, they used a fast film stock for Super 16mm cameras and then processed the footage on 35mm. Ackroyd (he serves as camera operator and director of photography) has said how he most often uses Eastman EXR 200T film 5293 and EXR 500T film 5298 because, 'it's got such good latitude you can shoot in very low light levels' (Ackroyd 1996: 17).

10 Sally Hibbin also says that the shooting ratio can be as high as 25:1 in Dobson (1993: 25). The total footage shot for *Raining Stones* was 86,230 ft (418 set-ups in 28 days). The length of the finished film is 8,153 ft or 91 minutes. Therefore, the average ratio is 10:1. Total footage and setups taken from *Raining Stones* Progress Report No.28, 23 October 1992. Finished film length taken from Turner (1993: 50).

11 Sally Hibbin speaking at the NFT 27 September 1994, with Rona Munro and Crissy Rock. I have read three drafts of Jim Allen's script: as in *The Big Flame* and *Days of Hope*, the actors speak the dialogue as it is written.

12 Saada (1993: 62).

13 An early scene in Luchino Visconti's *Ossessione* features a similar kind of camera and narrative movement, although it is a reverse movement, one that picks out the individual hero for us. As Bragana (Juan de Landa) stands talking to two truck drivers who have just pulled a drifter, Gino (Massimo Girotti), from their truck, the camera cranes up from the three men, over the truck, and focuses attention on Gino, whose back we see as he wanders into Bragana's *trattoria* and the life of Bragana's wife, Giovanna (Clara Calamai). In *Ossessione* the camera introduces us to Gino as if it is momentarily distracted from focusing on Bragana and his two customers; in its distraction the camera finds a story in the world. In *Raining Stones* the camera introduces us to the mother as if it too is momentarily distracted by events in the world: yet in both films the movement also alerts us to the hand of the director, carefully guiding our views of these worlds.

14 Smith, G. (1994: 59).

15 Jim Allen mentioned his lapsed Catholicism when talking about the first book he ever read, when he was in prison aged 21, in 1947. 'But he [a fellow inmate] talked to me about Jack London and he give me this book, *The Iron Heel*. So I sit in my cell, only one in a cell in those days. But I couldn't understand the words. So I'm back in and he give me a dictionary. But anyway he lit a light in a corner. And er, he said, go on, keep out of trouble, and blah, blah, blah. So I was a socialist. And then I came out. And the first collision was with the Church. And I walked out the church; long story.' Interviewed by the author, 30 May 1997.

16 Sarler (1994).

17 Smith, P. (1994); Allen (1994); Sally Hibbin speaking at the National Film Theatre, 27 September 1994.

18 'Susan' (1994).

19 Sally Hibbin spoke at the National Film Theatre on 27 September 1994. The treatment is in *Ladybird Ladybird* 'Early Draft' files, held at Parallax, London.

20 Fred Fever (1994), a man brought up in care, described the film as accurate, while social worker Mary Black (1994) argued that the film was inaccurate.

21 Walker (1993: 73) gives the adaptation of John Steinbeck's novel, *East of Eden*, by Paul Osborn and Elia Kazan as an example of how a long, discursive and detailed novel is turned into a 1950s Hollywood melodrama.

22 Neale (1986: 6–7).

23 See also Kaplan (1992).

24 Rona Munro speaking at the National Film Theatre, 27 September 1994.

25 Ciment (1994: 11).

26 All Loach's comments are taken from an early draft of the script. The script is not dated, but three later drafts, from which these scenes are cut, are dated 16 March 1993, 4 July 1993 and 18 August 1993. Scripts held at Parallax.

27 Pye (2000).

28 In a similar scene in an early draft of the script, Maggie's neighbours comment on her relationship with Simon after he has beaten her. In one flashback two neighbours have a long conversation about whether or not to report them or interfere. In his comments to Munro, Loach has written, sensitive to the possibilities of overstatement: 'Not sure this is needed – neighbours watching or listening will tell us as much.'

29 In another article, Caughie invokes the difference between the 'aesthetic logic' of *Cathy Come Home* and that of *Ladybird Ladybird*; yet, confessing that this 'logic' is 'extremely difficult to pin down' (Caughie 1996: 220), he makes little attempt to discuss it. Caughie also compares *Cathy Come Home* and *Ladybird Ladybird* as television event and art cinema, arguing that the latter entails a loss of national specificity (Caughie 1996: 219–21).

30 Undated treatment, p.4, held in *Land and Freedom* Script Files at Parallax, London.

31 These comments are from an eight-page fax sent by Ken Loach to Jim Allen on 9 January 1992, in which he comments on the second draft of *May Days* (*Land and Freedom*). *Land and Freedom* Script Files at Parallax, London.

32 Fax from Ken Loach to Jim Allen, 9 January 1992. *Land and Freedom* Script Files at Parallax, London.

33 Allen wrote the first draft of *Land and Freedom*, then called *May Days*, in early 1991. In a memo to Allen, Loach comments on this draft. Memo held in *Land and Freedom* Early Draft files, at Parallax Pictures, London. The note is not dated but it is placed next to scripts titled *May Days*, which indicate that it may be late 1991 or early 1992, when John Daly at Hemdale was still developing the film with Loach and Allen.

34 Fax from Ken Loach to Jim Allen, 9 January 1992. *Land and Freedom* production files at Parallax Films, London.

CONCLUSION

1 Walker (1982: 2 and 14).

2 Morrow (1974: 109). See also Preston (1996a: 181).

3 Esenwein and Shubert (1995). Letter to the author from George Esenwein, 15 March 2000.

4 See Cesarani (1997) and Braham (2000).

5 Interview with the author, 30 May 1997.

6 Durgan, *Land and Freedom*'s historical advisor, gives these details in Durgan (1996). See also Durgan (1999).

7 See Thomas (2001) on the ways in which Hollywood film melodramas use space to construct complex meanings.

8 Swallow and Lawson (1990).

9 Joe Ashton on *A Week in Politics*, tx: Channel 4, 25 February 1995, which showed the lobbying of the Heritage Select Committee in December 1994. VHS copy held by the NFTVA.

FILMOGRAPHY

Filmography of work directed by Ken Loach with writer in brackets. Both Graham Fuller's *Loach on Loach* and George McKnight's *Agent of Challenge and Defiance* contain full filmographies.

1964
Teletale: 'Catherine' (Roger Smith). BBC2, 24 January.
Z Cars: 'Profit by their Example' (John Hopkins and Robert Barr). BBC1, 12 February.
Z Cars: 'A Straight Deal' (Robert Barr). BBC1, 11 March 1964.
Z Cars: 'The Whole Truth' (Robert Barr). BBC1, 8 April 1964.
The Diary of A Young Man (Troy Kennedy Martin and John McGrath).
Episode 1 – 'Survival or They Came to the City'. BBC1, 8 August.
Episode 3 – 'Marriage'. BBC2, 22 August.
Episode 5 – 'Life or a Girl Called Fred'. BBC1, 5 September.

1965
The Wednesday Play: A Tap on the Shoulder (James O'Connor). BBC1, 6 January.
The Wednesday Play: Wear a Very Big Hat (Eric Coltart). BBC1, 17 February.
The Wednesday Play: Three Clear Sundays (James O'Connor). BBC1, 7 April.
The Wednesday Play: Up the Junction (Nell Dunn). BBC1, 3 November.
The Wednesday Play: The End of Arthur's Marriage (Christopher Logue). BBC1, 17 November.
The Wednesday Play: The Coming Out Party (James O'Connor). BBC1, 22 December.

1966
The Wednesday Play: Cathy Come Home (Jeremy Sandford). BBC1, 16 November.

1967
The Wednesday Play: In Two Minds (David Mercer). BBC1, 1 March.
Poor Cow (Nell Dunn).

1968
The Wednesday Play: The Golden Vision (Neville Smith). BBC1, 17 April.

1969
The Wednesday Play: The Big Flame (Jim Allen). BBC1, 19 February.
Kes (Barry Hines).
In Black and White aka *The Save the Children Fund Film* (Ken Loach). LWT, not transmitted.

1971
Family Life (David Mercer).
Play For Today: The Rank and File (Jim Allen). BBC1, 20 May.
Sunday Night Theatre: After a Lifetime (Neville Smith). ITV, 18 July.
Talk About Work (Ken Loach). Central Office of Information, never shown.

1973
Full House: A Misfortune (Ken Loach, adaptation of Anton Chekhov). BBC2, 13 January.

1975
Days of Hope (Jim Allen).
Episode 1 – '1916 Joining Up'. BBC1, 11 September.
Episode 2 – '1921'. BBC1, 18 September.
Episode 3 – '1924'. BBC1, 25 September.
Episode 4 – '1926 General Strike'. BBC1, 2 October.

1977
Play For Today: The Price of Coal (Barry Hines).
Episode 1 – 'Meet The People'. BBC1, 29 March.
Episode 2 – 'Back to Reality'. BBC1, 5 April.

1979
Black Jack (Ken Loach).

1980
The Gamekeeper (Barry Hines). ITV, 16 December.
Auditions. ITV, 23 December.

1981
A Question of Leadership (Barry Hines). ATV, 13 August.

1982
Looks and Smiles (Barry Hines). ITV, 19 May.

1983
Questions of Leadership. Central TV, not transmitted.
The Red and the Blue: Impressions of Two Political Conferences. Channel 4, 1 October.

1985
Which Side Are You On? Channel 4, 9 January.
Diverse Reports: The End Of The Battle ... Not The End Of The War (Editor Ken Loach, director Philip Clark). Channel 4, 27 March.

1986
Fatherland (Trevor Griffiths).

1989
Split Screen: Time To Go. BBC2, 9 May.
The Eleventh Hour: The View From The Woodpile. Channel 4, 12 June.

1990
Hidden Agenda (Jim Allen).

1991
Riff-Raff (Bill Jesse).
Dispatches: The Arthur Legend. Channel 4, 22 May.

1993
Raining Stones (Jim Allen).

1994
Ladybird Ladybird (Rona Munro).

1995
Land and Freedom (Jim Allen).

A Contemporary Case for Common Ownership. Defend Clause IV Campaign Video.

1996
Carla's Song (Paul Laverty).
The Flickering Flame: A Story of Contemporary Morality. BBC2, 18 December.

1998
My Name is Joe (Paul Laverty).
Another City: A Week in the Life of Bath's Football Club. HTV, 23 April.

2000
Bread and Roses (Paul Laverty).

2001
The Navigators (Rob Dawber). Channel 4, 2 December.

BIBLIOGRAPHY

A fuller listing of newspaper and magazine articles on Loach can be found in George McKnight's *Agent of Challenge and Defiance: The Films of Ken Loach* (1997).

Ackroyd, B. (1996) 'The Ken Loach Approach – and How to Film It', *InCamera*, Spring, 16–17.

Adorno,T., W. Benamin, E. Bloch, B. Brecht and G. Lukacs (1995) *Aesthetics and Politics*. London: Verso, first published 1977.

Akomfrah, J. (1994) 'For a Richer Vision of Poverty', *Vertigo*, 1, 3, Spring, 43–4.

Alba, V. and S. Schwartz (1988) *Spanish Marxism versus Soviet Communism: A History of the P.O.U.M.* New Brunswick and Oxford: Transaction Books.

Allen, C. (1994) 'A Social Sledgehammer', *The Times*, 26 September, 15.

Allen, J. (1975) *Days of Hope*. London: Futura Books.

Allen, R. (1995) *Projecting Illusion: Film Spectatorship and the Impression of Reality*. Cambridge: Cambridge University Press.

Andrews, N. (1993) 'Simply Horribly Funny', *Financial Times*, 7 October, 21.

Anon. (1926) [Editorial], *The Times*, 7 May, 3.

Anon. [J.A.D.] (1968) '*Poor Cow*', *Monthly Film Bulletin*, 35, 409, February 23.

Anon. (1969) 'Keeping Faith with the Viewer', *Radio Times*, 16 January, 4.

Anon. (1970) 'Tony Garnett Interviewed', *Afterimage*, 1, 1, April, 48–57.

Anon. (1975a) 'Does the Bias Run Both Ways?', *The Times*, 30 September, 13.

Anon. (1975b) 'History and the BBC', *The Daily Telegraph*, 27 September, 14.

Anon. (1978) 'French pull out of *Black Jack*', *Screen International*, 11 November, 1.

Armes, R. (1978) *A Critical History of British Cinema*. London: Secker and Warburg.

Arendt, H. (1994) *Eichmann in Jerusalem: A Report on the Banality of Evil*. Harmondsworth: Penguin; first published 1963.

Assayas, O. (1981) 'Le Gentil Proletaire', *Cahiers du cinéma*, 328, October, 60–1.

Aude, F. (1993) '*Raining Stones*: La Fierté de Bob', *Positif*, 392, October, 1517.

Auty, C. (1999) '*Une Femme Mariée*', in J. Pym (ed.) *Time Out Film Guide*. Harmondsworth: Penguin, 293.

Auty, M. and N. Roddick (eds) (1985) *British Cinema Now*. London: BFI.

Aziz, C. (1987a) 'Shoulder to Shoulder', *The Observer*, 22 March, 23.

—— (1987b) 'Soul Searching: Ken Loach and Trevor Griffiths Interviewed', *City Limits*, 26 March, 14–15.

Badder, D. (1978) 'Frears and Company: Conversations with Stephen Frears,

Baker, S. and O. Terris (1994) *A for Andromeda to Zoo Time: The Television Holdings of the NFTVA 1936–1979*. London: BFI.

Bakewell, M. (1966) 'The Producer and the Television Play', *The Listener*, 7 July, 9–10.

Barnett, A., J. McGrath, J. Mathews and P. Wollen (1976) 'Tony Garnett and Ken Loach Interview: *Family Life* in the Making', *Jump Cut* 10/11, June, 43–5, first published in *7 Days*, 12 January 1972.

Barr, C. (1975) 'Approaching Television', *Movie*, 20, Spring, 26–8.

—— (1984) 'A Conundrum for England', *Monthly Film Bulletin*, 51, 607, August, 234–5.

—— (1986) 'Television on Television', *Sight and Sound*, 55, 3, Summer, 157–9.

—— (ed.) (1992a) *All Our Yesterdays: 90 Years of British Cinema*. London: BFI; first published 1986.

—— (1992b) 'Broadcasting and Cinema 2: Screens within Screens', in C. Barr (ed.) *All Our Yesterdays: 90 Years of British Cinema*. London: BFI; first published 1986, 206–24.

—— (1996) '"They Think It's All Over": The Dramatic Legacy of Live Television', in J. Hill and M. McLoone (eds) *Big Picture, Small Screen: The Relations Between Film and Television*. Luton: University of Luton Press, 47–75.

Barry, M. (1960) *The Television Playwright*. London: Michael Joseph.

—— (1992) *From the Palace to the Grove*. London: Royal Television Society.

Bazin, A. (1967) *What is Cinema?: Volume I*. Trans. Hugh Gray. Berkeley and London: University of California Press.

—— (1971) *What is Cinema?: Volume II*. Trans. Hugh Gray. Berkeley and London: University of California Press.

Bennett A., B. Tufano and C. Menges', *Sight and Sound*, 47, 2, Spring, 70–5.

Bennett, T., S. Boyd-Bowman, C. Mercer and J. Woollacott (eds) (1981) *Popular Television and Film*. London: BFI.

Birch, H. (1993) 'Ken Loach: Very British Director', *Empire*, November, 59.

Bird, L. (1958) '"New and Original" is the theme for drama', *TV Times*, 12 September, 9.

Black, M. (1994) 'My Doubts on the Story', *The Guardian, Society*, 12 October, 3.

Black, P. (1972) *The Mirror in the Corner: People's Television*. London: Hutchinson.

Bolloten, B. (1991) *The Spanish Civil War: Revolution and Counter-Revolution*. Hemel Hempstead: Harvester Wheatsheaf.

Booker, C. (1969) *The Neophiliacs*. London: Collins.

Boulton, D. (1967) *Objection Overruled*. London: MacGibbon and Kee.

Braham, R. L. (2000) *The Politics of Genocide: The Holocaust in Hungary*. Detroit: Wayne State University Press; first published 1981.

Brandt, G. W. (ed.) (1981) *British Television Drama*. Cambridge: Cambridge University Press.

—— (ed.) (1993) *British Television Drama in the 1980s*. Cambridge: Cambridge University Press.

Bratton, J., J. Cook and C. Gledhill (eds) (1994) *Melodrama: Stage, Picture, Screen*. London: BFI.

Bream, P. (1972) 'Spreading Wings at Kestrel: Interview with Loach and Garnett', *Films and Filming*, 18, 6, March, 36–40.

Briggs, A. (1961) *The Birth of Broadcasting*. London: Oxford University Press.

—— (1995) *The History of Broadcasting in the UK: Volume 5: Competition 1955–1974*. Oxford: Oxford University Press.

Britton, A. (1978–79) 'The Ideology of *Screen*', *Movie*, 26, Winter, 2–28.

—— (1982) 'Metaphor and Mimesis: *Madame De …*', *Movie* 29/30, Summer, 91–107.

—— (1988) 'The Myth of Postmodernism: The Bourgeois Intelligentsia in the Age of Reagan', *CineAction!*, 13/14, Summer, 3–17.

—— (1988–89) 'The Philosophy of the Pigeonhole: Wisconsin Formalism and "The Classical Style"', *CineAction!*, 15, Winter, 47–63.

—— (1992) 'A New Servitude: Bette Davis, *Now Voyager* and the Radicalism of the Woman's Film', *CineAction!*, 26/27, January, 32–59.

Brooks, P. (1976) *The Melodramatic Imagination*. New Haven and London: Yale University Press.

Brown, R. (1983a) 'Continuing … the State of Things', *Monthly Film Bulletin*, 50, 588, January, 11.

—— (1983b) '*Looks and Smiles*', *Monthly Film Bulletin* 50, 588, January, 10.

Brunsdon, C. (1981) '*Crossroads* – Notes on Soap Opera', *Screen*, 22, 4, Winter, 32–7.

—— (1990) 'Problems with Quality', *Screen*, 31, 1, Spring, 67–90.

—— (1997) *Screen Tastes: Soap Opera to Satellite Dishes*. London and New York: Routledge.

Bullock, A. (1960) *The Life and Times of Ernest Bevin*. London: Heinemann.

Burch, N. (1990) *Life to those Shadows*. Trans. Ben Brewster. London: BFI.

Buscombe, E. (1980) 'Mannerism, But with Its Heart in the Right Place', *Tribune*, 29 February, 6–7.

—— (ed.) (1981) *Granada: The First Twenty-Five Years, BFI Dossier 9*. London: BFI.

—— (1991) 'All Bark and No Bite: The Film Industry's Response to Television', in J. Corner (ed.) *Popular Television in Britain*. London: BFI, 197–207.

—— (ed.) (2000) *British Television: A Reader*. Oxford: Clarendon Press.

Butler, A. (1992) 'New Film Histories and the Politics of Location', *Screen*, 33, 4, Winter, 413–26.

Carr, E. H. (1985) *What is History?*. Harmondsworth: Penguin; first published 1961.

Carson, B. (1998) 'Comedy, Sexuality and "Swinging London" Films', *Journal of Popular British Cinema*, 1, 48–62.

Casey, A. (1963) 'Blood without Thunder', *Screen Education*, 16, September–October, 25–8.

Caughie, J. (1980) 'Progressive Television and Documentary Drama', *Screen*, 21, 3, Autumn, 9–35.

—— (1981) 'Rhetoric, Pleasure and Art Television', *Screen*, 22, 4, Winter, 9–31.

—— (1984) 'Television Criticism', *Screen*, 25, 4–5, July–October, 109–22.

—— (1991a) 'Adorno's Reproach: Repetition, Difference and Television Genre', *Screen* 32, 2, Summer, 127–53.

—— (1991b) 'Before the Golden Age: Early Television Drama', in J. Corner (ed.) *Popular Television in Britain*. London: BFI, 22–41.

—— (1992) 'Broadcasting and Cinema 1: Converging Histories', in C. Barr (ed.) *All Our Yesterdays: 90 Years of British Cinema*. London: BFI; first published 1986, 189–205.

—— (1996) 'The Logic of Convergence', in J. Hill and M. McLoone (eds) *Big Picture, Small Screen: The Relations between Film and Television*. Luton: University of Luton Press, 215–223.

—— (2000) *Television Drama: Realism, Modernism and British Culture*. Oxford: Oxford University Press.

Cavell, S. (1979) *The World Viewed: Reflections on the Ontology of Film, Enlarged Edition*. Cambridge, Mass: Harvard Unversity Press.

—— (1995) *Must We Mean What We Say?* Cambridge: Cambridge University Press; first published 1969.

—— (1996) *Contesting Tears: The Hollywood Melodrama of the Unknown Woman*. Chicago and London: University of Chicago Press.

Cesarani, D. (ed.) (1997) *Genocide and Rescue: The Holocaust in Hungary 1944*. Oxford: Berg.

Christie, I. (1995) 'Film for a Spanish Republic', *Sight and Sound*, 5, 10, October, 36–7.

Ciment, M. (1994) 'Entretien avec Ken Loach: Le sentiment de l'inéluctable', *Positif*, 404, October, 8–12.

Citrine, W. (1964) *Men and Work: An Autobiography*. London: Hutchinson.

Clarke, J., C. Critcher and R. Johnson (eds) (1979) *Working-Class Culture: Studies in History and Theory*. London: Hutcinson.

Combs, R. (1994) 'Loach interviewed by Richard Combs', *The Guardian 2*, 6 January, 6–7.

Cook, A. J. (1926) 'Letter to the Editor', *The Times*, 13 May 1926, 4.

Cook, P. (ed.) (1985) *The Cinema Book*. London: BFI.

Cornell, P., M. Day and K. Topping (eds) (1996) *The Guinness Book of Classic British Television*. Enfield: Guinness.

Corner, J. (ed.) (1991) *Popular Television in Britain*. London: BFI.

—— (1995) *Television Form and Public Address*. London: Edward Arnold.

—— (1996) *The Art of Record: A Critical Introduction to Documentary*. Manchester and New York: Manchester University Press.

Cronin, J. E. (1979) *Industrial Conflict in Modern Britain*. London: Croom Helm.

Daney, S. and J-P. Oudart (1973) 'Sur *Family Life* (de Kenneth Loach)', *Cahiers du cinema*, 244, February, 44–8.

Davies, B. (1970) '*Kes*', *Monthly Film Bulletin*, 37, 435, April, 74–5.

Delmas, C. (1980) 'Un Grand Ken Loach Pour les Enfants', *Jeune Cinéma*, 125, March, 35–7.

Dixon, W. W. (ed.) (1994) *Re-Viewing British Cinema 1900–1992*. Albany: State University of New York Press.

Dobson, P. (1993) '*Raining Stones*', *Screen International*, 15 October, 25.

Dunn, N. (1962a) 'Out with the Girls', *New Statesman*, 18 May, 708–9.

—— (1962b) 'The Clip Joint', *New Statesman*, 28 December, 925–6.

—— (1963) 'Death of an Old Scrubber', *New Statesman*, 5 April, 487–8.

—— (1966) *Up the Junction*. London: Pan; first published 1963.

—— (1968) *Poor Cow*. London: Pan Books; first published 1967.

Durgan, A. (1996) 'The Hidden Story of the Revolution', *New Politics* 6, 1, Summer. On–line. Available HTTP: http://www.wpunj.edu/~newpol/issue21/durgan21.html (7 January 2000).

—— (1999) 'Freedom Fighters or Comintern Army? The International Brigades in Spain', *International Socialism Journal* 84, Autumn. On–line. Available HTTP: http://www.littleprints.free–online.co.uk/pubs/isj84/durgan.htm (11 January 2000).

Durgnat, R. (1970) *A Mirror for England: British Movies from Austerity to Affluence*. London: Faber and Faber.

Dyer, R. (ed.) (1981) *Coronation Street*. London: BFI.

Eaton, M. (1993) 'Writer's Block: Not a Piccadilly Actor in Sight', *Sight and Sound*, 3, 12, December, 32–3.

Ellis, J. (1981) *Visible Fictions: Cinema: Television: Video*. London: Routledge.

Elsaesser, T. (1987) 'Tales of Sound and Fury: Observations on the Family Melodrama', in C. Gledhill (ed.) *Home is Where the Heart Is: Studies in Melodrama and the Women's Film*. London: BFI, 43–69.

Elsaesser, T. and A. Barker (eds) (1990) *Early Cinema: Space Frame Narrative*. London: BFI.

Esenwein, G. and A. Shubert (1995) *Spain at War: The Spanish Civil War in Context*. London and New York: Longman.

Eyquem, O. (1980) '*The Gamekeeper* et *Prostitute*', *Positif*, 232/233, July, 76–7.

Fever, F. (1994) 'The Trouble', *The Guardian, Society*, 12 October, 2–3.

Fiske, J. and J. Hartley (1978) *Reading Television*. London: Methuen.

Franke, L. (1993) 'In the Frame: An Interview with Sally Hibbin', *FACT* 20, June, 10–12.

—— (1994) '*Ladybird Ladybird*', *Sight and Sound*, 4, 10, October, 46–7.

Friedman, L. (ed.) (1993) *British Cinema and Thatcherism*. Minneapolis: University of Minnesota Press.

Fudge, R. (1976) 'Speaking Directly to the People', *Jump Cut*, 10/11, June, 41–5.

Fuller, G. (ed.) (1998) *Loach on Loach*. London: Faber and Faber.

Fulton, M. (ed.) (1988) *Eyes of Time: Photojournalism in America*. New York: Little, Brown.

Furness, A. (1982) 'Young and In Love ... and Out of Work', *TV Times*, 15 May, 8–12.

Furst, L. R. and P. N. Skrine (1971) *Naturalism*. London: Methuen.

Galbraith, J. K. (1970) *The Affluent Society*. Harmondsworth: Penguin; first published 1958.

Gard, E. (1989) *Trade Unions in Britain*. Cambridge: Cambridge University Press.

Gardner, C. and J. Wyver (1983) 'The Single Play: From Reithian Reverence to Cost-Accounting and Censorship', *Screen* 24: 4–5, July–October, 114–29.

Garfield, L. (1971) *Black Jack*. Harmondsworth: Puffin; first published 1968.

Garnett, T. (1969) '*The Big Flame*', *Radio Times*, 13 February, 35.

Garnett, T., J. Allen, R. Battersby, C. Goodwin, K. Loach, J. MacTagart, R. Smith and K. Trodd (1969) 'Keeping Faith with the Viewer: A Letter to the Editor', *Radio Times*, 13 February, 2.

Garnett, T., J. Gould and R. Hudson (1972) 'Television in Britain: Description and Dissent', *Theatre Quarterly*, 2, 6, April–June, 18–25.

Gilbert, W. S. (1995) *Fight and Kick and Bite: The Life and Work of Dennis Potter*. London: Hodder and Stoughton.

Gledhill, C. (ed.) (1987) *Home is Where the Heart is: Studies in Melodrama and the Women's Film*. London: BFI.
Glynn, S. and A. Booth (1996) *Modern Britain: An Economic and Social History*. London: Routledge.
Goodwin, A., P. Kerr and I. MacDonald (1983) *Drama-Documentary, BFI Dossier 19*. London: BFI.
Goodwin, A. and G. Whannel (1990) *Understanding Television*. London: Routledge.
Grant, B. K. (ed.) (1986) *Film Genre Reader*. Austin: University of Texas Press.
Grant, B. K. and J. Sloniowski (eds) (1998) *Documenting the Documentary: Close Readings of Documentary Film and Video*. Detroit: Wayne State University Press.
Grant, D. (1970) *Realism*. London: Methuen.
Grant, S. (1987) 'No Place like Home: Interview with Trevor Griffiths on *Fatherland*', *Time Out*, 25 March–1 April, 24–6.
—— (1991) 'Troubles Shooter', *Time Out*, 2–9 January, 24–6.
Greene, H. C. (1969) *The Third Floor Front: A View of Broadcasting in the Sixties*. London: The Bodley Head.
Grierson, J. (1963) 'Grierson on Television', Contrast, 2, 4, Summer, 220–9.
The John Grierson Project, McGill University (1984) *John Grierson and the NFB*. Toronto: ECW Press.
Guard, C. (1995) 'Private View: *Riff-Raff*, Sight and Sound, 5, 1, January, 69.
Hacker, J. (1991) 'Discussion with Ken Loach', in J. Hacker and D. Price (eds) *Take Ten: Contemporary British Film Directors*. Oxford: Clarendon Press, 292–303.
Hain, P. (1986) *Political Strikes: The State and Trade Unionism in Britain*. Harmondsworth: Penguin.
Hall, J. (1991) 'Realism as a style in *cinéma-vérité*', *Cinema Journal*, 30, 4, Summer, 24–50.
Hammond, W. (1993) 'Estate of the Art', *Time Out*, 6 October, 22.
Hardy, F. (1979) *John Grierson: A Documentary Biography*. London: Faber and Faber.
Harvey, S. (1978a) *Independent Cinema?*. Stafford: West Midlands Arts.
—— (1978b) *May '68 and Film Culture*. London: BFI.
—— (1994) 'Channel 4 TV: From Annan to Grade', in S. Hood (ed.) *Behind the Screens: The Structure of British Television in the Nineties*. London: Lawrence and Wishart, 102–32.
Haskell, M. (1987) *From Reverence to Rape: The Treatment of Women in the Movies*. Chicago and London: University of Chicago Press.
Hattenstone, S. (1994) 'Rock Steady', *The Guardian 2*, 29 September, 10–11.
Hearse, P. (1994) 'Putting Politics on Screen', *Green Left Weekly*, 163, 19 October, 25.
Heilman, R. B. (1968) *Tragedy and Melodrama: Versions of Experience*. Seattle: Washington Press.
Higson, A. (1983) 'Critical Theory and "British Cinema"', *Screen*, 24, 4–5, July–October, 81–95.
—— (1984) 'Space, Place, Spectacle', *Screen*, 25, 4–5, July–October, 2–21.
—— (1992) '"Britain's Outstanding Contribution to the Film": The documentary–realist tradition', in C. Barr (ed.) *All Our Yesterdays: 90 Years of British Cinema*. London:BFI; first published 1986, 72–97.
Hill, J. (1986) *Sex, Class and Realism: British Cinema 1956–1963*. London: BFI.
—— (1996) 'British Television and Film: The Making of a Relationship', in J. Hill and M. McLoone (eds) *Big Picture, Small Screen: The Relations between Film and Television*. Luton: University of Luton Press, 151–76.
—— (1997a) 'Finding a Form: Politics and Aesthetics in *Fatherland, Hidden Agenda* and *Riff-Raff*', in G. McKnight (ed.) *Agent of Challenge and Defiance: The Films of Ken Loach*. Trowbridge: Flicks Books, 125–43.
—— (1997b) 'Interview with Ken Loach', in G. McKnight (ed.) *Agent of Challenge and Defiance: The Films of Ken Loach*. Trowbridge: Flicks Books, 160–76.
—— (1998) 'Every Fuckin' Choice Stinks', *Sight and Sound*, 8, 11, November, 18–21.
—— (1999) *British Cinema in the 1980s: Issues and Themes*. Oxford: Clarendon Press.
Hill, J. and M. McLoone (eds) (1996) *Big Picture, Small Screen: The Relations between Film and Television*. Luton: University of Luton Press.
Hines, B. (1969) *A Kestrel for a Knave*. Harmondsworth: Penguin; first published 1968.
—— (1979) *The Gamekeeper*. Harmondsworth: Penguin; first published 1975.
—— (1985) *Looks and Smiles*. Harmondsworth: Penguin; first published 1981.
Hirschhorn, C. (1967) 'The Seamy Tale of a Girl Seeking Happiness', *The Sunday Express*, 10 December, 22.
Hodges, A. (1981a) 'Ken Loach Interviewed', *Screen International*, 21 May, 11.
—— (1981b) '*Looks and Smiles*' *Screen International*, 30 May, 11.
Hoggart, R. (1962) 'Television in a Free Society', *Contrast*, 2, 1, Autumn, 6–11.
—— (1986) *The Uses of Literacy: Aspects of Working Class Life with Special Reference to Publications and Entertainments*. London: Peregrine; first published 1957.
—— (1995) *The Way We Live Now*. London: Chatto and Windus.
Hollander, A. (1991) *Moving Pictures*. Cambridge, Mass.: Harvard University Press.
Hood, S. (1983) *On Television*. London: Pluto.
—— (1994) 'Ken Loach Interviewed', in S. Hood (ed.) *Behind the Screens: The Structure of British Television in the Nineties*. London: Lawrence and Wishart, 194–201.
Horne, P. (1990) *Henry James and Revision: The New York Edition*. Oxford: Clarendon Press.
Houston, P. (1957–58) 'Captive or Free', *Sight and Sound*, 27, 3, Winter, 116–20.
Ibberson, J. (1969) '*Kes*', *Sight and Sound*, 38, 4, Autumn, 214.
Jacobs, J. (2000) *The Intimate Screen: Early British Television Drama*. Oxford: Oxford University Press.
James, H. (1949) *The Scenic Art: Notes on Acting and Drama 1872–1901*. Ed. Allan Wade. London: Rupert Hart-Davis.
James, R. R. (1969) *Memoirs of a Conservative: J. C. C. Davidson's Memoirs and Papers, 1910–37*. London: Weidenfeld.

Jeancolas, J–P. (1996) '*Carla's Song*: Managua mon amour', *Positif*, 429, November, 41–2.

Johnston, S. (1985) 'Film Narrative and the Structuralist Controversy', in P. Cook (ed.) *The Cinema Book*. London: BFI, 222–51.

Jones, D. A. N. (1975) 'Citrine on *Days of Hope*', *The Listener*, 9 October, 458–9.

Jones, N. (1986) *Strikes and the Media: Communication and Conflict*. Oxford: Basil Blackwell.

Jones, T. (1969) *Whitehall Diary: Volume 2, 1926–30*. Ed. Keith Middlemas. London: Oxford University Press.

Jones, T. (1998) 'How We Met: Ken Loach and Jim Allen', *The Independent on Sunday, Review*, 22 November, 92–3.

Kaplan, E. A. (1987) 'Mothering, Feminism and Representation: The Maternal in Melodrama and the Woman's Film 1910–40', in C. Gledhill (ed.) *Home is Where the Heart is: Studies in Melodrama and the Women's Film*. London: BFI,113–37.

_____ (1992) *Motherhood and Representation: The Mother in Popular Culture and Melodrama*. London and New York: Routledge.

Kay, G. (1994) 'Crissy Rock', *Empire*, October, 12.

Kemp, P. (1995) '*Land and Freedom*', *Sight and Sound*, 5, 10, October, 51.

Kennedy Martin, T. (1964) 'Nats Go Home: First Statement of a New Drama for Television', *Encore*, 48, March–April, 21–33.

_____ (1965–66) '*Up the Junction* and after', *Contrast*, 4, 5/6, Winter, 137–41.

_____ (1990) 'Sharpening the Edge of Television Drama', *The Listener*, 28 August, 9–12.

Kerr, P. (1986) 'The Complete Ken Loach', *Stills*, 27, May–June, 144–8.

Khan, M. (1994) 'Money/The Church/Family', *Vertigo*, 1, 3, Spring, 39–40.

Klevan, A. (2000) *Disclosure of the Everyday: Undramatic Achievement in Narrative Film*. Trowbridge: Flicks Books.

Knight, D. (1997) 'Naturalism, Narration and Critical Perspective: Ken Loach and the Experimental Method', in G. McKnight (ed.) *Agent of Challenge and Defiance: The Films of Ken Loach*. Trowbridge: Flicks Books, 60–81.

Klinger, B. (1994) *Melodrama and Meaning: History, Culture and the Films of Douglas Sirk*. Bloomington and Indianapolis: Indiana University Press.

Kohn, O. (1994) '*Ladybird*: Y a–t–il une "Loach touch?"', *Positif*, 404, October, 4–7.

Laing, S. (1986) *Representations of Working-Class Life 1957–64*. London: Macmillan.

_____ (1991) 'Banging in Some Reality: The Original *Z Cars*', in J. Corner (ed.) *Popular Television in Britain*. London: BFI, 125–44.

_____ (1997) 'Ken Loach: Histories and Contexts', in G. Mcknight (ed.) *Agent of Challenge and Defiance: The Films of Ken Loach*. Trowbridge: Flicks Books, 11–27.

LaJeunesse, J. (1981) 'Regards et sourires', *Image et Son/Ecran*, 365, October, 27–30.

Landy, M. (1991) *British Genres*. New Jersey: Princeton University Press, 1991.

Laverty, P. (1997) *Carla's Song*. London: Faber and Faber.

Laybourn, K. (1993) *The General Strike of 1926*. Manchester and New York: Manchester University Press.

LeFanu, M. (1983) 'Sur quelques films anglais contemporains', *Positif*, 271, September, 17–23.

Levin, B. (1970) *The Pendulum Years: Britain and the Sixties*. London: Jonathan Cape.

Levin, G. R. (1971) 'Tony Garnett and Ken Loach', in G. R. Levin, *Documentary Explorations: Fifteen Interviews with Film–Makers*. New York: Doubleday and Company Inc, 98–110.

Lewis, P. (1962) '*Z Cars*', *Contrast*, 1, 4, Summer, 307–15.

Loach, K. (1983) 'Broadcasters Who Uphold the Established Order through the Charade of Impartiality', *The Guardian*, 31 August, 9.

Loach, K., P. Laverty and S. Hibbin (1996) 'Commentaries on *Carla's Song*', *Vertigo*, 1, 6, Autumn, 14–18.

Lodge, D. (1963) '*Up the Junction*', *The Listener*, 21 November, 852.

London, J. (1957) *The Iron Heel*. New York: Hill and Wang; first published 1907.

Lounas, T. (1996) 'Raison et sentiments', *Cahiers du cinéma*, 507, November, 57–8.

Lovell, A. (1963) 'Television Playwright: David Mercer', *Contrast*, 2, 4, Summer, 220–29.

_____ (1975–76) 'Brecht in Britain – Lindsay Anderson', *Screen*, 16, 4, Winter, 62–80.

_____ (1984) 'The Context of British Social Drama', in R. Paterson (ed.) *The Boys from the Blackstuff, BFI Dossier 20*. London: BFI, 25–9.

Lovell, A. and J. Hillier (1972) *Studies in Documentary*. London: Secker and Warburg.

Lovell, T. (1980) *Pictures of Reality*. London: BFI.

_____ (1990) 'Landscape and Stories in 1960s British Realism', *Screen*, 31, 4, Winter, 357–76.

Low, M. and J. Brea (1937) *Red Spanish Notebook: The First Six Months of the Revolution and the Civil War*. London: Secker and Warburg.

Lyndon, N. (1975) 'Years of Promise', *Radio Times*, 6 September, 66–9.

McArthur, C. (1975–76) '*Days of Hope*', *Screen*, 16, 4, Winter, 139–44.

_____ (1978) *Television and History*. London: BFI.

_____ (1981) 'Historical Drama', in T. Bennett *et al.* (eds) *Popular Television and Film*. London: BFI, 288–301.

McAsh, I. (1978) 'One More Time', *Films Illustrated*, 8, 88, December, 154–5.

_____ (1980) 'Total Commitment to a Non–Star System', *Screen International*, 1 March, 15.

MacCabe, C. (1974) 'Realism and the cinema: Notes on some Brechtian Theses', *Screen*, 15, 2, Summer, 7–27.

_____ (1975–76) 'The Politics of Separation', *Screen*, 16, 4, Winter, 46–61.

_____ (1976a) '*Days of Hope* – A Response to Colin McArthur', *Screen*, 17, 1, Spring, 98–101.

_____ (1976b) 'Theory and Film: Principles of Realism and Pleasure', *Screen*, 17, 3, Autumn, 7–28.

—— (1981) 'Memory, Phantasy, Identity: *Days of Hope* and the Politics of the Past', in T. Bennett. J. S. Boyd-Bowman, C. Mercer & J. Woollacott (eds) *Popular Television and Film*. London: BFI, 314–18.

—— (1998) *Performance*. London: BFI.

MacFadden, P. (1997) 'Saturn's Feast, Loach's Spain: *Land and Freedom* as Filmed History', in G. McKnight (ed.) *Agent of Challenge and Defiance: The Films of Ken Loach*. Trowbridge: Flicks Books, 144–59.

McGivern, C. (1962) 'Let's Get it Moving Again', *Contrast*, 1, 3, Spring, 160–8.

McGrath, J. (1975) 'Better a Bad Night in Bootle…', *Theatre Quarterly*, 5, 19, September–November, 39–54.

—— (1977) 'T.V. Drama: The Case against Naturalism', *Sight and Sound*, 46, 2, Spring, 100–5.

McKnight, G. (ed.) (1997) *Agent of Challenge and Defiance: The Films of Ken Loach*. Trowbridge: Flicks Books.

MacMurraugh–Kavanagh, M. (1997a) 'The BBC and the Birth of *The Wednesday Play* (1962–1964): Institutional Containment Versus "Agitational Contemporaneity"', *Historical Journal of Film, Radio and Television*, 17, 3, August, 370–1.

—— (1997b) '"Drama" into "news": Strategies of Intervention in "The Wednesday Play"', *Screen*, 38, 3, Autumn, 247–59.

—— (1998) '"Kicking Over the Traces": An Interview with Tony Garnett', *Media Education Journal*, 24, Summer, 23–30.

Macnab, G. (1994) 'Loach on *Ladybird*', *Sight and Sound*, 4, 11, November, 12–14.

—— (1995) 'Raining Champion', *Time Out*, 25 October, 163.

Madden, P. (ed.) (1976) *Complete Programme Notes for a Season of British Television Drama 1959–1973, Held at National Film Theatre 11–24 October 1976*. London: BFI.

—— (1981) 'Jim Allen', in G. W. Brandt (ed.) *British Television Drama*. Cambridge: Cambridge University Press, 36–55.

Maddison, J. (1963) 'What is a Television Film?', *Contrast*, 3, 1, Autumn, 6–9 and 71–5.

Marris, P. (ed.) (1982) *Paul Rotha, BFI Dossier 16*. London: BFI.

Martin, A. (1992) '*Mise en scène* is dead, or The Expressive, The Excessive, The Technical and The Stylish', *Continuum: The Australian Journal of Media and Culture*, 5, 2, 87–140.

Mellencamp, P. (ed.) (1990) *Logics of Television: Essays in Cultural Criticism*. Indianapolis and London: Indiana University Press and BFI.

Mercer, D. (1973) 'Birth of a Playwriting Man', *Theatre Quarterly*, III, 9, January–March, 43–7.

Millar, G. (1980) 'Outlaws', *The Listener*, 103, 2651, 28 February, 279.

Mills, B. (1975) '*Days of Hope* – Going to Extremes', *The Listener*, 11 September, 337.

Monaco, J. (1972) *Loach/Hatton*. Programme Notes for film season at New School Department of Film.

Moretti, F. (1988) *Signs Taken for Wonders: Essays in the Sociology of Literary Forms*. Trans. Susan Fischer, David Forgacs and David Miller. London: Verso; first published 1983.

Morris, M. (1980) *The General Strike*. London and West Nyack: The Journeyman Press; first published 1976.

Morrow, F. (1974) *Revolution and Counter-Revolution in Spain*. New York: Pathfinder Press; first published 1936.

Mulvey, L. (1977–78) 'Notes on Sirk and Melodrama', *Movie*, 25, Winter, 53–6.

Munro, R. (1994) '*Ladybird Ladybird*', *Sight and Sound*, 4, 11, November, 11–12.

Murphy, R. (1992) *Sixties British Cinema*. London: BFI.

—— (ed.) (1997) *The British Cinema Book*. London: BFI.

—— (ed.) (2000) *British Cinema of the 90s*. London: BFI.

Naremore, J. (1990) *Acting in the Cinema*. Berkeley and London: University of California Press.

Nave, B. (1996) 'Rencontre avec Ken Loach', *Jeune Cinéma*, 240, November–December, 15–20.

Neale, S. (1983) *Genre*. London: BFI.

—— (1986) 'Melodrama and Tears', *Screen*, 27, 6, November–December, 6–22.

—— (1990) 'Questions of Genre', *Screen*, 31, 1, Spring, 45–66.

Newman, S., D. Potter, T. Garnett *et al.* (1964) 'Reaction to Troy Kennedy Martin', *Encore*, 49, May–June, 39–47.

Nichols, B. (1991) *Representing Reality: Issues and Concepts in Documentary*. Bloomington and Indianapolis: Indiana University Press.

—— (1994) *Blurred Boundaries: Questions of Meaning in Contemporary Culture*. Blooington and Indianapolis: Indiana University Press.

Nochlin, L. (1971) *Realism*. Harmondsworth: Penguin.

Nowell–Smith, G. (1967) *Visconti*. London: Secker and Warburg.

O'Hara, J. (1977) '*Days of Hope*', *Cinema Papers*, 12, April, 344–5.

Orbanz, E. (ed.) (1977) *Journey to a Legend and Back: The British Realistic Film*. Berlin: Edition VolkerSpiess.

Orwell, G. (1989) *Homage to Catalonia*. London: Penguin; first published 1938.

Ostria, V. (1994a) 'Entretien avec Ken Loach', *Cahiers du cinéma*, 484, October, 37–41.

— (1994b) 'Ken Loach, la logique du vivant', *Cahiers du cinéma*, 484, October, 35–41.

Otta (1967) '*Poor Cow*', *Variety*, 13 December, 6.

Paget, D. (1990) *True Stories? Documentary Drama on Radio, Screen and Stage*. Manchester and New York: Manchester University Press

—— (1998) *No Other Way to Tell It: Dramadoc/Docudrama on Television*. Manchester and New York: Manchester University Press.

Pannifer, B. (1991) 'Agenda Bender', *The Listener*, 3 January, 30–1.

Paz, A. (1976) *Durruti: The People Armed*. Montreal: Black Rose.

Perez, G. (1998) *The Material Ghost: Films and their Medium*. Baltimore and London: The Johns Hopkins University Press.

Perkins, V. F. (1978) *Film as Film: Understanding and Judging Movies*. Harmondsworth: Penguin; first published 1972.
—— (1981) 'Moments of Choice', *The Movie*, 58, 1141–5.
—— (1982) '*Letter from an Unknown Woman*', *Movie*, 29/30, Summer, 61–72.
—— (1990a) 'Film Authorship: The Premature Burial', *CineAction!*, 21/22, Summer/Fall, 57–65.
—— (1990b) 'Must We Say What They Mean? Film Criticism and Interpretation', *Movie*, 34/35, Winter, 1–7.
—— (1992a) 'The Atlantic Divide', in R. Dyer and G. Vincendeau (eds) *Popular European Cinema*. London: Routledge, 194–205.
—— (1992b) '*In a Lonely Place*', in I. Cameron (ed.) *The Movie Book of Film Noir*. London: Studio Vista, 222–31.
—— (1996) '*Johnny Guitar*', in I. Cameron and D. Pye (eds) *The Movie Book of the Western*. London: Studio Vista, 221–8.
—— (1999) *The Magnificent Ambersons*. London: BFI.
—— (2000a) 'Ophuls Contra Wagner and Others', *Movie*, 36, 73–9.
—— (2000b) '*I Confess*: Photographs of People Speaking', *CineAction*, 52, June, 28–39.
—— (2000c) 'Same Tune Again! Repetition and Framing in *Letter from an Unknown Woman*', *CineAction*, 52, June, 40–8.
Perry, E. (1994) 'Interview with Crissy Rock', *Time Out*, 28 September, 4.
Petley, J. (1981) 'DocuDrama: Truth or Fiction?', *The Movie*, 63, 1255–7.
—— (1982) 'An Interview with Ken Loach', *Framework*, 18, 9–12.
—— (1983a) '*Looks and Smiles*', *Films and Filming*, 341, February, 32.
—— (1983b) 'Ken Trodd: Drama in Crisis', *Stills*, 9, November–December, 60–3.
—— (1984) 'Union Blues', *Stills*, 14, November, 44–7.
—— (1987a) 'Future Film Policy', *Sight and Sound*, 56, 2, Spring, 86–90.
—— (1987b) 'Over the Top', *Sight and Sound*, 56, 2, Spring, 126–32.
—— (1987c) 'Ken Loach – Politics, Protest and the Past', *Monthly Film Bulletin*, 54, 638, March, 96.
—— (1987d) '*Fatherland*', *Monthly Film Bulletin*, 54, 638, March, 75–6.
—— (1988) 'The Price of Portraying a Less Than Perfect Britain', *The Listener*, 21 January, 14.
—— (1992a) 'The Lost Continent', in C. Barr (ed.) *All Our Yesterdays: 90 Years of British Cinema*. London: BFI; first published 1986, 98–119.
—— (1992b) *Ken Loach: La Mirada Radical*. Valladolid: Semana Internacional de Cine de Valladolid. [Page references from unpublished English manuscript].
—— (1993) 'Why Cathy Will Never Come Home Again', *New Statesman and Society*, 2 April, 23–5.
—— (1995) 'The Spanish Connection', *Living Marxism*, October, 38–9.
—— (1996) 'Fact Plus Fiction Equals Friction', *Media, Culture and Society*, 18, 1, January, 11–26.
—— (1997a) 'Factual Fictions and Fictional Fallacies: Ken Loach's Documentary Dramas', in G. McKnight (ed.) *Agent of Challenge and Defiance: The Films of Ken Loach*. Trowbridge: Flicks Books, 28–59.
—— (1997b) 'Ken Loach and Questions of Censorship', in G. McKnight (ed.) *Agent of Challenge and Defiance: The Films of Ken Loach*. Trowbridge: Flicks Books, 99–124.
—— (1997c) 'Ken Loach', in L. C. Hillstrom (ed.), *International Dictionary of Films and Filmmakers: Volume 2: Directors*. Detroit; New York; Toronto; London: St James' Press, 615–17.
—— (1997d) 'Us and Them', in M. Barker and J. Petley (eds) *Ill Effects: The Media/Violence Debate*. London and New York: Routledge, 87–101.
—— (1997e) '*Land and Freedom*', in N. V. Elert and A. Vasudevan (eds) *International Dictionary of Films and Filmmakers: Volume 1: Films*. Detroit; New York; Toronto; London: St James' Press, 553–5.
Petrie, D. (1991) *Creativity and Constraint in the British Film Industry*. London: Macmillan.
—— (ed.) (1992) *New Questions of British Cinema*. London: BFI.
Pilard, P. (1989) *Le Nouveau Cinema Britannique*. Paris: Editions Hatier.
—— (1993) 'Entretien avec Ken Loach: Vingt–Cinq Ans de cinéma', *Positif*, 392, October, 18–22.
—— (1994) 'A View from Paris', *Vertigo*, 1, 3, Spring, 40–1.
Pilling, J. and K. Canham (eds) (1983) *The Screen on the Tube: Filmed Television Drama*. Norwich: Cinema City.
Plantinga, C. R. (1997) *Rhetoric and Representation in Nonfiction Film*. New York and Cambridge: Cambridge University Press.
Porton, R. (1996a) 'The Revolution Betrayed: An Interview with Ken Loach', *Cineaste*, 22, 1, April, 30–9.
—— (1996b) '*Land and Freedom*', *Cineaste*, 22, 1, April, 32–4.
Preston, J. (1982) 'Looking Outwards', *Time Out*, 17 December, 32.
Preston, P. (1996a) *A Concise History of the Spanish Civil War*. London: Fontana Press.
—— (1996b) 'Viva La Revolucion', *New Statesman and Society*, 16 September, 18–21.
Prior, A. and J. Hopkins (1963) '*Z Cars*', *Screen Education*, 21, September–October, 7–16.
Pulleine, T. (1980) '*Black Jack*', *Monthly Film Bulletin*, 47, 555, April, 65–6.
Purser, P. (1961a) 'The Landscape of Television Drama', *Contrast*, 1, 1, Autumn, 11–20.
—— (1961b) 'Think–Tape – A Profile of Denis Mitchell', *Contrast*, 1, 2, Winter, 108–16.
—— (1962) 'Head of Drama', *Contrast*, 2, 1, Autumn, 33–6.
Pye, D. (1989) 'Bordwell and Hollywood', *Movie*, 33, Winter, 46–52.
—— (2000) 'Movies and Point of View', *Movie*, 36, 2–34.
Pym, J. (1992) *Film on 4: A Survey 1982/1991*. London: BFI
Quart, L. (1980) 'A Fidelity to the Real: An Interview with Ken Loach and Tony Garnett', *Cineaste*, 10, 4, Fall, 26–9.

—— (1995) 'Ladybird Ladybird', Cineaste 21:1/2, February, 84–85.
Ralling, C. (1968) 'The Truth about Documentary – or Documentary about the Truth', The Listener, 19 December, 826–8.
Remy, V. (1994) 'Entretien avec Crissy Rock', Télérama, 28 September, 30–2.
Ricks, C. (1984) 'Clichés', in C. Ricks The Force of Poetry. Oxford: Clarendon Press, 356–68.
—— (1998) 'Literature and the Matter of Fact', in C. Ricks, Essays in Appreciation. Oxford: Clarendon Press; first published 1996, 280–310.
Robinson, D. (1957) 'Looking for Documentaries: Part 2', Sight and Sound, 27, 2, Autumn, 70–5.
—— (1962) Contrast on Pilkington. London: BFI.
—— (1963) 'Shooting on Tape', Contrast, 3, 1, Autumn, 30–3.
—— (1967) 'The Dunn Cow', Financial Times, 8 December, 28.
—— (1968–69) 'Case Histories of The Next Renaissance', Sight and Sound, 38, 1, winter, 36–40.
Rosen, P. (ed.) (1986) Narrative, Apparatus, Ideology: A Film Theory Reader. New York: Columbia University Press.
Rosenthal, A. (1971) The New Documentary in Action: A Casebook in Film–Making. Los Angeles and London: University of California Press.
—— (ed.) (1988) New Challenges for Documentary. Berkeley and London: University of California Press.
—— (ed.) (1999) Why Docudrama? Fact–Fiction on Film and Television. Carbondale and Edwardsville: Southern Illinois University Press.
Rotha, P. (ed.) (1956) Television in the Making. London and New York: The Focal Press.
Rothman, W. (1997) Documentary Film Classics. New York and Cambridge: Cambridge University Press.
Royle, E. (1987) Modern Britain, a Social History. London: Edward Arnold.
Ryan, S. and R. Porton (1998) 'The Politics of Everyday Life: An Interview with Ken Loach', Cineaste, 24, 1, Winter, 22–8.
Saada, N. (1993) 'Travail au noir', Cahiers du cinéma, 472, October, 62–3.
Sackett, S. (1993) Prime Time Hits: TV's Most Popular Network Programmes: 1950s to the Present. New York: Billboard Books.
Sandford, J. (1973) 'Edna and Cathy: Just Huge Commercials', Theatre Quarterly, III, 10, April–June, 79–85.
—— (1976) Cathy Come Home. London: Marion Boyars.
Sarler, C. (1994) 'Nothing But The Truth', The Sunday Times Magazine, 14 August, 42–9.
Saynor, J. (1992) 'Writers' Television', Sight and Sound 2, 7, November, 28–31.
—— (1993) 'Imagined Communities', Sight and Sound, 3, 12, December, 11–13.
Scannell, P. (1979) 'The Social Eye of Television, 1946–55', Media, Culture and Society, 1, 1, 97–106.
Scannell, P. and D. Cardiff (1991) A Social History of Broadcasting: Volume One 1922–1939. Oxford: Basil Blackwell Ltd.
Shattuc, J. (1994) 'Having a Good Cry Over The Color Purple', in J. Bratton, J. Cook and C. Gledhill (eds) Melodrama: Stage Picture Screen. London: BFI, 147–65.
Sheperd, S. (1994) 'Pauses of Mutual Agitation', in J. Bratton, J. Cook and C. Gledhill (eds) Melodrama: Stage, Picture, Screen. London: BFI, 25–37.
Shubik, I. (1975) Play for Today: The Evolution of Television Drama. London: Davis–Poynter.
Slaughter, B. (1999) 'Jim Allen: A Lifetime's Commitment to Historical Truth', On–Line. Available http://www.socialequality.com/articles/1999/ aug1999/obit–allprn.shtml (11 January 2000).
Smith, G. (1988) 'Voice in the Dark: An Interview with Loach', Film Comment, 24, 2, March–April, 38–46.
—— (1994) 'Sympathetic Images: Ken Loach Interviewed by Gavin Smith', Film Comment, 30, 4, March–April, 58–67.
Smith, H. and A. J. Cook (1926) 'Letter to the Editor', The Times, 1 May, 14.
Smith, J. (1973) Melodrama. London: Methuen.
Smith, P. (1994) 'Filming Difficulties' The Sunday Times, The Culture, 18 September, 4.
Smith, P. J. (1997) 'Carla's Song', Sight and Sound, 7, 2, February, 38–9.
Stead, P. (1989) Film and the Working Class. London: Routledge.
Stephenson, W. (1973) 'Kes and the Press', Cinema Journal, 12, 2, Spring, 48–55.
Stern, J. P. (1973) On Realism. London: Routledge and Kegan Paul.
Stok, D. (ed.) (1993) Kieslowski on Kieslowski. London: Faber and Faber.
Stoddart, P. (1983) 'Off Air: What Has Happened to the Party Conference Season?', Broadcast, 21 October, 14.
Summers, S. (1996) 'Will Auntie Remain the Poor Relation?', The Observer, Review, 23 June, 10.
'Susan' (1994) 'The Ladybird Social Worker's Own Story', The Guardian Society, 12 October, 2–3.
Sussex, E. (1988) 'Getting It Right', in A. Rosenthal (ed.) New Challenges for Documentary. Berkeley and London: University of California Press, 110–21.
Sutton, S. (1982) The Largest Theatre in the World. London: BBC.
Swallow, N. (1966) Factual TV. London: The Focal Press.
Swallow, N. and A. Lawson (1990) 'Sydney Newman interviewed by Norman Swallow and Alan Lawson', ACTT [BECTU] Oral History Project 19/6/90. Copyright held by BECTU.
Tarr, C. (1985) 'Sapphire, Darling and the Boundaries of Permitted Pleasure', Screen, 26, 1, January–February, 50–65.
Taylor, D. (1990) Days of Vision: Working with David Mercer: Television Drama, Then and Now. London: Methuen.
Taylor, J. R. (1962) Anatomy of a Television Play. London: Weidenfeld and Nicolson/ABC TV Ltd.
—— (1964–65) 'Drama '66', Contrast 4:5–6, Winter–Spring, 132–6.
—— (1967) 'A Picturesque View of a Messy Life', The Times, 7 December.
—— (1970) 'The Kes Dossier', Sight and Sound, 39, 3, Summer, 130–1.

—— (1971) *The Second Wave: British Drama for the Seventies*. London: Methuen.

Taylor, R. (1991) *Kurt Weill: Composer in a Divided World*. London: Simon and Schuster.

Thomas, J. H. (1937) *My Story*. London: Hutchinson and Co.

Thomas, D. (2000) *Beyond Genre: Melodrama, Comedy and Romance in Hollywood Films*. Moffat: Cameron and Hollis.

—— (2001) *Reading Hollywood: Spaces and Meanings in American Film*. London: Wallflower Press.

Thompson, J. (1984) 'Loach "politically censored"', *Television Weekly*, 3 August, 6.

Thornett, A. (1979) *The Battle for Trotskyism*. London: Folrose; first published 1976.

—— (1987) *From Militancy to Marxism*. Oxford: Left View Books.

—— (1998) *Inside Cowley: Trade Union Struggles in the British Car Industry in the 1970s*. London: Porcupine.

Tracey, M. (1983) *A Variety of Lives: A Biography of Sir Hugh Greene*. London: The Bodley Head.

Tremois, C–M. (1980) '*Black Jack*', *Télérama*, 5 March, 101.

—— (1993) 'Les trois anglais sur le continent', *Télérama*, 26 May, 36–38.

Tribe, K. (1977–78) 'History and the Production of Memories', *Screen*, 18, 4, Winter, 9–22.

Trodd, K. (1999) 'Jim Allen', *The Independent, Review*, 6 July, 16.

Tulloch, J. (1990) *Television Drama: Agency, Audience and Myth*. London: Routledge.

Turner, J. (1993) '*Raining Stones*', *Sight and Sound*, 3, 10, October, 50–1.

Vahimagi, T. (ed.) (1994) *British Television: An Illustrated Guide*. London: Oxford University Press and BFI.

Wagstaff, C. (1996) '*Ladri di biciclette*', in D. Forgacs and R. Lumley (eds) *Italian Cultural Studies: An Introduction*. Oxford, and New York: Oxford University Press, 261–5.

Wainright, H. (1994) 'Political Sightings', *Vertigo*, 1, 3, Spring, 42.

Walker, A. (1974) *Hollywood England*. London: Michael Joseph Ltd.

—— (1985) *National Heroes*. London: Harrap.

Walker, J. (1985) *The Once and Future Film*. London: Methuen.

Walker, M. (1982) 'Melodrama and the American Cinema', *Movie*, 29/30, Summer, 2–38.

—— (1992) '*Kings Row*', *CineAction*, 26/27, Winter, 82–93.

—— (1993) 'Melodramatic Narrative: *Orphans of the Storm* and *The Searchers*', *CineAction*, 31, Spring–Summer, 62–73.

—— (1996) '*Dances with Wolves*', in I. Cameron and D. Pye (eds) *The Movie Book of the Western*. London: Studio Vista, 284–93.

Wallace, M. (1980) '*The Gamekeeper*', *Cineaste*, 10, 4, Fall, 30.

Warren, C. (ed.) (1996) *Beyond Document: Essays on Non Fiction Film*. Hanover, NH and London: University of New England.

Watt, H. (1974) *Don't Look at the Camera*. London: Elek Books.

White, C. with C. Thurlow (1982) *Carol Comes Home*. Sevenoaks: New English Library.

Whitehouse, M. (1967) *Cleaning Up TV: From Protest to Participation*.London: Blandford Press.

Willett, J. (1967) *The Theatre of Bertolt Brecht*. London: Methuen.

Williams, C. (ed.) (1980) *Realism and the Cinema: A Reader*. London: Routledge and Kegan Paul.

— (1994) 'After the Classic, the Classical and Ideology: The Differences of Realism', *Screen*, 35, 3, Autumn, 275–93.

Williams, R. (1974) *Television: Technology and Cultural Form*. London: Fontana.

—— (1977) 'A Lecture on Realism', *Screen*, 18, 1, Spring, 61–74.

—— (1977–78) 'Realism, Naturalism and their Alternatives', *Cine-Tracts*, 1, 3, Fall Winter, 1–6.

—— (1983) *Keywords*. London: Flamingo.

—— (1989) *On Television: Selected Writings*. London: Routledge.

Williamson, J. (1998) '*My Name is Joe*', *Sight and Sound*, 8, 11, November, 58.

Wilson, D. (1970–71) '*Family Life*', *Sight and Sound*, 41, 1, Winter, 50–1.

—— (1975) '*Days of Hope*', *Sight and Sound*, 44, 3, Summer, 160.

—— (1980) '*Black Jack*', *Sight and Sound*, 49, 2, Spring, 126–7.

—— (1991) '*Riff–Raff*', *Sight and Sound*, 1, 1, May, 61.

Wilson, D. A. (1975) 'Letters to the Editor: *Days of Hope*', *The Listener*, 16 October, 507.

Wilson, G. M. (1996) *Narration in Light: Studies in Cinematic Point of View*. Baltimore and London: The John Hopkins University Press; first published 1986.

Wood, R. (1989) *Hitchcock's Films Revisited*. London: Faber and Faber.

Worsley, T. C. (1970) *Television: The Ephemeral Art*. London: Alan Ross.

Wrigley, C. (ed.) (1997) *British Trade Unions, 1945–1995*. Manchester: Manchester University Press.

Wyver, J. (1983) 'Chris Menges: Seeing and Believing', *Stills* 6, May–June, 70–3.

INDEX